Gender Equality and Women Empowerment

A Comparative Study of Bangladesh, India and Sri Lanka Based on Women Representation and Participation in Politics

Gender Equality and Women Empowerment:

A Comparative Study of Bangladesh, India and Sri Lanka Based on Women Representation and Participation in Politics

Dr. Deepika Mann

KALPAZ

Published by

Kalpaz Publications
C-30, Satyawati Nagar,
Delhi – 110052
Ph.: 011-47034999, 9811692060
www.kalpazpublications.com
E-mail: kalpaz@hotmail.com

Distribution Network
gyanbooks.com
India, USA, Canada, UK, Australia, France

ISBN: 978-93-6433-521-8 (PB)
First Published, 2024

Printed at: Gyan Press, Delhi.

Gender Equality and Women Empowerment

Author: Dr. Deepika Mann

To the two who gave me life

And the one who made me free (Mr. Praveen Singh)

And definitely, for the women I have become through this process

Contents

Abstract

Gender Inequality (GI) or patriarchy is both ideological and structural. That is, ideological means the beliefs, norms, along with values regarding the status and roles of women in society. Structural refers to women's access to as well as positions within social institutions. In the academic arena, the research of women's socio-economic as well as political liberation is an important theme with incessant feminists' notions in the modern globe.

Women's liberation is determined by gender disparities that evolved by means of the socialization process, internalizing social norms, cultural values, along with expectations of concentrating the Asian patriarchal society, namely India, Bangladesh, and Sri Lanka. So, women were discriminated against from high positions in society, Political Leadership (PL), Decision Making (DM), together with economic top management in the conventional society. Nevertheless, a few educated women began to deal with women's problems as well as created a discourse concerning women's freedom in modern society by propagating feminist notions along with modifications that happened in Sri Lanka subsequent to the independence of the country.

A theme of Human Rights (HR), inclusive growth, as well as Sustainable Development (SD) is women's full and efficient Political Participation (PP). At all levels of DM and political involvement, the women's active participation on equal status with men is necessary for the accomplishment of equality, SD, peace, and democracy, along with the inclusion of their viewpoints and experiences into the DM processes. Empowerment of females permits them to transfer their own life, compose their agenda as well as organize and demand the support of the state and community for the transition. It can be noticed that a women's role is undividable from development same in several cultures, yet it sometimes doesn't emphasize a similar position that matters for males. As a result, it is assumed that females need more help for their immense position in DM along with social development.

Individual empowerment is focused on by the rhetoric of female empowerment, thereby, ignoring the problem of women in power. The women's representation amongst heads of state as well as members of Parliament remains less when analogized to their population share even though they have experienced noteworthy gains in literacy and Educational Attainment (EA). In spite of a nation's level of Economic Development (ED) along with a near-universal accord

on women's political rights, the lack of female leadership is common in countries around the globe. For controlling women in these three countries, an increase in the utilization of religion as a political tool contributes to an increase in GI. Household and politics are the immediate authoritative patriarchal domains that constantly talk about "protecting" women by ignoring their voices and requirements. Thus, this probably creates a loss of agency amongst women.

Scrutinizing the problem of GI from an International viewpoint is the major objective of this research. By considering the parameters, namely Gender-related Development Index (GDI), Gender Empowerment Measure (GEM), GI in education, GI in economic activity, and Women PP (WPP), a comparative study of the Gender disparity amongst South Asian Association for Regional Cooperation (SAARC) countries (India, Bangladesh, and Sri Lanka) has been conducted. The secondary study is done, and in diverse regions, the ways are examined in the results. The outcomes exhibit that organized collective participation of women was more efficient only in social welfare, livelihood, together with social security than WPP. The low- level of PP by women is attributable to economic, religious, as well as political factors, as per the research. On the whole, it is discovered that women have a deficiency of space for PP even though they are curious about participating in local governance.

In brief, a provisional outlook of what can be perceived as notions of empowerment in the WPP context has been made.

List of Tables

List of Figures

List of Symbols and Abbreviations

IR	International Relations
CEDAW	Convention on The Elimination of Discrimination Against Women
GII	Gender Inequality Index
HDR	Human Development Report
GEM	Gender Empowerment Measure
GDI	Gender Development Index
HDI	Human Development Index
NPWA	National Policy for Women's Advancement
NCWD	National Council for Women Development
SAARC	South Asian Association for Regional Cooperation
TTP	Tehrik-E-Taliban Pakistan
UNIFEM	United Nations Development Fund for Women
INSTRA	International Research Training Institute for Advancement Of Women
ESD	Education for Sustainable Development
NAWP	Newham Asian Women's Project
CSW	Commission on the Status of Women
SAARC	South Asian Association for Regional Cooperation
WPP	Women Political Participation
OTI	One-Text Initiative
OBC	Other backward classes
RPO	Representation of People Order

OSCE	Organization for Security and Co-Operation in Europe
IPU	Inter Parliamentary Union
SDGs	Sustainable Development Goals
IPV	Intimate Partner Violence
UNGA	UN General Assembly
WIN	Women In Need
SSA	Social Scientists' Association
SGBV	sexual and gender-based violence
WDN	Women's Democracy Network
FSLGA	Federation of Sri Lanka Government Authorities
UN	United Nations
VAW	Violence Against Women
BMP	Bangladesh Mahila Parishad
GBV	Gender Based Violence
NAPs	National Action Plans

Chapter - 1

Introduction

1.1 PREFACE

Inconsistency is signified by Asian women in politics. In several levels of government, women just hold a fraction of appointive together with elective political offices whilst including half population (Iwanaga, 2008). Recently, women have consolidated various voting power as a group; however, regarding political representation, disenfranchised concurrently. When democracy is spreading globally as a government system, the question arises as to how they are grossly under- depicted at every government level in Asia. For the questionnaires from various perspectives, that volume is an effort of offering probable answers. The 21st century unrevealed a few huge problems dealing with scholars as well as political leaders alike in Asia. Several elements of continuity, modification in WPP, along with representation are explored.

Various countries, a multitude of societies, political systems, together with different phases of democracy as well as socio-ED are covered by Asia, which is a vast and diverse region (UNESCO World Report, 2009). Thus, the term 'Asia' is referred to as East Asia, South-East Asia (SEA), together with South Asia. Nevertheless, the South Asian (SA) region is aimed. When weighed against women of industrial democracies, the right to vote along with stand for election was hugely received by women in Asia. While European countries along with the United States (US) had empowered women shortly after the 1st World War, before the 2nd world word initiated, just '3' Asian countries had endorsed female suffrage (Schaeffer, 2020). In permitting women to vote, Sri Lanka was the 1st nation in Asia in 1931 subsequent to Thailand in 1932 and Myanmar in 1935 (Bowie, 2010). In most Asian countries, Women's Political Representation (WPR) sustains to lag although with a few progress. (Sultana, 2010) There was a low incremental growth of women in politics even in many affluent Asian societies like (a) Japan, (b) Taiwan, (c) South Korea, (d) Singapore, along with (e) Malaysia in which they are extremely successful in higher educational institutions along with professional occupations (Booth, 1999). In a few poor nations like Vietnam, Laos, Pakistan, China, and the Philippines, the proportion of women in parliaments is extremely superior. In forms like quota or reserved seat systems, ideological commitments to Gender Equality (GE) or the endorsement of an extra egalitarian political culture that might be owing to the utilization of several assenting action policies, which promote women's parliamentary representation.

Major women are marginalized as of partaking in mainstream politics even though little elite of highly educated women has acquired the highest positions in governments in Asia. Even with the fact that Asia is experiencing fast socio-economic changes along with political restructuring wholly, the glass ceiling appears to stay unbroken for the major Asian women in politics (Women's HR, 2022). The women's political situation in various Asian societies hasn't been changed by years of fast socio-economic developments; in addition, various difficulties persist in preventing women as of entering public office. Constraints are imposed on women in Asia along with recognize the various political chances accessible to them due to the factors like religious and other cultural variables. The women's political status in Asia is anything uniform. From country to country, the women's chance varies significantly. Regarding WPR, a few countries have advanced faster than others.

Reading descriptive and substantive terms, there was comparatively small written particularly regarding Women's Empowerment (WE) along with political representation in less urbanized countries when weighed against the propagation of studies probing women together with politics in superior industrialized democracies (Asiedu et al, 2006). For appraising the policy effect of electing women, the shortage of women in national parliaments makes it challenging. Due to fewer women legislators, it is more challenging to appraise the effect of women's existence in politics on the political structures in Asia (Atske et al, 2019).

Political perspectives along with challenges that are weakly depicted will be generated by the women legislators, which were deduced by the women's numerical presence. For the equivalent existence of women along with men in political bodies, the supposition of female legislators acting on the sake of women, or articulating women's interests, creates arguments' necessity along with the legislature (Franceschet & Piscopo, 2008). Female politicians have a gendered knowledge, which controls them to act consequently in particular manners, which was signified by the indispensable representation of women's interests. Could we suppose that women politicians have a shared experience along with viewpoint, which joints them grounded on their gender? As per (1) ideological, (2) ethnic, (3) religious, (4) economic, (5) social, together with (6) other differences, there are differences amongst women politicians, which might be detected (Chakrabarty, 2008). In shaping the priorities in policy problems, a few women politicians deny gender as a factor. Other significant factors like party policy along with party discipline, which have a high influence on their political DM, are pointed out by them. For promoting women's interests, a few male politicians as well progress women's interests together with construct alliances with women politicians. It is significant not to ignore the thought that women politicians signify disparities amongst women even though they share similar gender for recognizing whether women do symbolize women's interests.

1.2 GENDER EQUALITY

Gender isn't going to be "an explanatory framework". Relatively, it signifies explanatory frameworks, which people previously have, along with the ones those International Relations (IR) theorists believe that they must have. Gender isn't either explanandum (explained) or explanans (explaining) (Carver, 2003). On its own or in conjunction with other factors it might be either or both. Persuading that gender matters might be essential for some researchers. Since the cause and effect are connected, gender is going to be in explanandum along with explanans; in addition, the linkage is a key part of what persuades that the explanation is a pre-eminent one certainly. For instance, voting Republican or Conservative (an effect) possibly does something with Republican or Conservative values or beliefs (a cause), but certainly, it might also be explanatorily joined with income along with wealth and with parental voting (Republican or Conservative), with geographical residence (where there are many Republicans or Conservatives), etc. Although gender is not the framework itself it could operate within a framework. "to gender" a study and "to having gender into the explanandum or explanans, or possessing it figure in some diverse way in both might be regarded.

GE has established extraordinary awareness at international forums from the 1980s (Kardam, 2002). There was a developing international comprehension that GE is a qualification to attain human along with SD. GE is personified in an international legal instrument, the Convention on the Elimination of Discrimination Against Women (CEDAW) that became effective in 1981 along with has been approved by 174 nations in '2' decades betwixt Mexico City and Beijing (Riggin, 2011). A set of norms as well as rules associated with GE are encompassed in the Ratification of CEDAW, which becomes signatories to diverse platforms of action along with other regional. Could this comprise a novel global framework for GE? If yes, what are the circumstances under which collaboration amongst associated actors takes place? What does 'GE' mean in different social along with political contexts? Even though there is a budding global regime on GE? At national and local levels along with diverse institutions, how are they interpreted along with applied?

1.3 CONCEPT OF GENDER EQUALITY

The GE concept is identified as the main element for attaining progress in every area. Society's every member is concerned by the GE along with engenders the foundation of a mere society. To maintain peace along with prosperity of a just society, HR problems that impact women play a key role. Society is not able to boast where there is total GE still now. The GE question was still a topic of theoretical discussion. Things are modifying but slowly. In the United Nations (UNs) Charter of 1945, the prohibition against sex discrimination was articulated initially; then, later restated in the Universal Declaration of HR of 1948 (UDHR). Against discrimination, every HR instrument has reinforced and extended protections. For both sexes, equal protection was warranted by the International Covenant on Civil along with Political Rights adopted in 1966. In 1966 promised women equality of status, International Covenant on Economic, Social, along with Cultural Rights was also espoused (General Assembly (GA) resolution 2200A, 1966). By reaffirming GE as a fundamental pre-requisite for Social Justice (SJ), the Fourth World Conference (FWC) of Women detained in Beijing in 1994 caused further updates.

GE and WE are '2' sides of the same coin, which was signified by paring '2' concepts of WE and GE into one MDG implicitly. WE are required for progressing toward GE. In figure 1.1, the WE requisites maximization in GE.

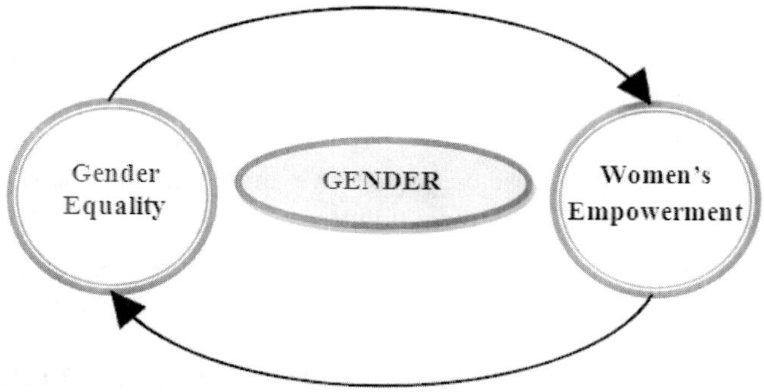

Figure 1.1: Structure of Gender Equality

Women and men interact along with function as GI and women‘s disempowerment take place in every diverse domain, both concepts are multi-dimensional. Thus, huge potential indicators are initiated. For analogizing the Status of Women (SW) as well as men on specific characteristics of interest, indicators of GE /inequality are designed typically; while, indicators of empowerment/ disempowerment lean not to be virtual by definition. For measuring the roles, attitudes, and rights of women and sometimes men, indicators of empowerment are designed (Gupta, 2014).

In spurring the women's development movement, The UN's International Women's decade, which was initiated in 1975, played a significant role (World Conferences on Women, 1995). The government committed itself to the WE at the Social Summit in Copenhagen in 1993 along with the International Conference on Population as well as Development in Cairo in 1994 (UNs publication, 1994). At the FWC on Women in Beijing in 1995, that commitment was operationalized along with originated into a clear action plan (Beijing and its Follow-up, 1995) in which Governments devoted themselves to the 'empowerment along with the progression of women like the right to liberty of thoughts, conscience, religion, together with belief; hence, the moral, (ii) ethical, (iii) spiritual, together with (iv) the intellectual requirements of women and men are contributed separately or in society along with shaping their lives following their objectives.

Explanations of Gender Equality

While there are several explanations for women's status in society, our analyses concentrate on 4 dominant themes in the literature:

- The typical modernization viewpoint aims on ED,
- Gender-egalitarian attitudes and self-expression values are raised due to more recent human enhancement targeting emancipative cultural changes.
- The historical legacies perspective highlights the persuade of cultural as well as political traditions,
- The institutional design view, which is significant as of a political engineering standpoint.

1.4 EMERGENCE OF CONSTRUCTIVIST INTERNATIONAL RELATIONS

The main axis of the inter-paradigm debate—the so-called Third Great Debate in the 1980s in the area of international relations (Weber, 2014)—was between rationalists and early critical international theorists (Jung, 2019). In his 1988 talk to the ISA Annual Conference, Robert Keohane noticed the existence and legitimacy of a new paradigm, which he termed "reflectivist." In this process, the rationalists-versus-constructivists dispute had progressively become the primary line of contention, as a constructivist approach to the study of international relations (IR) rose to prominence in the 1990s. Three mutually reinforcing elements led the current research emphasis on the reorientation of critical international theory, which resulted in the "constructivist turn in IR." First, there was "the response of neoliberals and neorealists to critical theorists' criticisms." As Keohane previously stated, many acknowledged the promise of the reflectivist critical international theorists as a new source of alternative insights into the intersubjective foundations of international relations (IR). The second element was the end of the Cold War, which revealed "the inability of the mainstream rationalist theories" to explain such a profound international transformation. Third was a generational shift of IR experts who were profoundly enlightened by the critical theories of the Third Debate (Theys, 2018).

1.4.1 GENDER AND THE CONSTRUCTIVIST PERSPECTIVE

The establishment of a regime is one thing, but maintaining it is another. The "translation" of international standards to national and local levels remains hard, and there are significant implementation gaps between global norms and local responses. The gender rule was not a product of state initiative. It was imposed on them by global non-governmental actors (Kardam,2004), international governmental organizations, and some industrialized western governments through bilateral aid agencies.

Even though there may be powerful national women's movements that use CEDAW to strengthen their positions and hold states accountable, states are frequently hesitant to 'do' things if it requires budgets, staff, and targets. If the judges, the police, and the court system have not changed their behavior and are guided by a distinct set of standards, gender-sensitive laws may not be applied.

Moreover, even if laws are approved, women may not be aware of their rights, and even if they are, they may be impotent in the face of opposing social norms of gender that promote women's inferiority to males (Sultana, 2010). How can gender equality be "owned" at the national and local levels if the gender equality regime is primarily viewed as an externally imposed political agenda and CEDAW lacks clear and effective monitoring and compliance mechanisms? This needs the interpretation of nebulous and general global rules and ideas so that people can comprehend them (Andrew and Freeman, 2012). It also necessitates an appreciation and open discussion of opposing gender norms and identities, as well as rival concepts of 'gender equality' supported or promoted by various institutions (the legal system, the bureaucracy, the market, religious establishment, or kinship and family systems). Otherwise, there is a risk that states will continue to go through the motions of "doing something," no matter how little, in order to appease global monitoring committees and international aid organizations.

Constructivists contend that international life is social, as it is governed by the norms and laws that comprise social structures (Guzzini, 2000). The success of regimes, according to constructivists, is determined not just by external incentives but also by fundamental principles. These laws do not "explain" in the positivist sense, but they are the basis of all other phenomena. These structures can only reproduce as a result of the actions of knowing agents (Guzzini, 2005). Structures and agents cannot coexist in isolation.

1.4.2 GENDER AS A SOCIAL CONSTRUCT AND CONTESTED GENDER NORMS

A substantial body of feminist literature is predicated on the idea that interests and identities are socially formed (Karen, 2011). Feminist constructivists (Goertz and Mazur, 2008) dispute the notion that gender is inherent, unchanging, and based on biology, asserting instead that gender is a social construction. Then, gender identity becomes debatable. As a result, it permeates all levels of society, from the domestic to the international and global: social interaction enacts gendered scripts; social institutions establish gendered norms; and social communication follows gendered rules (Halpern and Jenkins, 2016). Thus, combining gender with a constructivist perspective in international relations yields a research agenda that can focus on contested norms such as human rights, or investigate how the concept of human rights may be based on a western notion of self, and how the public/private distinction has prevented domestic violence from being defined as a violation of human rights (Tickner J, 1992). Such a study agenda may investigate how gender identities are formed, contested, and negotiated within various institutions on a global and local scale.

In institutions such as marriage, the legal system, politics, and religion, a specific society may have varying and occasionally contradictory or complimentary gender norms (Dietrich et al, 2021). In a country like Turkey, where multiple traditions and worldviews coexist and where global influences undermine and transform local institutions, conflicting norms may be especially pertinent. According to some feminist social scientists, such dissonance can create space and opportunity, particularly if it coincides with material conditions that create an opening (Kardam,2017). Since all of these institutions are interconnected in society, changes in the gender relations or gender regime in one set of institutions can affect the gender relations or regimes in other sets of institutions. A constructivist method permits the investigation of contested norms, their interaction with one another, and the power relationships that legitimize those norms.

1.5 INTERNATIONAL FACILITATORS

A system of several factors, which influence women's representation in national parliaments, is represented by the introduction's remaining portion for depicting the features of WE and legislative representation (Strengthening women PP, 2016). By utilizing the international facilitator concept, the factors that optimistically sway women's participation together with representation in politics is evaluated, which is useful to address the women politicians' paucity.

In politics, women's engagement is contributed by those inputs as of the external environment, which enters into the political system. Governments continuously empathize with novel conditions and opportunities offered by the external environment (Bridging the digital gender divide, 2018). For coping with the international influences, they frequently change their gender policies (Sen & Ostlin, 2007). In the international environment, there were several changes caused by the Women's Movement (WM) and organizations, which have come out across the globe from the 1970s.

The enterprise of enormous women's organizations along with networks worldwide emerged in UN Decade for Women (1976–85). Thus, WPP has emerged. The women's organizations targeted the strategies, which maximized female representation in DM positions in the FWC (UNs, 1995) on Women in Beijing 1995. The states are stimulated for establishing quotas for women in politics by the Beijing Platform's call for assenting action gauges like the statutory quotas' obligation to deal with GI. By several international women's organizations, namely the SA Network for Political WE together with the Center for Asia-Pacific Women in Politics, other sources of international facilitators are depicted. In public DM, those organizations have aimed at the women's problem along with have endorsed activities to ameliorate the number of women into legislative bodies.

By deploying the usage of quotas like (a) constitutional, (b) electoral, or political party quotas, which guarantee women's access to DM institutions, women's presence in politics is maximized. There is a consensus among scholars that, on the represented women, gender-centric quotas could have a constructive along with great effect. For maximizing women's participation along with representation in elective along with appointive positions in public office, quota systems are the most effectual and expeditious affirmative action policies (Dahlerup, 2020). Several sorts of quotas raised unfavorable socioeconomic together with cultural conditions. Women's agendas are augmented to a greater priority level owing to the augmentation in the numbers of women in political DM positions. While ample women are in public office, one could expect that the political agenda will broaden along with encompass problems previously ignored by male-dominated policymaking bodies.

1.5.1 CONCEPTS OF LEADERSHIP IN PUBLIC RELATIONS

"A dynamic process, which includes an intricate blend of individual skills along with personal attributes, values, as well as behaviors, which always generate ethical together with effectual communication practice" is termed leadership (Sharma & Jain, 2013). (i) Individual characteristics, (ii) power associations, or impact on attitudes along with (iii) behaviors differ in approach relying on environmental factors. By environmental factors like broadcasting, reception of information, the growth of social media-centric communication, rapid-moving crises, along with modifying gender as well as generational dynamics, leadership's definitions are shaped constantly (Place & Winter, 2017).

1.5.2 GENDER GAP AMONG LEADERS IN PUBLIC RELATIONS

Women just take 20% of the senior leadership positions still even though the maximizing value is kept on "feminine" leadership styles along with they cover 75% jobs in the public relations industry. Besides, in huge public relations firms, women cover less than half of the executive committee positions; in addition, more than $100 million were made in global revenue since just '4' women lead public relations agencies. Regarding (a) leadership qualities, (b) leadership efficacy, or leadership preferences, new public relations scholarship has detected no considerable discrepancies betwixt men and women although women lack leadership presence.

1.6 WOMEN AND POLITICS IN GLOBAL PERSPECTIVE

Devoid of women's participation in the political system, a truthfully democratic and representative government can't be recognized. The actions of people who desire to influence or support the government and politics are termed the PP. PP could be conventional and unconventional (Logan, 2017).

Voting, operating for office, making offerings to candidates, or reporting members of Congress are the traditional methods that are widespread and broadly acknowledged. Unconventional participation is low broadly accepted as well as often contentious. Generally, it entails utilizing strategies, namely marching, boycotting, rejecting to follow laws, or protesting. Individuals along with groups have thrived or are unsuccessful in utilizing both kinds of participation.

People participate in politics for several reasons like,

- to prove support for the country;
- to attain a few merits for themselves;
- to influence broad public policy

Women must have the same rights as PP and exercise their rights fully in a democracy. The world of government and politics is dominated by men everywhere historically. In national legislatures, vote less, and women are less depicted; in addition, do not examine policies endorsed that address their requirements along with circumstances. Male dominates highly in parliament as other state structure does. Men generated parliament for men with some regard for women. Parliament came out as a crucial political institution along with integral organ of democratic government fashioned in western countries.

In the national parliament, France women's representation sustains much below that of a few developing nations such as (a) Uganda, (b) Tanzania, (c) Vietnam, together with Cuba in a few developed democratic countries namely the U.K., Switzerland, the US, as well as France. Similarly, betwixt countries, there were huge differences; for example, when weighed against Rwanda, Cuba, along with Bolivia in which female representation rates are the highest, the USA, and the UK has pretty low female participation rates in parliament (Ranked together with mapped which countries have the many women in parliament, 2017). In Latin America, (i) Bolivia, (ii) Cuba, along with (iii) Mexico are the '3' top '10' countries in 2019. Over years, Americans have seen a huge aggregate change.

1.6.1 GLOBAL WOMEN'S MOVEMENT

The central function of non-state actors in the spread of regimes is depicted by the literature on international regimes, especially from the cognitive viewpoint. In regime formation, the intellectual school deals a stronger role in transnational Social Movements (SM); in addition, the essential content of regime rules as well as why they thrive, are elucidated. 'Structural' along with 'intellectual' leadership in the GE norms' codification was found, together with promoted a collective understanding since the appearance of the global GE regime owes a plenty to the leadership of a global WM and its related NGOs. The individuals that transform power grounded on material resources as well as bargaining leverage are termed, structural leaders. The individuals who could utilize the ideas' power for shaping institutional bargaining and for initiating the partaker's view about accessible options are termed, intellectual leaders. Each hue in the notion rainbow – (a) secular, (b) religious, (c) radical, (d) conservative, (e) grassroots as well as elite – was mobilized by several women. They were local, national, regional, along with international. To go through arranging, lobbying, together with legislating problems at every level, their target was to bring women jointly to distribute information, resources, along with strategies as well as to engender other spaces.

Via policy advocacy, global women's networks molded the global GE regime. Particular skills and strategies are required by advocacy: for supporting one's claims or preferred policy modifications, 'expert' information grounded on academic research has to be collected; structuring one's viewpoints in ways, which policy-makers would understand; recognizing along with accepting that one has to work within the organization to modify it (UNs, 2018). Knowing how to dispute a case along with exhibiting tangible information to back arguments together with make the case a robust one as well as the political adeptness to lobby, construct alliances, together with influence decision-makers is encompassed in advocacy.

1.6.2 EMPOWERING WOMEN IS A LONG-TERM AGENDA OF THE REGION'S SOCIAL TRANSFORMATION

For grouping, the ASEAN Economic Community (EC) launch in December 2015 was indicated as a crucial occasion. Nevertheless, the detrimental effect will be caused to women across South- East Asia by the regional economic integration (Hakura et al, 2016). Since women are not located in those sectors that are positioned to develop, a significant study was reported by the ASEAN Secretariat, which designed the depicted gender effects of the ASEAN EC (World investment report, 2020).

Hence, the prevailing substantial gender inequalities will be exacerbated by the ASEAN EC. One among the measures, which record data for almost all '10' ASEAN nations, is the GI Index (GII) that was generated by the UNs Development Program. In attainment betwixt women and men across Reproductive Health (RH), empowerment, along with economic positions, it is a complex gauge of inequality. The occurrence of GIs across South-East Asia is highlighted by the GII. Major ASEAN countries cluster at the bottom-end of the rankings, with Cambodia, placed lowest at 112 of 159 nations.

Other inequalities, which are harder to constantly gauge across countries, are not encompassed in GII while considering the starker gaps betwixt women and men; starker gaps betwixt women and men. When analogized to men, the women are surlier to be vulnerable to deployment and to be contributing unpaid labor via domestic work. Gender-centric violence is experienced by 40% of women in South-East Asia (UNs, 2020).

Several actors have gathered around the program of authorizing women regarding the constant and invasive gaps betwixt women along with men beside the projected negative effects of the ASEAN- EC. Via several projects, ASEAN, donors, NGOs, together with organizations in South-East Asia are supporting this target.

Concept of Power and empowerment: definitions, meanings, and applications

WE might be a litigious design; however, feminist economists along with scholars of Gender as well as Development share that,

(a) To make planned life choices in GI, WE encompass their attainment of resources maximized agency, along with the capability.

(b) For acquiring change via Collective Action (CA), WE encompass the enhancement of awareness or 'the power within' and the direct exercise of power; those processes merge in the systemic or structural conversion of women's status.

(c) WE are multidimensional along with takes place at various levels like at the individual, in interpersonal associations, as well as via group mobilization or CA.

For altering power structures, the accent on entrepreneurship along with self-sufficiency in the typical development policy agenda along with associated economics research fails. Depoliticization of the collective change schedule is caused by the techniques. Authorizing women for progress aim as well as stress on gauging empowerment 'findings' has depicted empowerment 'operationalized' as a programmatic goal along with intervention design.

Feminist fears that the technocratic turn in 'empowerment' uncovered its unavoidably transgressive along with political content (Batliwala 2007), not just in the SA context. We have constrained huge overall development discussions to narrow discussions on women's Economic Participation (EP), even though those are significant by the accent regarding paid work along with regulate of income in development literature together with programming (Buvinic & Nichols, 2014). For transformations required at the individual, interpersonal together with collective levels, women's economic contribution is not adequate.

1.6.3 POLITICAL OPPORTUNITIES AND CRITICAL JUNCTURES FOR WOMEN'S EMPOWERMENT

With education, gendered norms might commute slowly. The generations evolve as professional together with working women in social spaces grounded on routine. When analogized to Bangladesh, India, or Pakistan, women's Labor Force Participation (LFP) rates are greater in Sri Lanka along with Nepal; however, women were not present in education along with paid work on a considerably huge scale (Nazneen et al, 2019). The work, which requires deep attention, has a long process of modification. For representing agendas, which might have no possibility of success, various contributions highlight extra more periodic type of modification, determining vital moments or serious junctures, which engendered political breaks for activists. For opposing WE, a target was made on the state as an actor along with its function in constructing space. In feminist literature, the state's role along with the WM is a greatly argued problem. Thus, recently, the state's role has come under issue. The state's regulatory power as well as ability to offer the most marginalized citizens is reduced due to the amount of corporate authority, especially those of social media firms, and the rollback of state provisioning (Burke & Stephens, 2017). Since laws and civil liberties are shortened known to maximize security pressure from fanatic forces along with the augment of religious, populist forces that maintain the state's securitization, various states have as well acquired power over common people's lives. The WM's weak existence is depicted; thus, they demand GE, which doesn't have problems with the SA states. Nevertheless, in making a few yields by utilizing the state machinery, WMs are victories. It mobilizes against state control at other times.

How the WM has wielded public interest litigation as a stratagem along with courts as places for recourse on guaranteeing equal rights in Pakistan are recognized by Khan, Malkani, along with Yousuf on the Pakistan problem (Aziz & Sicangco, 2021). For highlighting women's rights as vital problems and for educating the wider public, the WM has wielded court cases. Sexual as well as reproductive rights, PP, fortification against discriminatory laws, along with socio-economic rights are the '4' main areas in which the Pakistani WM made development. Centered on the executive, conventional authorities, together with the military, the state isn't monolithic; in addition, by the states' other parts, the state could be employed for countering excesses. Incentives and interests, which wander as of the political elite, might be encompassed by the state officials or agencies. For attaining justice, the VM's capability for navigating interests along with recommending interests, which are considered counter-cultural or marginal, sustains a vital pathway.

1.7 WOMEN'S EMPOWERMENT THEORY

Maximizing women's economic and social standing via raised education, employment opportunities, and political representation is termed WE (Bayeh, 2016). Engendering a climate where women have equivalent access to along with control over resources as males is the aim. WE are termed as providing women the power to partake in social, economic, along with political activities on their terms and with total autonomy. For the empowerment concept, the mechanics of lawful power-sharing, distribution, and redistribution are significant.

The capability of surpassing the personal along with social hurdles is offered for women by empowerment (Cornwall, 2016). Negotiating power in household DM is one among the women's autonomy's negotiating power (Bloom et al, 2000). Empowerment helps women's spiritual, social, political, psychological, and economic strength (Sohail, 2014). Empowered women raise confidence on account of their greater capabilities. Providing women, the necessary rights and responsibilities for them to befall self-sufficient along with enjoy the same advantages as men are termed, WE. In every society's organization and structure, women could fight gender-centric discrimination.

A bottom-up procedure of modifying gender power relations by maximizing women's awareness of their subordination along with strengthening their capability to challenge it is WE (Stamarski & Hing, 2015). Several topics like economic independence, efficient communication, distinct thinking, etc, are covered by it. Thinking freely, making decisions on their own, having freedom of movement, and being free from every form of abuse and violence are the qualifications of an empowered woman. The women's capability for making decisions in the social, economic, and political spheres is termed empowerment. Women's indulgence of socio-psycho-cultural and political injustices they might undergo in their families and communities are raised by empowerment. As per the freedom, women who are empowered could choose and act. In the literature, there are several interpretations of "WE". Some of them are as follows,

- Via the growth of choice and action, maximized women's authority, control over the resources along with decisions affects their lives.
- For making decisions in the social, economic, and political spheres, women are empowered.
- For supporting their well-being, challenge prevailing conventions and culture.
- Guarantee that she has equal admittance to resources and that she has more opportunities in society.

To grant DM power or autonomy, compulsion or accountability should not be used. Figure 1.2, the UNESCO report defines WE as follows (Stantilin, 2000):

- Possessing the potential to make decisions about their own lives
- Having admittance to related knowledge and resources for making informed decisions.
- Having several options from which to choose (rather than just yes/no or either/or).

- The capability to be aggressive when making group decisions.
- Having a positive outlook about one's ability to change.
- The ability to add novel abilities, which will help one's personal or collective power grow.
- Demonstrated ability to influence others' perceptions via democratic means.
- Participating in the never-ending and self-initiated process of growth and transformation.

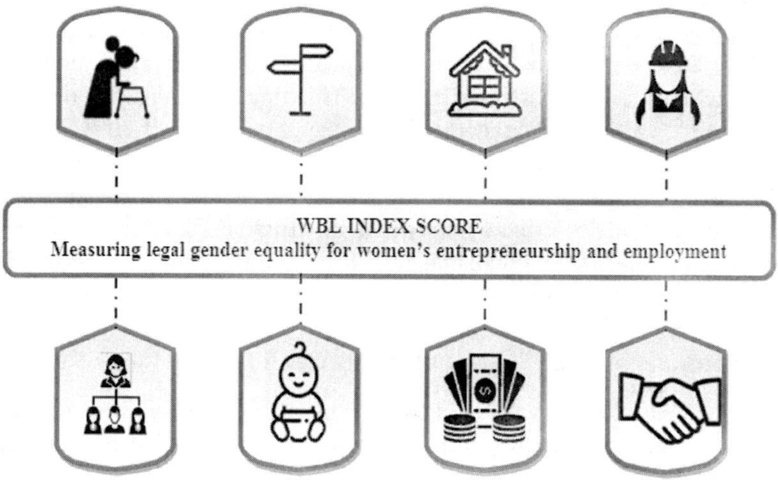

Figure 1.2: WBL Index Score

1.7.1 DIFFERENT DIMENSIONS OF WOMEN'S EMPOWERMENT

There is no single metric, which can be used to appraise how far women have progressed and how far they still have to go to attain GE (Rajput & Singh, 2022). To modify cultural norms in support of women's rights, recognizing the various aspects of WE is critical for developing policies that promote GE and begin. Economically, socially and culturally, legally, politically, and psychologically are the '5' by which WE can be measured.

Economic self-sufficiency: Economic WE require equal access to economic resources and earning ability. Since they are underpaid, women's contributions to home economic activities are always overlooked; thus, they do not have access to the money generated by these activities. Women who work for a living are the mere ones who are counted. For Economic Empowerment (EE), such unpaid activity should be appraised and recognized since it affords them some financial freedom and DM capacity. In participation in economic activities, access to savings along with credit, and control over income as well as productive assets namely land, business, together with industry, women's EE manifests itself (Andrea & Marie 2005).

Employment, asset ownership, and financial DM should be given equal importance. Regarding the total female population and the overall worker population, it is a proportion of women in paid employment.

- Attaining senior or DM positions in the organization
- Taking employment as a career choice rather than by force or owing to family circumstances
- Acquiring family support while managing work-life balance like several women who are motivated to pursue (not forced) their career by family members
- Taking advantage of service benefits and given equal opportunities in promotions
- Having complete control over their income and being involved in family financial decisions like investments made with the family's income.

For enhancing the living conditions and overall well-being, women's employment is significant. To protest, enter the labor force, along with have an equal opportunity to reach positions of economic power as a result of EE, women gain financial independence, family respect, confidence, and courage. Industrialized countries are permitted to embark on a path of faster growth since women's involvement rates have increased (The Economist, 2006). If they work in low-paying, distress-inducing jobs women's economic well-being and welfare might not enhance (Srivastava & Srivastava, 2009).

Empowerment on a social and cultural level: There is no discrimination against women, they have autonomy over their bodies, they are free from sexual and domestic abuse, they have access to family planning facilities, they have more visibility in social areas, and cultural norms, which place women in a subservient position to men, are changing (Kim et al, 2018). Social and cultural empowerment is required by women not just to have control over their bodies, but also to have access to education to improve their life. Creating an environment in which her dignity as a human being is valued is required for women's social empowerment. Regarding society's male members, in particular, it is the eradication of women's submissive status.

- Maximized sex ratio in society
- Augmented proportion of women in education and areas of work regarded male- dominated or not for women
- Number of women-headed families
- Women in influential positions in SMs
- Number of women able to choose on family planning and child spacing

Legal empowerment: Women's legal rights understanding and knowledge are maximized since legal empowerment creates a framework for legislation. By leveraging the court system to effect change from the top down, this permits women to mobilize for stronger women's rights laws.

- The Child Marriage Restraint Act of 1929
- The Factory Act of 1948 -Hindu Succession Act of 1956
- Immoral Traffic (Prevention) Act of 1956
- The Dowry Prohibition Act of 1961
- The Maternity Benefit Act of 1961
- Medical Termination of Pregnancy (MTP)Act of 1971
- Equal Remuneration Act of 1976

Political empowerment: In WE, maximizing women's political engagement and representation is a significant step. Women's participation in SMs via Non-Governmental Organizations (NGOs), active participation in local political fronts, the right to vote, awareness of along with the capability to participate in the political system, and depiction in local as well as national governments are included in it. By the 73rd along with 74th constitutional Amendment Acts of 1993, women's effective involvement in Panchayat Raj institutions and municipalities is ensured; hence, special reservations are made for women. Women are provided a fresh sense of empowerment and self- assurance by the blockade to women's participation at the grassroots level. For augmenting women's participation in politics, Political Empowerment (PE) ensures that the Gender Gap (GG) in women's engagement in all political matters is narrowed from the top. In the democratic institutional system, GE is a precondition for women's successful involvement. Gandhi stated that 'as long as women in India don't partake in public life; there can be no redemption for the country,'. Nevertheless, women's representation in politics is sometimes near. Because of their inadequate awareness of the law as well as social concerns, their male partners mislead them. From the women's reservations' establishment in politics, women's representation has become mandatory. But women represent but work as per their husbands or other male family members, defeating the entire objective (Dahlerup & Freidenvall, 2005).

- Women's political knowledge like the names of local councilors, MLAs, and MPs
- Women's representation in local councils'/ DM bodies as a percentage of total seats
- Women's percentage in Local Government (LG) DM positions
- Women's Percentage in the local civil service
- Percentage of women/men registered as voters/ percentage of qualified women/men who vote
- Percentage of women/men in senior/junior DM positions inside unions
- Percentage of union members who are women/men

Psychological empowerment: It has been scientifically proven that even though women have their physical weaknesses; they are psychologically stronger than men. Psychological empowerment of women is caused by the acknowledgment of women's rights along with their inclusion in society. It is the outcome of their EE, participation in DM, and level of DM freedom, as well as their freedom of movement. The characteristics of psychological empowerment are (1) self-awareness, (2) high self-esteem, (3) self-confidence, (4) courage, (5) perception of own rights, (6) privileges, (7) roles, (8) responsibilities, (9) power of self-determination, (10) positive attitude, risk-taking ability, (12) the capability to face daily challenges, (13) acquisition knowledge and novel ideas and skills, (14) great relief as of mental stress and anxiety, and (15) leading the confidence to face discrimination or criticism is provided to women by Psychological empowerment along with facing discrimination or criticism and the strength to stick to their convictions if they are correct.

- The number of married women or widows pursuing higher education, undergoing a training program, or taking paid employment
- The number of women who have shown the courage to go forward after being victimized

- The number of women who have set their career after facing rejection from their husband or family

'4' important components of human progress in the Human Development Report (HDR-1995) are WE, productivity, equity, and sustainability. The GEM along with the Gender Development Index (GDI) are the '2' novel indices offered by the report for measuring WE. For taking merits of life's opportunities, the GDI is concerned with the augmenting women's capabilities; the GEM is concerned with the application of those capabilities. In paid work, GEM considers women's engagement. In DM positions, the contribution to national income, as well as their representation is regarded. The GEM complements the Human Development Index (HDI) by adding another measurement metric to gauge development. To access a country's social and economic progress, the HDI is a hugely wielded composite index. The country's Life Expectancy (LE), EA, and income are integrated into it. This was engendered for measuring development as more than only economic progress and income growth, but also as improvements in people's lives. Since development encompasses a wide range of other criteria that can be used to assess human well- being, the HDI is limited (Dahlerup 2007).

At three different levels, WE can be studied and measured, each with its own set of indicators:

- Individual
- Community
- National

WE at each of these levels lead to their empowerment at the following level.

(a) On an individual or family basis

- In key DM processes, equal entrance to resources and participation are necessary.
- To all of the family's resources, like money for school supplies or a school bag, and the ability to choose which school to attend, both the girl and the boy in the family have equal access. Likewise, women in the family should have equal rights to family resources as their male counterparts.
- Personal liberty like freedom of movement and choice.
- The level to what a woman exercises control over her reproductive functions; in addition, detects her family size.

- The extent to which a woman has control over how her earnings are spent.
- To pursue her personal goals, the opportunity is required to forge her own identity and receive unwavering support from her family. For instance, a woman should get unconditional support from her husband and other family members if she wishes to continue her education, (both financially and in terms of housework) until she achieves the necessary degree of education.

(b) There are women's groups at the community, institution, or organization level; monies are allocated to women as well as women's projects; women have equal opportunity in DM and representation in policy choices.

- To preserve their safety and legal and social rights, permanent cells are present.
- Contribution in community programs, business ventures, politics, and cultural events

(c) Public awareness campaigns to safeguard her social along with political rights on a national level.

In the overall national development plan, women's representatives are included. Implementation of women's welfare programs and policies; and appreciation of women's contributions on an equal footing with men that is equal weighting in reward and award distribution (Shah 1975).

1.8 THE NATIONAL POLICY FOR WOMEN'S ADVANCEMENT (NPWA)

For women's progress, the Ministry of Women along with Children Affairs engendered a national policy, after a comprehensive consultation with various women's organizations, HR, along with civil society representatives. Over the past 30 years 194, it was grounded on the Beijing Platform for Action (BPA) along with the hard-won victories of the Bangladeshi WM; in February 1997 it was approved at the 1st meeting of the National Council for Women Development (NCWD) along with declared on March 8, 1997, International Women's Day. Eliminating inequalities in private and public life is the key goal.

The Women's Advancement Policy, amongst other things, warrantees' equality of women along with men in every sphere of private as well as public life, broadcasts suitable gauges for eradicating discrimination against women, espouses the spirit of HR and liberties in every sphere of women's lives; in addition, guarantees to bring equality in the economic, social, together with cultural sectors subsequent to the principle of opportunity equality. For conducting campaign programs aimed at cheering women to participate actively in politics, NGOs like women's organizations are encouraged by the art 8 of the NPWA. For sustaining straight elections in expanded reserved seats in the National Parliament, it was initiated after the present term ends in 2001. Under Article 9 of the NPWA like Bangladesh high commissioners, university grants commissions, planning commissions, and the judiciary, NPWA Women is appointed to high posts. NPWA 1997 initiated every essential step to appoint women to 30% of positions at every DM level namely policy- making, to guarantee their equal along with complete participation, grounded on UN Economic along with Social Council recommendations. The sickness is prevented along with the supply of safe drinking water is warrantee since Article 10 of the NPWA makes sure rights to health services, and lowers the infant and Maternal Mortality Ratio (MMR). For working employees, and elderly women, the residential accommodation plans under Art 11 of the NPWA are for the construction of hostels and dormitories. In agriculture, fishery, livestock, along with forestry, NPWA Article 12 Encourages and gives equal chances for women; in news, and other programs, and stresses specific opportunities for troubled women, asserts women's role in the media along with gender-sensitive coverage of women.

Nevertheless, the essential principles of equality of women along with men ensured by CEDAW and the Bangladesh constitution like the provision of women's constitutional rights in place of equal rights in the formulation along with execution of economic policy in the NPWA of 2004 are violated as subsequent governments made specific changes to the NPWA of 1997 in 2004. Full together with equal opportunity as well as control over the (i) right to land, (ii) earned property, inheritance, (iv) property, (v) credit, and (vi) technology are offered by NPWA 1997 that are vital to women's EE; in addition, to put these rights into practice, essential novel laws are enacted, however, complete and equal opportunity along with authority over only earned property, etc, are offered by NPWA 2004.

1.9 DEMOGRAPHIC PROFILE OF SOUTH ASIA

The SAARC members are the '7' countries; in addition, it has a merged population of about 1.5 billion people. The below-table depicts the population distribution. Different proportions of the population in each country, as well as a different amount of the gross domestic product, is accounted for by agricultural and animal husbandry. Islam is the main religion in Pakistan, Bangladesh, and the Maldives regarding religion. Hinduism is the dominant religion in India and Nepal. Buddhists make up the majority of the population in Bhutan and Sri Lanka. When weighed against roughly 2 years in the other countries, the Maldives and Sri Lanka have an average of 4.5-5.5 years of schooling along with considerable percentages of female illiteracy. Each country has a low-income economy. The population of SAARC countries doubled between 1950 and 1990. 3.63 percent was the annual growth on average. India accounted for more than 75% of the SAARC population in 1990. In 1950, 1970, 1980, and1990, the fall of Sri Lanka's, India's, Bangladesh's, and Maldives and Nepal's fall began. There is no evidence of population reduction in Bhutan. Owing to the lack of habitable land, Bhutan has a low population density. The highest population density is in Bangladesh subsequent to the Maldives, where Male is home to 26% of the entire population. In every country, rural areas were home to more than 68 percent of the population in 1990. The demographic shifts projected by 2025 differ by country.

Each country has above 35 percent children and 40-48 percent dependents except Sri Lanka. Until 1990, males outnumbered females. Only Sri Lanka and Bhutan had a gender balance in 1990. Sri Lanka has the highest number of single males and females, as well as the lowest proportion of ever-married girls aged 15-19 years. In 1990, just Sri Lanka had fertility that was near to replacement (2.5). Fertility rates in India ranged from 3.9 to 5.9 in Bhutan.

1.10 OVERVIEW OF SOUTH ASIAN POLITICS

With the availability of '2' nuclear-armed along with hostile states violent intra-state ethnic conflicts, south Asia is the globe's volatile areas. Grounded on (i) class, (ii) gender, (iii) religion, language, (v) ethnicity, along with (vi) caste, states share assured chief features like (a) post-colonial state creation, (b) centralized governments, (c) socioeconomic inequalities, (d) intra state divisions as well as conflicts (State of the world's indigenous peoples, 2009).

How several governments or opposition movements in Northeast, Southeast, along with South Asia have guided or sustained be owned by women is incredible. In SA countries like (i) Bangladesh, (ii) India, (iii) Pakistan, along with (iv) Sri Lanka in which women have whispered posts as Prime Minister (PM) or president enormous times or are the 2nd ones in line, the female politicians' phenomenon is predominant. (a) Sheikh Hasina Wajed, Begum Khaleda Zia (Bangladesh), (b) Sonia Gandhi (India), (c) Wan Azizah Wan Ismail (Malaysia), (d) Aung San Suu Kyi (Burma),

(e) Benazir Bhutto (Pakistan), (f) Megawati Sukarnoputri (Indonesia), (g) Corazon C. Aquino, Gloria Macapagal-Arroyo (Philippines), along with Chandrika Kumaratunga (Sri Lanka) are the famous top female politicians in Asia who are alive still (Huis et al, 2017). As everyone was confirmed in their formal or informal position via elections, all those women have the democratic legitimization generally that is a recognizing activity. Due to their descent as of influential families, a rather classic occurrence in Asian politics, those women have expanded their existing position as presidents, PMs, or opposition leaders. By gaining the political position in a hereditary-like way they shared a dynastic descent since they are daughters or widows of previous government or opposition leaders.

Asia's women politicians are depicted at the top by the analysis of socio-political and biographical characteristics and are rather a deviant case of general female PP (Thompson 2007). They are featured as traditional along with non-egalitarian as well as even misogynist grounded on behaviors to women in politics since those women reached top political office in socio-political contexts. Democratic legitimation is available in these women instead of their political systems. However, due to their descent from influential families, all of those have gained their existing position, which is a common phenomenon in Asian politics. Similar patterns concerning political along with social biographies such as descent as of the national political along with societal elite ((i) political dynasty, (ii) wealthy backdrop, together with (iii) university education, frequently at international elite universities), a lofty societal rank, which ends up in publicly attributed proficiency along with legitimacy to guide, and a group of satisfactory behaviors along with accessible space for agency different as of their female colleagues in other sections of community, are depicted by the women politicians who are under review.

Women Political Leaders (WPL) isn't frequently raised to power 'in times of social or political distresses in evolving countries. During social and political turmoil in Bangladesh, Khaleda Zia along with Sheikh Hasina was raised to power. In other Asian countries namely the Philippines, Sri Lanka, Indonesia, India, and Pakistan, the women leaders like Corazon Aquino, Sirimavo Bandaranaike, Megawati Sukarnoputri, Indira Gandhi and Sonia Gandhi, together with Benazir Bhutto attained higher positions.

1.11 WOMEN'S EMPOWERMENT IN SOUTH ASIA

Debates are located in the power in the structures of class, caste, geography, along with gender norms and also relations, which shape women's choices since the WE in South Asia together amounts to a more political discussion of WE (Abbas & Muneer, 2019). The power across scales is traced; also, in a few instances over time. About WE in South Asia, '4' key interventions are made by the articles into a debate with the conversation of each other along with the wider literature they reference. Initially, a few mechanisms are specified clearly via which the paid works merge as a significant site of resists for WE. Since the habitually low-paid, low-quality jobs various SA women could get are life-changing in themselves, those don't evolve. Actually, in securing households against poverty or vulnerability, they are paid poorly. Paid work provides more; however, not basically improved choices for various women in poverty. When weighed against compatibility with women's own health along with wellbeing, such paid work frequently demands several women's resources along with capacities. A few paid workers such as garment factory jobs in Bangladesh are dangerous. Even in fast-growing South Asia, these women value such jobs and show not their empowering potential although the revoltingly restricted choices various face. It spreads around women's home lives, combined interests as workers, as well as general concerns as women in the public space, which positions paid work at the centre of women's authority it doesn't work hugely. Women are pressed to 'balance' their household with their work-related duties, which requisites the work's renegotiation at home. The routine anguish of Sexual Harassment (SH) is suffered by various SA women at or going to work; in addition, owing to the public presence, the threat or actuality of aggression is faced by them. For arranging the basic rights of pay, decent working situations, along with protection at work via trade unions, which are intended together executed by as well as for male workers, women workers suffer. It is how women could arrange along with construct relations with other radical actors around those questions, which could be understood that the mechanisms together with conditions where the paid work could authorize women across the scales as well as levels of power that stuff. Repositioning power as a political instead of individualized economic force in the process of WE is the 2nd intrusion. In molding the policies, which own women's lives, state political power matters hugely. For reframing debates around women's rights or GE along with exploiting the political chances that emerge, whether and how the WM and its allies are successful in capturing that power relies on its abilities. However, counter-forces have materialized against (a) women's unionization, (b) public mobility, (c) occupation of 'good' men's jobs, along with common absence of subordination to patriarchal precepts since power is a protean force, as well as activists have pressured for women's rights along with resources. Devoid of a recognizing backlash it creates; in addition, the series of contention that engenders advance together with recoil in the WM, the WE evaluation is incomplete: Action produces a reaction.

The endeavors fighting efficacy were depicted recently; however, in Asia and the Pacific, there is still room for development. Across the world's '8' region, the GG has developed at various levels along with speeds, which was started by the World Economic Forum's (WEF) Global GG (GGG) Index 2021 (the better will be the GE if the higher the percentage is). The GG in EP along with opportunity sustain the 2nd largest of the '4' main gaps with 58.3% still; in addition, it is expected for another 267.6 years for closing that gap amongst every GG like EP and opportunity, EA, health, and survival, as well as PE. with a narrow GG of 73.5% in EP along with opportunity after North America (75.3%), Central Asia and Eastern Europe is ranked 2nd subsequent to Western Europe (70.0%). With 69.6%, East Asia and the Pacific are ranked 4th. 33.8% is the hugest GG evident in South Asia, almost 1/4 point below the world average, which is depicted in Table 1.1.

Table 1.1: Regional Performance 2021, by Sub index (%)

Regions	Economic participation and opportunity	Education	Political Empowerment
Western Europe	70.6	99.8	43.8
North America	75.3	100.0	33.4
Latin America and the Caribbean	64.2	99.7	27.1
Eastern Europe and Central Asia	73.5	99.7	14.2
East Asia and the pacific	69.6	97.6	13.5
Sub-Saharan Africa	66.1	84.5	20.8
South Asia	33.8	93.3	28.1
The Middle East and North Africa	40.9	94.2	12.1
Average	58.3	95.0	21.8

1.12 GENDER DISPARITY IN SOUTH ASIA

From DM, women in South Asia are mainly excluded, having constrained access to as well as to control over resources, are constrained in their movement and are commonly threatened by male relatives. Sons are viewed as having economic, social, or religious value; while owing to the dowry system, daughters are usually seen as a financial obligation. When weighed against affluent countries, gender imbalance is at its worst in SA countries. huge differences in GI within countries, such as across Indian states or else Pakistan provinces require more local explanations when GGs in health along with education outcomes are higher on average in South Asia when analogized in other countries. In those countries, the amount of GG differs by region.

GDI, GEM, LE, Adult Literacy Rate (ALR), projected earned income, and HDI rank is the '6' parameters that will be discussed by the researchers for demonstrating the extent of the GG in South Asia. In Sri Lanka and Nepal, the overall HDI rank for the south ranges from 99th and 142nd. India that makes up 85 percent of South Asia ranks 128th on the HDI up from 105th in 2000. On the GDI, India ranked 112 in 2005. Regarding gender empowerment, the '3' Muslim countries like the Maldives, Bangladesh, and Pakistan ranked top. 0.97 is the female to the male ALR of Sri Lanka that is considerably higher when analogized to the other countries. Females have a LE of 63.3 years in India that is significantly less than in Sri Lanka in which females have a LE of 75 years that is equal to industrialized countries. As earned income for women in Sri Lanka was 2193 USD in 1999, compared to USD 1195 for Indian women, for improvement in all of the above characteristics, earned income of women appears to be favourable. The SW in South Asia, except for Sri Lanka, is not so excellent on many fronts when analogized to women born in industrialized nations. Gender stereotyping is caused in South Asia by pre-existing gender conventions and attitudes.

Women are less likely to seek appropriate and early disease treatment because of the existing GI.

Nevertheless, the burden of disease, morbidity, health-seeking behaviour, social and economic causes, and the quality of care offered to women, among other things, are not well recorded in South Asia, the frequency with which such care is necessary. Further explanation on a local level is required for the gender disparity between states and provinces within the area. Over 97 percent of the population is required in South Asia, India, Bangladesh, and Pakistan; while, India accounts for 85 percent of the region. Thus, India is chosen to concentrate on as it has considerable internal disparities.

1.13 ANALYSIS OF WOMEN EMPOWERMENT IN SOUTH ASIAN COUNTRIES (INDIA, BANGLADESH, AND SRI-LANKA)

"GI" is the main problem of human beings, particularly for women's development. Since economic liberalization, women have done key developments, yet, they don't have similar opportunities (Rubery & Koukiadaki, 2016). In many developing and underdeveloped countries, GI is still a huge issue. A chief source of inequity is the less accessibility of opportunities for women. For the expansion of women's abilities and their liberty of selection, numerous development dimensions, like health, education, representation in politics, the labour market, etc., have been utilized for women's discrimination with negative consequences.

The difference in opportunities and contribution of males and females in development is implied as GIs. Measuring GI globally and offering a solution for the upliftment of the female situation in society regarding men at large is the reason behind the construction of GII. For gauging the position of women in 159 countries, the GII was utilized; it gauges GIs in main fields of Human Development (HD). To critically examine the policies for WE and proffer options to re-alter the policy, GII aids for the women's betterment. Centered on '3' dimensions: RH of women, WE, along with Participation in Women in the Labor Market, GII is created.

Two indicators describe RH:

- MMR
- Adolescent birth rate

Two indicators describe Empowerment:

- Female parliamentary seat occupancy
- ALR in secondary education

1.13.1 WOMEN EMPOWERMENT IN INDIA

On account of the religion, Indian culture orally admitted the women's adoration because their religious practices glorify women as a creator or the ones who give them life as well as adore them (Abbas, 2019). Also, Manu Shastra, a religious book, stated that God feels joy when women have been honored. However, this exalts the status of females in society is not exercised, along with restraint of women continues in kind of sati, female infanticide, devadasi system, along with child marriages in several underdeveloped regions of India. Nevertheless, owing to active HR, international organizations, NGOs, and the diffusion of education, opportunities were unlocked for women at the end of the twentieth century. Even the Constitution of India, a sacred document, interprets the women's protection under Article 15. State lawmakers are authorized by clause 3 of Article 15 to construct special provisions to safeguard women.

WE opportunities are explicated in articles 16, 23, 39, and 42. India, the largest in South Asia, has only 12% of women's representation in parliament, which is lesser than the global average of 22%. The Women Reservation Bill is still pending in the parliament, which was put forward fifteen decennia before which women had 30% seats in the parliament (Abbas & Muneer, 2019).

It is essential to safeguard their rights and elevate their position to a social class to facilitate women for self-contained and confidence. Hence, the Government of India (GoI) has novel legislations that offer security to protect women like the National Commission for Women Act (1990), which check all the matters associated with the legal rights of women, i.e., the Protection of Women from Domestic Violence Act (2005) along with Sexual Harassment of Women at Work Place Act (2013) (Singla & Tulsyan, 2020). Numerous activities were done via workshops, conferences, and public meetings to increase awareness regarding WE and to boost their social position.

Feminist organizations emerged in 1991, and they began their endeavors in Bombay under the term "Stree Muktisanghtan□, in Pune "Purogaminstree Sanghtan" and Delhi "Socialist Women Group", along with "Stree Sanghtan" elevated their voices for women. Several women, namely (a) K. Beddi, (b) Y. Kookhay, Bechandri Pal, (c) Kalpana Chawla, (d) P.T. Usha, (e) Aroondhaty Roy, et cetera, have contributed commendably in diverse sectors are from India. As their status is observed from the developmental viewpoint, the GoI has created an efficient approach to reinforce WE in society. "Mahila Kosh Yojna□, Training and Employment Plans for Women, and "Rashtriy Mahila Kosh" are a few of the initiatives taken by the Indian government for WE, and these are to develop self-employment prospects and increase self-belief amongst women to admit social along with economic transformation together with it improve economic efficiency by offering finance in diverse sectors to women. Furthermore, some of them are the (i) Rajiv Gandhi Scheme for Empowerment of Adolescent Girls, (ii) Central Social Welfare Board, (iii) Indira Gandhi Matritva Sahyog Yojana, along with (iv) Swadhar, which generate Empowerment Opportunity (EO) for women's growth as well as self-help groups with financial support for women.

1.13.2 WOMEN EMPOWERMENT IN BANGLADESH

Since the independence of following GE via different development agendas along with government and non-government institutions, Bangladesh has encompassed the majority of the Muslim populace.

Bangladesh is far superior at exhibiting women's status when weighed against other SA countries. The Constitution of Bangladesh has clearly stated the WE's status that guarantees women's rights. Women's contribution in every level of life is protected by Article 10. Equal opportunities and eradication of socio-economic discrimination are ensured by Article 19. Next, the protection of fundamental rights for women is corroborated by articles 17, 18, 27, 28, and 29. Women are free to politically partaking, along with offering reserved seats for women are mentioned in article 65 (Report, 2016). Converting Bangladesh into a middle-income nation by 2021 (called Vision 2021) was the goal set by the Bangladesh government development plan of 2011-2015 (Rahman & Siddiqui, 2015) that regarded women's involvement in political together with economic activities with WE as one of the major determinants of transformation. Women's contribution to the economic activities of Bangladesh is aiding to boost the nation's economy. About 65%, 22%, and 13.32% are their contributions to the agriculture field, service sectors, and industry as labour, respectively. The garment industry is the main contribution of women, i.e., they comprise over 80% of the industry's labors.

1.13.3 WOMEN EMPOWERMENT IN SRI LANKA

With respect to the high literacy rates of women, Sri Lanka is deemed to be one of the most advanced of the SA nations. Because of its prolonged civil conflict along with for electing the world's 1st woman PM, Ms. Sirimavo Bandaranaike, in 1960, Sri Lanka acquired world glory. When weighed against the other women in the SA areas, Sri Lankan females have relished more liberty and independence. Article 12 of the Constitution of Sri Lanka has acknowledged women's protection and their equality, and it authorized equal protection of the law and outlawed prejudice centered on religion along with caste. Also, it guaranteed unique benefits for women, as well as this organized affirmative state activities. Liberty from cruel treatment is offered by article 11. Sri Lanka has espoused the Women Charter, which is the state's major policy statement under Article 16 with respect to women's rights. This charter is a "Bill of Rights" for women, which ensures (a) political along with civil rights, (b) the right to education as well as training, (c) the right to economic activity along with advantages, (d) the right to protection as of social bias as well as Gender Based Violence (GBV) by accomplishing GE (Research Directorate, 1993) (Staniland, 2020). The government of Sri Lanka is taking definite gauges, namely the endorsement of structural reforms along with legislative reforms in the law enforcement tool to address Violence Against Women (VAW) for achieving these rights. Likewise, the Ministry of Child Development and Women

Affairs, "the Women's Bureau of Sri Lanka", together with "The National Committee on Women" is the state institutions that are running to protect women's rights and verify their empowerment.

1.14 CHALLENGES STILL FACING WOMEN IN ASIA

The SA area has turned out to be a core of interest in discussions of several social and political thinkers. A lot of concentration is given to the problems associated with the WE's status, and South Asia can't escape as of it. The focus will be given to the comparative investigation of WE in South Asia in this research regarding Bangladesh, India, and Sri Lanka. In a few Asian countries, women can access commanding positions, but that doesn't indicate they are free from impediments. Female politicians encounter partialities and double standards. Several battles have been fought by women to be regarded as political leaders. Owing to the sex to which they are designated at birth, their abilities are frequently questioned. For instance, Tsai Ing-Wen, the president of Taiwan, contested for the presidency in 2016, and her political party allies questioned her capability to be a president and a commander-in-chief since she belongs to the sex that wears skirts. Asian women should have more credentials to display that they are qualified to be leaders besides disobeying Gender Stereotypes (GS). For instance, women are required to be greatly educated at a younger age, as per the current national elections in South Korea.

Even when women come to power, they continue to encounter double standards. Former president of South Korea, Park Geun-Hye's impeachment made women's groups worry about her negative effect on GE in the nation. She was the daughter of a former dictator. Her electoral campaigns largely ignored women's problems. This paved the way for men (and women) to say that females are not competent leaders. The dishonor could discourage others from electing another woman again – an issue that is hardly ever viewed when men are entailed in scandals as they persist to be preferred by voters. Likewise, it was also viewed as Thailand's PM, Yingluck Shinawatra, who escaped the nation subsequent to she was tried in 2016 when the court found her guilty of accusations of misuse of authority over the removal of the national security chief. These kinds of scandals as well deteriorate people's faith in women as leaders. When compared with men, women might not inevitably be better. However, women encounter more severe standards and inspections than their males when they are proven dishonest. Furthermore, the general public is likely to ascribe this corruption to their gender instead of their characteristics.

1.15 POLITICAL VIOLENCE IN SOUTH ASIA

Anti-state rebellions were a widespread aspect of South Asia's political backdrop in the 1st decade of the 21st century. Grave challenges in India have been exhibited by separatist and revolutionary insurgencies. For challenging a long-complacent Pakistani security establishment, Tehrik-e- Taliban Pakistan (TTP), as well called the Pakistani Taliban, rose with terrifying speed. Maoist rebels rallied against the Nepali government; the Liberation Tigers of Tamil Eelam (LTTE; "Tamil Tigers") established a de facto state in northern Sri Lanka; along with a few anticipated an increasingly aggressive Islamist surge in Bangladesh. Also, there were fears of partial or whole state collapse in intense circumstances. In extreme events, there were fears of partial or complete state failure.

However, the state will be dominant in South Asia by 2020. The majority of anti-state riots across the subcontinent have been devastated, demobilized, or controlled. The chief rebels in India have seen a descending trend in fatal cruelty; the TTP are poorly tarnished; the Tamil Tigers are demolished; Nepal's Maoists are integrated into a new Nepali political system, along with Bangladesh's advance into "competitive authoritarianism" has been severely escorted by a decrease in direct anti-state violence.

1.16 ISSUES CONCERNING WOMEN AT THE INTERNATIONAL LEVEL

Six critical areas were pointed out by UN document Women in 1991, which was universal for developing and developed countries. They were legal literacy, health, education, employment, politics, and violence. Regardless of the country's economic status, there was an incidence of self-sufficiency throughout the world; this circumstance is greatly apparent in the event of the US and India. In the US, 50,000 women were raped, and in India, owing to dowry, the death toll of women augmented to 9,000 in 1993. From 1991, WPP was obvious, and this indulgence was vital to handling women's intimidation and enhancement of women's position. Out of the whole world's cabinet ministers, only less than 4% were women in 1990, and regarding the heads of the states, only 7 countries had women heads. In the 20th century, this case was modified marginally so that only 8 countries were without any women legislatures.

An important role has been played by WPR in the global state of affairs. Main international conferences on women's status have been arranged by the UN for the last 40 years. A few of the main conferences were conducted in 1957, 1966, and 1975 and the most recent of all was conducted in Beijing in 1995. In Mexico, the 1st ever global conference on women was conducted in the year 1975, which marked the commencement of global awareness on women's problems. At this conference, the 1st World Plan of Action for Advancement of Women was generated, and 1975 was affirmed as the "International Women's Year". Furthermore, "Equality, Development, and Peace" was the theme for the decade 1976 to 1985, which was the UN's decade for women. This decade caused the creation of '2' bodies, particularly concerning only women, i.e., UNIFEM (UNs Development Fund for Women) along with INTRA (International Research Training Institute for Advancement of Women).

Gender discrimination: From the instant women are born until they die, they encounter discrimination. When analogized to the birth of a girl, the birth of a male as a first child is more extensively celebrated, and parents are relieved to have a child to carry their future generation.

- **Women's health and nutrition:** Women's health is a forecaster of a healthy future generation. Girls obtain less attention to Health Care (HC) than boys in rural areas. It has also been perceived that mothers who give birth to a girl child are mistreated and denied prenatal treatment. Devoid of sufficient rest, they are compelled to partake in routine housework.
- **Education:** In schools and universities, girls are also affected by discrimination. Boys are enrolled in superior private schools, whilst girls are enrolled in government schools with insufficient facilities and safety.
- **Work and job opportunities:** Every time women are expected to prioritize their families over their careers, and also they are compelled to accept low-level positions with low pay. Owing to family shifts, they are forced to leave or budge jobs or places of work; consequently, they lose career perks and promotions. At work, they also face discrimination from their male co-workers. Particular DM positions are rejected to them. When analogized to men, women are always underpaid.
- **Participation in social and political activities**: When it comes to partaking in social and political activities, women experience hostility from family members. Women were taken for granted by male members or their family members and dominated their role in the DM process. Women are designated insignificant portfolios in politics, namely "social welfare".

- **Crimes against women:** One of the most common kinds of crime against women that augments gradually is cruelty by husbands.

1.17 HISTORICAL PERSPECTIVE OF REPRESENTATION OF WOMEN IN THE DECISION-MAKING PROCESS

"Women all over the globe persist to be chiefly marginalized as of the political field, often on account of discriminatory laws, practices, attitudes along with GS, low levels of education, deficiency in access to HC, along with the disproportionate impact of poverty on women", which was affirmed by the 2011 UNGA resolution on WPP. Thus, a multi-pronged method should be espoused to remove multidimensional issues like GI; political WE could serve as a catalyst amongst the diverse initiatives. More opportunities are engendered for women by PE and consequently, develop a level playing field for them.

Worldwide, to accomplish GE, many international commitments have been conducted, and these have highlighted enriching WPR. Whilst women's rights are upheld by the CEDAW along with the BPA called for eliminating obstacles to equal participation. Women's representation is also considered by the Millennium Development Goals (MDGs) in parliament to gauge development towards GE.

GGs have narrowed in several areas like education, health, employment, legal rights of women, participation in governance, etc, recently. However, substantial inequalities persist across every area across countries with changing degrees even with enhancement. For every international commitment mentioned above, India is a signatory. Nevertheless, regarding the representation of women in political DM, India is far behind in acquiring GE.

1.18 MOTIVATION

In politics, women are breaking all barriers; however, the voices still go useless along with their contributions are frequently side-lined. In perceived male-oriented areas like finance, energy, ED, climatic variations, foreign affairs, defense, trade, along with infrastructure, women are still viewed as incompetent of taking on accountability. This is in which the women are offered 'women's only' portfolios or only permitted to sit in women's committees; in addition, are being alienated as of the other committees due to their gender.

Asian countries had to do additional than merely get more women representatives and leaders elected. Imagining the empty seats around the

DM table is easy when considering WPP; in addition, for getting into these seats, it is challenging to picture various many obstacles and challenges women face. In 2020, women are marginalized as of politics along with public life in elections recently. Though women are still far behind those men, they are putting themselves forward for elections hugely. Why is this case? Women sustain to be side-lined in DM although it is extensively accepted that development, peace, along with prosperity in societies can't be attained without half of the world's populace. In politics, the stigma against women is present still. Structural, socioeconomic, institutional, and cultural barriers are constantly faced by them.

For acting in the interests of women, female MPs are usually imagined hugely; in addition, it is a signal for the public that they are able to lead as men. It could motivate other women could work actively in politics. For other women and girls, female MPs are the main role models in various parts by inspiring them to envisage themselves as equal to men and by extension to enter political life. These positive impacts are hard to see in various parts of Asia. Hence, that motivated to research on WE in political representation.

1.19 OBJECTIVE OF THE STUDY

Detecting women's representation as well as participation in the political spectrum in South Asia amongst '3' regional SAARC countries like Bangladesh, India, and Sri Lanka is the goal. A paradoxical image of women's representation along with participation is signified by the SA region. Only a fraction of women holds positions in politics whilst they comprise half of the total populace. South Asia has had the states' highest female heads of any region as of Srimavo Bandaranaike to (a) Chandrika Kumaratunga, (b) Khaleda Zia, (c) Sheikh Hasina, (d) Indira Gandhi, along with (e) Benazir Bhutto (Basu Amrita, 2005). In South Asia, India, Sri Lanka, and Pakistan are evolving countries. It is unconducive to conduct research and gather relevant information regarding the study owing to existing diplomatic deadlock and unstable relations with Pakistan. Since Bangladesh, which is the least evolved nation, is the only country in which women lead parliament and the opposition, it is selected in place of Pakistan. To find out the factors which are liable for the stagnation of WPR along with WPP in politics, a comparative study of the three countries will be conducted. Various factors will be taken into consideration to study this phenomenon. Women's representation and participation in politics are the dependent factors; while, the political system of the country, social fabric of the country, culture, religion, political lineage, and education are encompassed in the independent factors. The justice argument and the utility argument are the '2' arguments of women's representation, which will be targeted. Men and women must be represented equally in politics since women make up half of the populace of each country as per the justice argument of women's representation. The usefulness of having WPP is addressed by the utility argument. The quality of deliberation will be increased by increasing women's participation; in addition, for other younger women, visible women in politics could act as role models.

For women's under-representation in politics in '3' countries, by conducting that research, the actual reason could be evaluated. It could not just benefit these three countries but also the SAARC region at large. Individual countries could determine the mechanisms for improving the number of women in political representation and would be able to alleviate the prevailing GI gap by detecting the disadvantages.

The SD Goal's (SDGs) aim is to attain GE and WE, which will be planned. To promote GE, there is a double rationale. The matter of HR and SJ is the equality betwixt women and men- equal rights, opportunities, along with responsibilities. Next, for (effectual indicator) sustainable people- centered development, huge equality betwixt women and men is a requirement. Since the (a) perception, (b) interests, (c) needs, together with priorities of women and men are essential for enriching the enhancement process, they shout be considered not just as a matter (Bonner M, 2019). To narrow down the GI through education, the GE aspect of SDG will focus on WE. For deciding the advantages themselves and for acting on those decisions, Education for SD (ESD) targets to aid people in maximizing their attitudes, skills, and knowledge (UNESCO). Thus, the target will be on bringing WE via PP as a vital process attaining GE along with, via that, SD. respective independence of the three countries- Bangladesh 1971, India 1947, and Sri Lanka 1948 will be assumed by the study's timeframe.

1.20 RESEARCH QUESTIONS

1. What is the stagnation factor for women's participation in India, Sri Lanka, and Bangladesh in politics?
2. Why is it challenging for women to go into politics without the political support of family?
3. How does having women in positions of power influence the style of politics?
4. Will the novel public space for women make a difference in women's participation?

5. How does education play a chief function in women's representation?
6. How do social constructs affect women's participation in politics?

Chapter - 2

Literature Review

2.1 INTRODUCTION

For modern states, women's PE is progressively identified as decisive. A connection betwixt women's PE and results for women, children, and society is viewed collectively as the same by Scholars and practitioners (Alexander et al, 2016). The academic literature examining economic and social development has progressively dealt with the advantages of empowering women (Branisa et al, 2013). Regarding DM bodies, WPP worldwide still remains relatively invisible (Mahavidyalaya, 2016). Worldwide, women form below 10% of the world leaders (WPP, 2011), i.e., only one in five members of a parliament is a woman. In the political arena, women's leadership is evinced to be socially valuable (Schwab et al, 2017) as well as is a subject of women's right to equal opportunity along with access. WPP is augmented as the BPA in 1995, whilst in the Asia Pacific region, the area lags behind global trends: women's parliamentary representation in Lower or Single House in the region is 20%, but the global average is 25%. Diverse problems have been caused by socio-cultural occurrences, namely gender, caste discrimination, and religious beliefs, which infringe basic HR. A large gap betwixt men's and women's functions has been shaped by the different roles of men as well as women, which are centered on social and economic background in the country.

For the international community, focus on gender is also more vital. Urging member states to accomplish a lowest of 30% women in every elected position is done by the declarations of an extensive variety of international bodies—guided chiefly by the UN, however, encompassing the Inter-Parliamentary Union (IPU), (b) African Union, Common Wealth (CW), (c) Council of Europe, (d) European Union, along with (e) Organization of American States (Towns, 2010). Inside the family and community, the diverse roles and opportunities are accessible to women and men, and a societal structure is well established in the conventional culture. The main problems in SA countries are social boundaries that affect the attitude of the whole society and community. Women's PE is an urgent problem in international development cooperation with the insertion of WPR along with the empowerment of women and girls in the 5th SD Goal (SDG). So, for diverse stakeholders like (i) sponsorship organizations, (ii) scholars of development studies, or government officials, the problem of women's PE is of high interest. One of the proudest and most widespread forms of injustice prevailing since times immemorial is termed GI. Inequality in the political sphere is one of the most well-known amongst the several forms of GI. Democracy acts as a platform for GI and equal opportunities for all out of the diverse prevailing forms of the political system. In attainting the SDGs by 2030, women are necessary. Nevertheless, at all levels of DM worldwide, women are underrepresented, and accomplishing gender parity in political life is far away, as per data. There are a few facts about women in executive government positions (Un Women 2021):

- Twenty-six women are acting as Heads of State and/or Government in 24 nations from 1 September 2021. For another 130 years, GE in the highest positions of power will not be accomplished at the present rate
- Only ten nations have a woman Head of State; 13 nations have a woman Head of Government.
- Only 21% of government ministers were women, with just fourteen nations having accomplished 50% or more women in cabinets. Gender parity in ministerial positions will not be accomplished prior to 2077, with an annual augment of only 0.52% points.
- (a) Family/children/youth/elderly/disabled, (b) social affairs, (c) Environment/natural resources/energy, (d) Employment/labour/vocational training, together with (e) Women affairs/ GE are the '5' most held portfolios by women ministers.

Additionally, a fundamental degree of control over resources promotes empowerment. The freedom as of forced labour along with the right to employ in paid labour is involved in the control over resources but also the freedom to possess property (Driscoll & Kraay, 1998). The economic power along with the capability to put into effect choice in a gamut of domains is broadened if women possess control of property, land, together with loans (Burroway, 2012). Lastly, access to justice is decisive for the preference dimension of women's PE grounded on the viewpoint that women's rights are HR. The conventional practices that limit women's preference stay unaltered if women are not capable of fighting against attacks to their ratification of regular practices in daily life via the justice system. Formal legal rights would be less significant if a judicial system doesn't execute equivalent rights for women to have property or to succeed to resources in their rulings (Benschop, 2002).

2.2 LITERATURE REVIEW

A multidimensional concept that is defined with many dimensions, namely "rights, resources, and voice", is Women's Empowerment (WE). The field for societal DM is termed politics. Scarce resources like tax revenues and direct resources are allocated by individuals who possess formal as well as official positions in government to a few groups at the cost of others and possess the power to implement their decisions, eventually with force. Individual choices are influenced by decisions taken by politicians by persuading a few behaviours and forbidding others. Those with formal or informal political authority dominate over other social organizations, namely the family or education, as well as are capable of codifying specific practices into law. The comprehensive literature is given below.

2.3 WOMEN AS POLITICAL CREATORS

Afridi et al. (2017) concentrated on whether as well as how political reservations for women in village councils had an effect on the supremacy of India's most motivated antipoverty program to date NREGA utilizing data as of Andhra Pradesh. The development done by WPL was not just counteractive but entailed quick and whole overtaking, as per the panel data investigation. Once these initial gendered drawbacks reduce, WPL didn't enforce superior or worse than men. The study recommended judgments with regard to the costs together with entire impacts of Gender Quotas (GQs) reliant on the leadership performance's time trajectory. (Burchi & Singh, 2020) deployed econometric methods to a dataset acquired by combining individuals with district-level political data. It deduced that an augment of 10% points in WPR generates an augmentation of 6% points in the likelihood of children finishing primary school. Next, it was discovered from the gender-discriminated outcome: that when analogized to boy's education, WPR influences girls considerably. Although a rise in school infrastructures didn't seem to be a significant mediating factor, the association works partially via the enhancement of women's access to educational programs, namely the Mid-Day Meal scheme. Even though data limitations restrain the comprehensive comprehension of the routes via which women's representation in politics affects children's education, the outcomes allude to the significance of the 'role model' influence.

Chattopadhyay & Duflo (2004), employing statistics that the author amassed on 265 city committees in West Bengal along with Rajasthan, it is far viewed that the reserving of a board seat had a direction on the relationship of public merchandise with woman pioneers positioning highly in open merchandise honored by humans (an instance, drinking water). It exhibited that the council seat's reservation impacts the kinds of public goods offered. Particularly, investing more in infrastructure by leaders would be directly pertinent to the requirements of their own genders. (Figueras, 2012) put forward that the educational levels of individuals were affected by the politician's gender that existed in the districts in which these politicians were elected. By means of cohort and district of residence, an exceptional dataset amassed on politicians in India was paired with individual data. The recognition of close elections betwixt women and men was permitted by means of the political data that produce quasi-experimental election findings wielded to approximate the fundamental impact of the politician's gender. The chance that an individual would attain primary education in an urban area was increased if the female political representation was increased. However, it was not the case in rural regions and the sample taken together.

Park & Liang (2019) evaluated whether government leadership's gender representation in the legislative along with executive branches ameliorated social equity associated with women's social results as well as how this consequence was restrained by the eminence of democracy. The investigation exhibits that in non-OECD nations, political gender representation had a noteworthy, positive effect on women EA along with GE, whilst bureaucratic gender representation was important for EA only by utilizing a panel dataset on 135 OECD along with non-OECD nations as of 2005 to 2015. Political representation had a constant impact on EA, LFP, and overall GE for OECD countries; however, there was no proof of bureaucratic representation. In moulding the connection betwixt institutional representation along with women's social results in non-OECD nations and their OECD fellows, democratization plays a highly vital role, where GE was ascribable to wider social, economic, along with cultural factors.

Bannor (2019) concentrated on examining WPP in Ghana in the context of SD, an endeavour for identifying factors that contain optimistically impacted WPP, difficulties encountered by women occupying, as well as aiming to occupy political positions, along with pioneering ways of handling these complicities. An online assessment with deliberately chosen members of the common public as well as interviews with (i) female parliamentarians, (ii) district assembly, (iii) unit committee members, (iv) political party executives, along with (v) representatives as of non-governmental institutions were entailed in the technique, which is qualitative in design. The study was dependent on secondary data as of prevailing literature to bolster the work besides Primary Data (PD) from respondents. The research discovered that the statistics are still less at national together with Local Government (LG) levels with a marginal increase, chiefly in the contestants for elective positions in spite of domestic together with international obligations as well as efforts to augment WPP. Female's representation in the national parliament had been less than 13% since 1992. The research demonstrated that owing to the patriarchal society, women occupying along with aiming to occupy political positions countenance the same; sometimes peculiar difficulties that encompass extreme monetization of politics, political party gate keeping along with the 'godfather' syndrome, as well as absence of bolster as of family, media, along with society. It is a warning for (a) the entire stakeholders, (b) government, (c) women's groups, (c) NGOs, (d) civil society, (e) customary as well as religious leaders, (f) development partners, along with women themselves to collaborate.

Bhalotra et al. (2017) evaluated that the event of women being solitarily elected as state legislators promotes succeeding PP amongst women. It was revealed that female incumbent was more likely than male incumbents to recontest along with there was refusal in the entry of fresh women candidates utilizing a regression discontinuity design on Indian constituency level data. This turn down was most noticeable in states with deep-rooted gender bias along with male-dominant parties, recommending a strengthening of barriers against women in these regions. The existence of institutionalized demand-side barriers instead of gender-specific choices and limitations was specified as the same outcomes for (majorly male) Muslim candidates. From 1992-2012, it proffered proof on information for 4,265 get-together votes to cast public in India, and it was found that women directors improved economic execution in their constituencies by approximately 1.8% points annually over male legislators.

Chandrika (2019) scrutinized the difficulties that female encountered in obtaining their socio- economic along with political freedom in Sri Lanka. Also, explored how feminists participate in accomplishing equal rights for females. This work was grounded on secondary data amassed as of the literature review, which were directly associated with the problems handled. The research exhibited that the factors impacted bias of females as of socio-economic along with political domains compared to males in the society. In comparison with men, conventional women possess much low social, economic along with political, together with household power in Sri Lanka. Nevertheless, consecutive governments had dedicated very much to education, health, along with welfare programs subsequent to independence. The prominence of females in Sri Lanka had been modified radically owing to this condition. Similarly, feminist scholars demonstrated that women play a vital part in the family as homemakers along with working women's involvement in the country's ED. Also, the significance of equal rights for females in socio-economic, political domains along with women's freedom against the patriarchal viewpoints in society was highlighted. Yet, on account of unequal opportunities for PP, labour force, and DM in the country, women are experiencing numerous issues. It is vital to augment feminist activities along with must modify their direction to authorize females in the entire sections via policymakers in the nation to tackle these conditions.

2.4 WOMEN PARTICIPATION IN POLITICS IN INDIA, SRI LANKA AND BANGLADESH

Both for support by an agency along with as a control device by the law-makers, women's contribution may be utilized. Participation might be direct or indirect, formal or informal; it might be political, social, or administrative. There are several forms of women's participation in PRIs. It implies all the activities that exhibit the female's participation in the processes along with administration, i.e., contribution to policy formulation along with programme planning, execution, assessment of policies together with programmes intended for the development target groups. Since the pre-independence phase, 'seven' Indian women have been related to politics. Both as volunteers and leaders, they were part of the freedom movement. Several governments or opposition movements in Northeast, southeast along with South Asia has been headed or persists to be headed by females, which is extraordinary.

Especially in SA nations like (a) Bangladesh, (b) India, as well as (c) Sri Lanka, the phenomenon of female politicians is principal, where females had held position as PM or President a lot of times or are the 2nd one in order (Iwanaga, 2008).

According to the literature on women's representation together with involvement, there are '3' main factors that are accountable for women's under-representation, and they are: social-structural factors that talk about the availability of women, political factors that concentrates on the straightforwardness of the political structure to women and ideological factors talk about the role of women in politics (Kenworthy, 1999; Paxton, 1997). The study exhibits that ideology plays a significant role in explicating low scales of WPR amongst the '3' factors (Chowdhury, 1994; Rule & Zimmerman, 1994). Simultaneously, the "supply" of female candidates together with the "demand" for female candidates is the '2' factors on which women's participation in legislature depend (Norris, 1997). All women are politicized within their families and have acquired leadership owing to their family connections, which is the common factor that SA women in politics share (Jahan, 1987). A male relative mediates the power presumed by them. The overriding sexual division of work in which women are expected to deal with domestic work and the political parties are subjugated by men are the other factors accountable for women's political under- representation (Lama, 2001). If the position is higher, then the women will be few, which are the common rule in South Asia (Chawdhury, 2009).

A stupendous act for this area is that every woman has their democratic legitimization mutually because each of them had been corroborated in her formal or informal status via elections. On account of descent from powerful families, all of these females have acquired their present positions as Presidents, PM s, or Opposition Leaders– a somewhat distinctive occurrence in Asian politics. Every one of them is a daughter or widows of previous government or opposition leaders; thus, they convey a dynastic descent, having earned their political status in a hereditary-like way (Locher & Prugl, 2002). With respect to attitudes towards women in politics, women PMs, Presidents, or opposition leaders had been thriving in socio-political contexts, which usually had been distinguished as conventional as well as non-egalitarian (even misogynist). Countries like Pakistan ranked forty-four out of the sixty-two nations examined and Bangladesh 43, as per the current World Values Survey (1995–2001). Therefore, regarding the recognition of Female PL (FPL), these countries graded at the low end of the spectrum. The socio-political data of countries with FPL (Butler, 1993) is elucidated in table 2.1.

Table 2.1: Socio-Political Data of Countries with Female Political Leadership

COUNTRIES	RELIGION	POLICY	POLITICAL RIGHTS
BANGLADESH	(State religion: Islam) Muslim (83%), Hindu (16%)	Parliamentary democracy	4
INDIA	Hindu (81%), Muslim (12%), Christian (2%)	Parliamentary democracy	2
PAKISTHAN	Hindu (81%), Muslim (12%), Christian (2%)	Military	6
SRILANKA	Hindu (81%), Muslim (12%), Christian (2%)	Residential parliamentary democracy	3

Sri Lanka, during the regime of Chandrika Kumaratunga (mother, Sirimavo Bandaranaike acted as PM of Sri Lanka until her death in 2000) regarded as a 'defective democracy' owing partially to the Tamil clash, which Kumaratunga promised to solve, augmented its ranking by concerning '1' digit towards a freer as well as democratic humanity. Amid the Asia crisis of 1998, at the end of the Suharto rule, a slow, intricate, along with conflicting democratization process brought the nation as of the verge of an autocratic rule (categorized as a varied sort of militaristic-Sultanistic polity) to a similar hierarchy as Sri Lanka together with Nepal. Since Bangladesh's dictators were defeated in 1990–1991, it made the biggest leap to democratization in the 1990s, converting as of a military rule into a 'defective democracy' under a steady female premiership.

A similar question is applied to the '2' countries with a negative record. Majorly owing to failed democratic governance, Pakistan worsened as of 'partly free' to bordering on 'not free'. During the Asian crisis in 1997–1998, the thriving autocratic rule in Malaysia, categorized as a 'partly free' semi-authoritarian country, was agitated; however, in contrast, Indonesia, Malaysia handled to re-stabilize its political rule subsequent to cleansing former vice-premier Anwar Ibrahim for suspected corruption as well as homosexuality.

Rameez et al., (2018) concentrated on the degree of female's involvement in local governance along with investigated why there was a low-level of PP of women in local governance. Here, quantitative together with qualitative techniques encompassing questionnaire surveys, interviews, as well as focus group discussions were utilized. The outcomes exhibit that merely in social welfare, livelihood along with social security, structured collective involvement of women was more efficient than PP. A low level of PP in female is ascribable to (i) economic, (ii) biological, (iii) religious,(iv) psychological along with (v) political factors, as per research. On the whole, women lacked space for PP even though they were ready to partake in local governance.

Abidi (2013) concentrated on the involvement along with representation of Muslim Women in Politics regarding India, Bangladesh, and Pakistan. The role of Muslim women and their participation in political stability, democracy, secularism, HR, and external/internal security circumstances were addressed in this work. In modern society, how gender discrimination turns out to be an obstacle in playing a positive role in political problems was stated. (Chowdhury, 2009) suggested that Bangladeshi women must battle to develop an environment in which women of every class could be elected to the parliament along with could convey the interests of every woman. For considering women as human beings, they should fight against patriarchy. Simultaneously, for political institutionalization, women should also fight that would avert violence and corrupt practices. After that, the chief factor in electoral politics in Bangladesh was coherent debate regarding the critical problems of the individuals, not money or muscle power. Women could partake uniformly in the DM process of Bangladesh if reason turned out to be a chief factor.

Worldwide, women's under-representation is based on several factors, namely shortfall of education, economic incapability, family duties, religion, stereotypes in society, electoral system, party principles, psychological obstacles (lack of self-confident power, low self-worth), et cetera. The majority of developing countries were battling to eradicate these obstacles. The subsequent questions were dealt with by (Kabir & Haque, 2014). Why were so few women appointed to public office in Bangladesh? What were the hurdles to female's partaking in politics? Could theories advocated in the Western liberal democratic states elucidate the lower level of WPR along with government of Bangladesh? What schemes had the government espoused for augmenting WPR? What progression had been made toward women's involvement in social life? A comprehension of the current condition of Bangladeshi female's contribution in politics and the national policy- making process was contributed by the research.

Abbas & Muneer (2019) examined that Pakistan in the South Asia area was a country that followed the global trend of providing women participation in all aspects of life and rejuvenated the lost SW more vigorously. Since the struggle for independence, women of Pakistan evenly partake. To reveal the nation in several political and economic issues, several women in the history of Pakistan offered their worth able services and incredible capabilities. Pakistan was a lively country that empowered women in its army, judicative and legislative actions, as well as appreciated women's function in the economic along with political strengthening of the country's structure.

Mondal et al., (2020) put forward the GI in the SAARC location by considering the parameters, namely EP as well as opportunity, EA, health and survival, along with PE. The GGG Report 2020 of the WEF had been wielded for the investigation. There existed substantial disparity with respect to EP and PE, although women have encountered noteworthy enhancement in literacy and EA. A substantial scope prevailed to enhance the economic, social, and political outlooks of females in this area, according to the research. For accomplishing GE, constant policy action at the national and regional levels was needed.

Karim et al., (2013) performed research on any '1' country they had to go via with the entire area to obtain a clear description. Since Bangladesh's inception analogizing to other countries in this area, in this work, Bangladesh and its socio-economic and political development were highlighted. This nation had a huge potential to evolve as a glorious nation, but simultaneously it had multidimensional burdens, according to several political and social scholars. These scholars attempted to reveal the socio-economic along with political expansion of Bangladesh as well as its diverse burdens analogized to other countries. This research was completely centered on secondary sources like books, articles, and information acquired via the internet.

2.4.1 GENDER-RELATED DATA OF COUNTRIES WITH FEMALE POLITICAL LEADERSHIP

The World Bank Group's inclusive source for the most recent sex-disaggregated data together with gender statistics encompassing (i) demography, (ii) education, (iii) health, (iv) economic opportunities, (v) social life, (vi) DM, along with agency is Gender Data Portal. The gender-related data of countries with FPL (Butler, 1993) is explicated in table 2.2. The notion of socially built gender obstacles (like stereotypes along with accessible resources) in a predominantly gendered environment where women politicians require verifying themselves is focused on by the chief drift of the gender associated leadership literature. The processing along with examining of gender- related data proffered by the HDI are needed for a comparative investigation of such phenomena. Table 2.2 portrays GDM: Gender Development Measures.

Table 2.2: Gender-Related Data of Countries with Political Leadership of Women

COUNTRIES	GDI* RANK	GDI* VALUE	GDM* RANK	GDM* VALUE	WOMEN ELECTED IN LOWER HOUSE	FEMALE SUFFRAGE (ACTIVE/ PASSIVE)
BANGLADESH	110	0.499	76	0.218	Elections 2001: 6 of 300 (2,0%). Ministerial level 9,5%	1972
INDIA	103	0.572	-	-	Elections 2004: 45 of 545 (8,3%). Ministerial level 10,1%	1950
PAKISTHAN	120	0.471	64	0.416	Elections 2002: 72 of 342 (21,1%).	1947
SRILANKA	73	0.738	74	0.276	Elections 2004: 11 of 225 (4,9%)	1931

With respect to the favorable gender composition of the socio-political surroundings, these Asian nations with long-lasting experience in women's authority display deprived ratings according to the values. On deeming equal growth options (GDI) and empowerment opportunities for women (GEM), India, Bangladesh, and Pakistan are in the bottom 3rd out of 144 countries. Truly, all these countries, encompassing Sri Lanka, lag considerably behind other nations that are deficient in female governance or PL, even though they have enhanced their GDI and GEM rankings.

2.4.2 ELECTORAL PERFORMANCE OF WOMEN POLITICIANS

Furthermore, in the democratic modifications of the countries, female leaders in (i) Bangladesh, (ii) Burma, (iii) Indonesia, (iv) Malaysia, (v) Pakistan, along with (vi) Philippines was greatly entailed or were otherwise still occupied in battling autocratic rules; so these women were and are critical transition agents.

Elections for national parliament or head of state/government were conducted amid Asia's 'super election' the decennia of 2004 in '5' of the '8' Asian countries with women political positional leadership, while elections were conducted in '9' nations- (i) Afghanistan, (ii) Hong Kong, (iii) India, (iv) Indonesia, (v) South Korea, (vi) Philippines, (vii) Malaysia, (viii) Sri Lanka, along with Taiwan. This election year was distinguished by the supremacy of top women politicians either as opposition leaders or as PM or President, a few on their way to the 2nd term in office in '6' out of '9' nations. Democratic legitimacy accomplished via elections was shared by the entire Asian WPL in government and as of the opposition, with a few possessing a victorious record of electoral performance. The electoral performance of top Asian women politicians (Butler, 1993) is explicated in table 2.3.

Table 2.3: Electoral Performance of Top Asian Women Politicians

COUNTRIES	WOMEN POLITI-CIANS	POSITION AND PARTY	ELECTION RESULT
INDONESIA	Megawati Sukarnoputri	National Parliamentary Elections (NPEs) (2nd time) with Party of Democratic Struggle (PDIP)	Electoral loss: 18,53% of votes (1999: 33,7%) analogized to 21,58% of strongest party Golkar (1999: 22,5%)
INDIA	Sonia Gandhi	PM in NPEs (2nd time) with Indian National Congress Party – a post she afterward refused, selecting rather than fit her own favorite	Electoral victory: 220 seats out of 541 (1999: 154 seats) analogized to 185 of chief opponent party (1999: 280)
MALAYSIA	Wan Azizah	Opposition leader in NPEs with National Justice Party (inside Barisan Alternatif). She presently served her 2nd term in parliament (1999–2004, 2004–).	Electoral loss: 21 out of 219 seats (33,6% of votes, 1999: 43,5%, 45 seats) for Barisan Alternatif, encompassing one for herself as well as her own party (1999: 5 seats
SRI LANKA	Chandrika Kumaratunga	President in direct elections (1st time subsequent to being Vice President as of 1998–2000 along with acting president as of 2001–2004 subsequent to the impeachment of elected president Estrada), K4-Coalition	Electoral victory: 39,12% of votes analogized to 35,72% of opponent Ferdinand Poe Jr

PHILIPPINES	Gloria Macapagal Arroyo	NPEs - subsequent to her own prelude presidential dissolution - where she served as front runner for her Freedom Party (within United People's Freedom Alliance). She serves her 2nd term as president (1994–1999, 1999–)	Electoral victory: 105 out of 225 seats (46% of votes, 2001: 93 seats) analogized to 82 of competitor United National Party (38% of votes, 2001: 109 seats)

An exceptional electoral performance was possessed by the female opposition leaders, with none of them ever possessing had to run more than twice prior to endearing the preferred political office (for example: Sonia Gandhi, Wan Azizah, together with Megawati Sukarnoputri) along with being re-elected subsequent to defeat (for example: Benazir Bhutto along with Sheikh Hasina). The gap betwixt successful female politicians accomplishing the maximum political offices; in contrast, the common women under-representation in parliamentary along with ministerial posts at lesser political levels is a prominent feature.

Hillman (2017) evaluated the evolving political context where the GQ works to dispute that regular support programs developed to increase the GQ's effect on women's representation were inadequately aimed at the main barriers. In the interest of lawmakers as well as public sector professionals functioning to expand gender equity as well as students of democratization, representation, along with gender politics in Asia, the outcomes would be made.

Matland (1998) denoted that there was the lowest level of development (encompassing women's LFP), which was required to develop the basis for other variables, namely electoral systems, to have an impact. The factors that help women in acquiring representation in highly developed nations merely have no influence devoid of this foundation. The forces lined up against female political activity were very great to allow only minimum representation in the majority of less developed countries. Nevertheless, cultural modifications begin to happen as development augments. Also, women started to obtain the resources like education, experience in the salaried labor force, and training in the professions that dominated politics that required becoming politically authoritative. This engendered the creation of a crucial mass. The women with the essential resources started to become an efficient interest group insisting on greater representation and effect in DM when they became considerable. A vital part of this process is development.

Kunovich & Paxton (2005) concentrated on '3' results for females: the percentage of women political party leaders, the proportion of women candidates in a country, along with the proportion of females elected. The cross-national gauges of women's insertion in political parties were created together with scrutinized in a cross-national, path-analytic model of women in politics to discover that (1) female's position in party picks interpreted into gains for female as candidates merely under proportional representation systems, (2) females' position in party pick augment the probability that women candidates would be elected just in non-proportional representation systems, along with (3) parties might be excessively receptive to the observed accountability of female as candidates when actually, female had success as candidates across all areas of the globe.

Bird (2005) evaluated political representation amongst evident racial minorities in France, Denmark, along with Canada. Extracting as of these events, it propounded a common system to analogize patterns of visible minority representation. Citizenship regimes, institutional features, along with interest constellations was the '3' factors that interacted for shaping the political opportunity structure for ethnic minority representation. The outcome had diverse levels of representation from one country to another and significant local dissimilarities in every country since these factors differ across and within countries. There was an influence on the plan of action of individual ethnic candidates and ascertained the style as well as substance of cultural representation in every nation owing to the configurations across these '3' factors.

Norris (2006) put forward the effect of electoral systems on gender representation, corroborating that considerably more women were normally elected in systems utilizing party-list proportional representation, particularly in the Netherlands, which had a huge district magnitude analogized to majoritarian electoral systems utilizing single-member districts. In the Netherlands, any modification that retreated as of countrywide PR would thus possibly decrease the women's proportion in parliament if no other compensatory actions were considered. Statutory quotas controlling the candidate selection process for the entire parties (for instance, as utilized in Belgium), the function of reserved seats in legislatures, as well as the usage of voluntary quotas in candidates selection rules executed by specific parties were scrutinized as the alternative strategies that could be espoused.

Agarwal (2009) mentioned that gender and political literature had discussed extensively how female's proportional strength influences policy formulation in legislatures. Women's restricted contribution in local establishments was concentrated by research on gender and environmental governance. However, both bodies of function's vital aspects were left undiscovered. The intermediate process and the effect of women's numbers on their efficient participation, namely attending along with asserting at meetings along with holding office, were neglected by the former. What effect would augment women's percentage have on involvement, together with what proportions were effectual were the questions neglected by the latter. The study centered on PD for community forestry organizations in India along with Nepal and statistically experimented if a group's gender constitution impacted female's efficient involvement as well as if there were any decisive mass effects for handling these gaps. The widely highlighted proportions of 1/4th to 1/3rd were bolstered by the findings; however, women's economic class as well matters, as do a few factors other than women's numbers.

As created in Hanna Pitkin's seminal work centered on the notion of representation, it is an intricate structure whose numerous dimensions were assumed to be intimately interlinked. Nevertheless, the incorporated character of the representation was neglected by most empirical work and scrutinized its many dimensions in isolation. The image of representation outcomes was not so much inaccurate as unfinished. An incorporated system of representation links formal, descriptive, substantive, along with symbolic representation was affirmed by (Schwindt-Bayer & Mishler 2005). The interconnections amongst the numerous dimensions of representation were confirmed by data on the women's representation in thirty one democracies. Dominant influences on women's descriptive as well as symbolic representations were put forth by the electoral system's structure. Legislatures' receptiveness to women's policy concerns was augmented by descriptive representation and enriched insights of legitimacy. Nonetheless, the impacts of substantive representation were far lesser than the theory foresees.

Paxton et al., (2006) enquired how the development and dialogue of the international WM impacted female's achievement of political power. They utilized event history methodologies to handle female's political representation in over one hundred and fifty nations, more than 110 decennia (1893–2003). Female suffrage, the 1st female parliamentarian, along with the attainment of 10, 20, as well as 30% women in a country's nationwide legislature were taken into account. The outcomes exhibit that augmenting global stress for the addition of women in intercontinental politics along with the varying dialogue of the global WM aids to elucidate women's acquirement of these numerous political results. Moreover, the experts reveal that country-level political, social structural together with cultural features engendered nations to serve in cooperation with, or against, these worldwide stresses by appending these notions to conventional domestic systems of women in politics. For the 1st time, this study on women in politics had regarded such an inclusive list of countries, time points, and results.

Wang (2007) intended to elucidate the correlations amongst political thoughts, Internet usage, and PP and to create a pathway model where interrelationships amongst diverse concepts could be explained and altered to proffer a highly incorporated theoretical formulation. Here, '2' path models are encompassed. Demographics caused political attitudes, political usage of the Internet, and PP, which were presumed in the 1st model. Political usage of the Internet led to political attitudes, and then attitudes engendered PP in the 2nd model. The outcomes display that the data correspond superior to the 2nd model than to the 1st; political usage of the Internet endorses political interest and thoughts of trust as well as efficiency and constructs an individual more probable to partake in campaigns as well as politics.

Choi (2018) emphasized the gap betwixt normative theories as well as an elite-biased empirical research of female's political progression and the circumstances, processes, along with findings perceived across many SEA nations. This work identified '3 main pathways through which women in SEA had strived for election along with re-election to political office by pulling on an innovative ethnographic study in Indonesia, the Philippines, Thailand, together with Vietnam.

2.4.3 POLITICAL REPRESENTATION OF WOMEN IN COUNTRIES WITH ELECTIONS

The regional average of women representation at 15.2% was conquered by only '1' of the '5' countries, with '4' other countries functioning even worse. As of the existence of women PMs along with Presidents to announcing the political space for female along with supporting more of them to contest elections, one could forecast a dropping effect. The gender-associated democracy shortage intensifies in table 2.4 as it is viewed as the case for those nations with a long-lasting custom of over a decade with FPL, namely India, Sri Lanka, and Bangladesh. Years are named as YRS and seat is named as ST in the table 2.4.

Table 2.4: Female Political Representation in Countries with Elections

COUNTRIES	PARLIAMENT				SENATE			
	YRS	ST	WOMEN	% WOMEN	YEAR	ST	WOMEN	% WOMEN
INDONESIA	Apr-04	541	45	8.30%	Nov-02	240	25	10.30%
INDIA	Apr-04	550	61	11.10%	-	-	-	-
MALAYSIA	Mar-04	219	20	9.10%	2003	70	18	25.70%
SRILANKA	Mar-04	220	36	16.40%	May-01	24	3	13%
PHILIPPINES	Apr-04	225	11	4.90%	-	-	-	-

Lies with quota regulation, a regular electoral instrument to cancel the gender-associated democracy shortfall in the political field are the general features of the '3' countries with double digit representation-Pakistan, Philippines, along with Indonesia. Since February 2003, an obligatory quota of 30% of females on party lists has been specified by the new Indonesian election system of proportional representation. Theoretically, in every election, each has to make sure that this quota is met on its candidate lists; however, this doesn't essentially guarantee an augmented women's representation as party officials might just append the 30% of women candidates to the end of the list rather than launching a more improved system of cross nomination.

2.4.4 GENERAL PATTERNS OF PP OF WOMEN IN ASIA

In the arena of PP, the delineated dichotomy betwixt victorious women governance and a marginalized majority of politically active women turns out to be chiefly obvious. In every form of formal politics in the 1st and 3rd World, men and women partake diversely, whether acquiring problems on the political agendas or in policymaking and execution. In contrast, the difference betwixt European and (East) Asian PP is emphasized by the prevailing studies owing to the public- private dichotomy that highlights socio-cultural organization, which causes Asian women being selectively incorporated as women into politics.

As a result, owing to problematic GS, women politicians become restrained that further restrains their potential as well as agency to rather inferior positions. By participating public meetings as well as rallies, being members of elective bodies along with political mass organizations, and participating in political struggles as well as movements (for example: independence along with pro-democracy movements as seen in (a) India, (b) Pakistan, (c) Burma, (d) Malaysia, along with (e) Indonesia), Asian women partake rather uniformly in elections in typical politics. The parliamentary gender ratio in Asia between 1975 and 1998 (% of women) (Butler J, 1993) is explicated in table 2.5.

Table 2.5: Parliamentary Gender Ratio in Asia 1975 and 1998 (% of women)

COUNTRIES	LOWER/ SINGLE 1975	HOUSE 1998	UPPER HOUSE 1975	RANK 1975	RANK 1998
INDONESIA	7.20%	11.40%	-	7	6
INDIA	4.10%	8.10%	7.00%	11	8
MALAYSIA	3.20%	7.80%	3.30%	13	10
SRILANKA	3.80%	5.30%	-	12	15
PHILIPPINES	2.80%	12.40%	12.40%	14	5
BANGLADESH	4.80%	9.10%	-	10	7
BURMA	-	-	-	-	-
ASIA	14.30%	14.10%	6.20%	-	-
PAKISTHAN	4.10%	2.30%	2.20%	11	21

In relation to the country's party systems that are stated, the outlined gender-specific dichotomy doesn't alter. Regarding affecting party policies, commencing agenda problems, or partaking in top-level DM processes, female party members have barely any say even though outstanding women politicians leading parties in every South as well as SEA nations are found. Because only 5.1 percentages of executive council posts are owned by females, Bangladesh is commendable for the area.

The situation in Pakistan is very bad, i.e., below 5% of the entire political party members were female, along with the numbers of women decision-makers were even more insignificant. In 1999, just three out of twenty-one members of the central executive committees were female; in the Muslim League-Nawaz Group, only five out of forty-seven (ibid.) in the Pakistan People's Party, headed by Benazir Bhutto. Amid the 1990s election, a similar trend existed in SA electoral politics, an average of 6.53% of candidates were women in India, 3.9 percentage in Sri Lanka, 1.69 percentage in Bangladesh, along with 1.71 percentage in Pakistan (modified with the initiation of a quota system in the 2002 elections).

To elucidate this event, there are '2' chief socio-cultural reasons wielded. Initially, politics is observed as a male field owing to its public nature, so restricting culturally satisfactory forms of female agency (deficiency of mobility, communication with male counterparts) as well as partaking options. Hence, on account of observed the electorate's gender bias, parties may be unenthusiastic to selecting a female candidate; thus, damaging a woman's potential as a 'winning candidate' together with impeding essential financial (party) support in governing for election.

2.5 IMPORTANCE OF WOMEN'S POLITICAL PARTICIPATION

There have been several initiatives to augment WPR by the decentralization of power in diverse Local Self-Government (LSG) institutions of India subsequent to independence in 1947. The commitment of marginalized sections of society, encompassing women in the DM function in political institutions, has been augmented by the act of PRIs. By utilizing the qualitative techniques, namely document investigation of the PRIs amendment act together with adept interviews with elected female representatives in '1' district of the Kerala, (Varghese, 2019) tried to discover the FPL in LSG institutions. Identifying the difficulties of FPL positions in India, the biggest democratic country, is the aim of the work. There is substantial growth in women's parity in the leadership position; nevertheless, there is a specific critical hindrance that still prevails for women to be energetic in the political arena.

A basic aspect of contemporary democratic governance is GE in PP. In every aspect and at every level of political processes, men and women must have equal rights under international standards. Women encompass below 11% of the Members of Parliament even though women have accomplished a big leap forward in acquiring a vote along with the right to be selected to political offices in several nations (Sindhuja & Murugan, 2017). Gender disparity still prevails predominantly in the political field, although diverse legislative enactment and diverse commissions were set up to promote GE.

One of the areas of focus of WE is promoting women's partaking in politics. Not only the social, political, and economic position of females is enhanced by the presence of females at the DM levels, but it also reinforces democratic institutions by making them highly comprehensive and significant. Women or women's problems are not promoted by Male-dominated political institutions of government. Therefore, highlighting that female themselves should systematize and assemble their networks, learn to converse their interests with diverse organizations, and advocate mechanisms to improve their own representation become very important.

Pankaj Kumar (2017) discovered that there were still several nations where women's representation was absent, for example: women's involvement in the Arab nations, namely Yemen, Kuwait, et cetera, is the lesser in the globe. In contrast, women's contribution in the parliament of Nordic countries like Sweden, Iceland, and Denmark was superior. It was discovered that illiteracy had ended up an obstacle to women's paths. On account of lack of education, women were not competent enough to utilize their rights correctly. The government must take efforts for educating women. Actually, it is essential to alter normal people's life to alter their thinking as well as status by converting the women's lives could be the women's liberation.

Sahu & Yadav (2018) scrutinized the connection betwixt education level and PP of women. The membership in a political party, voting in elections, the political post's occupation, means of a political post's occupation, along with degree of occupation of a political post's scale of occupation was encompassed in the PP's index. The findings displayed that females of the South West region of Cameroon were quite well open to Formal Education (FE) as just 4.1% sampled populace had no FE. The propensity to partake in politics in regions of voting in elections along with occupation of the political post either via elections or appointments at every level of government was more if the level of women's FE was high. (1) Accessing WPP and DM, (2) finding the opportunities for WPP, (3) ascertaining the level of opportunities for WPP and DM were the goal of the research. To comprehend the requirement for females to partake in politics and governance, this work suggested that the government, civil society, along with women activists necessitate seeking sensitization along with awareness construction amongst the community.

Fanny & Oluwasanumi (2014) scrutinized the association betwixt education level and PP of female in the South West area of Cameroon. To choose the study's sample population, the multistage cluster sampling method was wielded. The sampled population encompassed a whole of 222 women. Utilizing a structured questionnaire, data were amassed. Utilizing descriptive and inferential statistical tools, data investigation was performed. The finding displayed that female of the South West area of Cameroon were quite well open to FE since just 4.1% of the sampled population had no FE. The propensity to partake in politics in regions of voting in elections along with the political post's occupation either via elections or appointments at every level of government was more if the level of women's FE was high.

Munir et al., 2014 intended to discover modifications that happened in media patterns along with messages in relation to women in politics and their effect on society embracing as of 2002 to 2012 grounded on

'Media Investigation of WPP'. When the PPP-led democratic government substituted the Musharraf-led government, the women politician's coverage by the media augmented subsequent to 2008, as per the findings. However, since the media greatly and normally depicted women politicians as fashion celebrities or in television debates as senseless politicians, this augmentation could barely impact the women politician's reception in society. The media couldn't provide as preferred with respect to removing obstacles of gender, class, and personal power, even though it proffered extended space to women politicians, as per the study. There were restricted chances for women politicians as of the lower middle class together with low allure to obtain their due share in politics and society evincing via the media despite a few women politicians possessing influence and from the wealthy class obtained space in media. It couldn't connect the gap betwixt society and these women parliamentarians as they didn't have their constituencies and were not responsible to the masses/society. This is because society and the populace barely took them as powerful in politics along with DM; the media also provided them coverage in the interest of exposure. In line with their own ambitions, (Singh, 2016) mentioned that enriching the improvement and empowerment of women around the globe, encompassing the right to freedom of thought, principles, faith, along with belief, therefore, led to men, independently or in community with others. Thus, it ensured them the likelihood of understanding their complete potential in society along with molding their lives.

Mohammed et al., (2017) ascertained WPP and DM in Somalia. (1) Appraising WPP and DM, (2) finding the opportunities for WPP, (3) ascertaining the level of opportunities for WPP and DM in the dawn of the Somali political landscape, (4) Authorizing women to partake in politics and DM process intended for discovering solutions towards political inequity in Somalia. By employing quantitative and qualitative study approaches with a '2' parts questionnaire and a '1' part interview schedule for amassing data from the respondents, this research was done via a descriptive- analytical survey. Random sampling methods were wielded to choose a sample of (40) from a population size of (50). Also, the study suggested scrutinizing the civil society organization's participation in the endorsement of WPP and HR, assessing the policy gaps regarding gender equity in governance together with politics for WE, and the inference of culture on WPP and DM.

Saidon et al., (2019) debated the association betwixt leadership and gender in WPP in Malaysia as of 1980 to 2013. Displaying women's capability to administer leadership as Elected Representatives (ER) in their constituencies, political parties, communities, and the country, was the goal. The hurdles to WPP in Malaysia were inspected. The examination and interviews with 15 respondents were chosen regarding WPP. Moreover, in the qualitative investigation, secondary data and information from the earlier study were merged with primary sources. A legal-rational leadership theory as well as the notion of the social creation of gender was the conceptual outline utilized. Educational, economic, social, health, and environmental were the factors that affected the WPP. On account of a few limitations like education, religion, culture, social, etc., the level of WPP occurred in stages. Gender didn't affect the capability of women's leadership but also impacted the leadership style. In doing the job and their male counterparts, Female Members of Parliament were capable and competently knowledgeable regarding diverse problems and had a greater level of political awareness.

Khodair & Hassib (2015) attempted to appraise the efficacy of the function of NCW in elevating WPP in the origin of the revolutions regarding the 2015 parliamentary elections. Owing to '3' factors, the responsibility of NCW was slightly restricted, and they are: limitations in the NCW institutional framework, limitations in the Egyptian legal/ constitutional framework, along with limitations in the Egyptian societal and cultural heritage.

Stockemer & Byrne (2011) put forward that female's contribution to the workforce affects parliamentary representation. For every 'ten' points, women narrow the gap in how much they provide to a nation's GDP per capita, and women's representation augments by 2% points, which is signified by this system. Women only contributed about half of the men to nation's GDP per capita by considering the world average, and it augmented the women's LPF, which could have a strong optimistic effect on the further progress of the proportion of women associates in nationwide groups. One of the requisites for acquiring high female's incidence in politics was designating an equal playing domain for men along with women in the labor force. It exhibited that the insertion of female's involvement in the workforce in any system on female's parliamentary representation was critical.

Beauregard et al., (2016) evinced that long-standing influence of women's representation were vital than temporary gauges in comprehending GGs in various political activities. The GGs were explicated to a broader level than the women's presence in the legislature and cabinet at a certain time as women had acquired access to the political system. When inspecting the impact of female's representation, the research evinced the kind of political action matters.

Sharma & Zangmo (2019) inspected the cause behind the women populace's passive participation in LG activities in the Sarpang district. Qualitative and quantitative techniques of investigation were wielded. For revealing the causes of women's less involvement in government creation, the Field Questionnaire Survey (FQS) was wielded. 80 women respondents were selected for the research, and they were split into 10 respondents equally as per '8' sub-districts of the Sarpang district. The partaker's age range varied from 20-70 years. The reasons exhibited by the research were the financial issue, shortage of uphold as of the family, absence of knowledge and information, social bias, domestic responsibilities, and fear and dishonor of losing the election, limiting their vigorous contribution to the institution of government. Promoting more women's participation by proffering them free social skills training, performing free workshops on political education, seminars on alertness of women's rights, together with the function of women in constructing government were some implications that were presented.

2.6 FACTORS INFLUENCING WOMEN POLITICAL PARTICIPATION

These are engendered by several factors. In every SADC country, political, socio economic along with cultural obstacles chiefly limit or avert women's contribution. Patriarchal elements of conventional cultural systems along with male-headed structures of contemporary governance are still a factor, according to the SADC (2016), even though this also is varying in a few parts of the area and more gradually elsewhere. Continuing structural firmness inside political parties and deficiency in political will at different levels are the other constraints (Baylis et al., 2008). Several factors serve as obstacles to WPP. Women's participation is chiefly limited or averted by political, socio-economic, along with cultural obstacles.

2.6.1 VIOLENT CONFLICT, SEXUAL VIOLENCE AND WAR

Politics is spoiled by aggression, harassment, terrorization, along with torture in several African states. It exhibits specific obstacles to women's commitment and PP whilst both genders are victims. An Afro-barometer survey exhibited that women experience "a sense of susceptibility to political threats along with violence", as per the UN (2015). For example, 64% of women utter that they are very worried regarding political threats, as per this survey. Even after the battle ends, the impact of war will be endless. Women along with girls are frequently the 1st to lose their rights to education, PP, as well as livelihoods, amongst other rights, being frankly infringed whilst all communities undergo the effect of armed dispute.

Nevertheless, to deal with the miseries of war, others dispute that females might choose to connect more vigorously in public life or partake in politics. The occurrence of war and disagreement is positively associated with PP, which is exhibited by quantitative research. In short, a greater degree of civic along with political commitment after the disagreement is exhibited by individuals who are subject to wartime violence. For instance, higher PP and political awareness were caused by conflict-associated displacement along with deaths in Sierra Leone. Likewise, proof for an association linking earlier violence in Northern Uganda to augmented commitment in politics amongst (debatably) arbitrarily seized ex-combatants was put forward by the author. Also, women retreating as of armed groups in Uganda regenerate socially along with are flexible. The materialization of women's organizations together with networks as conflict's survivors was caused due to the growth of female's roles in Post-Conflict (PC) renewal. Women assemble to join together a gendered viewpoint as well as WPR in peace negotiations along with throughout the PC time via these institutions and networks.

2.6.2 ELECTORAL CONTESTS: VOTER INTIMIDATION, PERSECUTION, ARBITRARY ARRESTS AND ASSASSINATIONS

A vigorous as well as purposeful plan wielded by political actors—office holders and opposition parties—to promote their interests or accomplish particular political objectives regarding an electoral contest is known as election violence. Therefore, to either win the election or reinforce their post-election negotiating position, several politicians' recourse to illegal electoral tactics and utilize (i) militant youth wings, (ii) militias, or the state security forces. One issue that had been recognized as a blockage to the healthy involvement of female in the political process along with governance is Electoral Violence (EV).

A targeted and detrimental tool that is wielded in diverse modes throughout the electoral cycle to discourage females as of partaking as election administrators, voters, along with candidates is VAW. Also, it is mentioned that VAW in elections could be obvious or quiet; above the violence that does physical injury, there is aggression displayed with respect to gender-centered hatred oration, with the wicked goal of dissuading females as of showing themselves as nominees or voting elections. If these electoral obstacles are not handled, it develops an ambiance that leads females to carry a negative attitude toward political activities. With respect to Political Violence (PV) along with the social disgrace, politics is a grimy game and is a further obstacle for women to enter politics.

2.6.3 INSTITUTIONAL FACTORS: PARTY POLITICS

Institutional is another method via which aggressive battle can persuade structural variations that impact the contribution of women politicians. The obstacles that are encompassed in the Institutional limitations are political systems that function via rigid schedules that don't consider female's household duties along with the kind of electoral quotas wielded.

Women's entry into politics is enabled by embracing fresh electoral or party policies amid or following the war. In resolving prevailing codified institutions for encompassing women in PL together with achieving GE in global politics, sufficient support structures are deficient. As political parties fear that they would lose political assistance along with eventually political supremacy, they don't like to execute reforms. Thus, alterations are opposed by them, which are probable driving them to yield power. This was because they would be working in political parties, which were patriarchal as well as carried out grimy politics. Several people followed political leaders blindly without knowledge of what was going on.

2.6.4 CULTURAL AND TRADITIONAL NORMS

Women's capability in engaging politically inside as well as ahead of the voting booth, chiefly as community organizers as well as elected officials, were frequently created by norms that force broader social structures, as per (George, 2019). A deep-rooted patriarchal system where family control and DM powers are with males was the limitation faced by women.

Especially in rural regions, conventional faiths and cultural perspectives—particularly regarding female's roles along with status in society stay tough. Conventional functions along with the division of labor were still evidently gendered. It was more complex for females to abscond their customarily household functions for more public functions exterior of the house owing to social norms. Women's gender individuality is still chiefly devised as being domestic in nature along with persists to serve as a deterrent to female's access to formal politics.

2.6.5 ECONOMIC FACTORS

For improving the participation along with representation in political

DM bodies, the socioeconomic position of women to a larger level plays an imperative role. The economic foundation of women is deficient, which would enrich their PP. A factor in women's contribution is the lack of an economic base, and the shortage of it in politics is due to the high cost of campaigning. Offered the costs related to elections, a lack of financial resources could restrict participation. For conquering the obstacles to PP, independent funding and fixing limits on campaign expenditure might bolster women. Accessing power inclines to evolve from family, communal, and economic linkages. Then, these factors might aid to explicate outlines of participation.

2.7 EDUCATION MAJOR ROLE IN WOMEN REPRESENTATION

Since educated women can play an imperative function in the growth of the nation, women education in India has been a chief concern for the government along with civil society. As education facilitates retorts to the challenges, it is a milestone for WE to tackle their conventional role and alter their life. Hence, in accordance with WE, one cannot ignore the significance of education. Also, recently, India balanced to turning out to be a superpower. For transforming the position in society, the education of women is the most influential tool. An urgent necessity is female's education in India since education is a keystone for WE. As a way to enhance their status inside the family, education causes a decrease in imbalances and roles and creates the notion of participation (Ahmed et al., 2001).

2.7.1 WOMEN EMPOWERMENT THROUGH EDUCATION

The crucial part of any society, state, or country is WE. It is a woman who plays a leading role in the fundamental life of a child. A vital part of society is women. A positive attitudinal transformation can be engendered by education as a way of WE. Thus, it is critical for the socioeconomic and political development of India. For endorsing the approaches to empower women, the Indian constitution strengthens the state to espouse positive gauges. A significant difference is made in women's lives by education. The spearhead of several formal and informal campaigns is WE, which is a universal problem and discussion on women's political rights. In 1985, at the international women's conference at NAROIBI, the concept of WE was launched. Since education facilitates women to react to difficulties and aid in tackling the customary role and changing their life, education is considered a milestone for WE. Regarding WE, one cannot ignore the significance of education. As stated by UNIFEM, the word WE implied:

- Obtaining knowledge and comprehending of gender associations as well as the ways wherein these associations may be altered.
- To safeguard preferred modifications along with the right to rule one's life, creating a sense of personality and faith in one's capability.
- To develop a more just social and economic order, countrywide along with worldwide, for creating the capability to arrange and impact the social change's direction.

Therefore, a psychological sense of personal control or authority along with concern with authentic social effect, political authority, and legal rights is called empowerment. It is a multi-level construct implying people, institutions, and societies. It is an international, continuing process grounded in the local community, entailing shared respect, decisive reflection, along with gentle group participation.

The women's equal status in India was not still accomplished after 68 years of Independence, despite constitutional promises, law's enactment, and social reformer's initiations, measures by the government via diverse schemes and projects, along with U.N.O.'s directives. 74.04% of the populace was illiterate, composing 65.46% females along with 82.14% males, as per Census 2011. Women comprised 48% of the inhabitants in India, out of this, 29% was the nationwide workplace, along with 26% of females had access to formal credit, in accordance with a report by UNDP 2013 on HD Indicators. This made (Bera, 2016 & Krook, 2017) discover efficient gauges for women's upliftment. So, to portray the current situation of WE, feasible determinants, and how education could be utilized as a tool of WE, an endeavor is made. At last, it was recognized that education facilitated females not only to obtain knowledge but as well assisted them in accomplishing (a) economic security, (b) social position, (c) self-confidence, (d) courage, along with (e) inner strength to countenance difficulties in life as well as decrease inequalities and misuse on them. Ultimately, for WE, a stratagem of the wide educational program and constructive attitudes had been suggested.

Manas (2014) tried to examine "WE via Higher Education in India". Since the beginning of civilization, women in India have been undergoing diverse statuses. The masculine principles made the women endure a lot, although women construct half of the populace. Equal chances and significance were denied to women. India was the same as the remaining world. For years, women in India had been fighting for equal rights. So, in India, women's history was very momentous. The women's status was solved slowly by the revolt of diverse female reform movements that occurred throughout the nation. Nevertheless, females in India, during ancient times, were designated specific rights. Fascinatingly, in Ancient India, women's education was increased. Centered on age, education, employment status, household DM power, and liberty of movement of women significantly differ. Approval of unequal gender norms by women still existed in society. To comprehend the issue and viewpoint of WE and try to scrutinize the WE's position in India utilizing diverse indicators, namely women's household DM power, legal Policies for WE, and the function of Judiciary and Awareness, Rajesh Kumar 2016 put forward the study.

2.7.2 EDUCATIONAL EQUALITY

The area of enrolment of boys and girls in schools is the other region wherein women's equality has exhibited a chief enhancement on account of adult literacy programs. The GG in literacy levels is slowly getting decreased because of women's greater participation in literacy campaigns. When analogized to the non-literate householders, inequality in enrolment of boys and girls in neoliterate households is considerably lower. Equality in primary education betwixt girls and boys is accomplished by the world. Yet, some countries have accomplished that objective at every level of education. The WPP keeps augmenting. Over 30% of members of parliament in minimum '1' chamber were women in January 2014 in 46 nations. GI continues, and women persist to experience inequity in access to education, work together with economic properties, and involvement in government in several countries.

In all fields, females encounter obstacles and drawbacks. 62 million girls are not in school around the globe. Worldwide, in women's lifetime, 1 in 3 women will undergo GBV. 1 in 7 girls is married before 15 years of age, with a few child brides as young as 8 or 9 in the developing countries. 99% of them in developing countries expire as of pregnancy along with childbirth-associated problems, i.e., every year over 287,000 women. Only 3 to 20% are landholders whilst women compose greater than 40% of the agriculture labour force. Women-owned establishments constitute as little as 10% of every business in Africa. But, in South Asia, it is only 3%. Women compromise below 20% of the world's legislators in spite of expressing half the global populace. The power to convert each domain is done by placing females equal to men. The GE and WE is not only a part of growth but also the heart of development. For fastening the involvement to bolster women and girls, a few educational awareness programs on GE and WE is done to avoid the above-mentioned.

2.8 SOUTH ASIA, POST-COLD WAR AND POLITICAL VIOLENCE

A sort of intrastate violence that had changed extensively in South Asia together with the post- Cold War period of global economic unity along with political honesty was termed Domestic terrorism (Wollack, 2002). How economic integration and the rise of democracies were associated with domestic terrorism in South Asia? It was debated that retreating to terrorism was a coherent option when individuals and groups' cost of heterogeneity—deficiency as of public goods owing to geographical along with ideological distance—augments; the chance was proffered by democratization as well as integration into the worldwide economy. For the time betwixt 1990 and 2007, the testable assumptions obtained as of the theory were empirically examined on a dataset of '5' SA countries. In the greatly heterogeneous SA countries, the findings exhibit that minority bias and the incidence of unconnected democratic organizations augmented terrorism. Home- based terrorism had been augmented by global trade in the incidence of minority inequity; however, foreign direct investment neither augmented nor reduced such happenings.

Joberg (2012) dealt with the study question: how did the smallest states in the SA zones handle obtaining a considerable number of investments as of China together with India devoid of lapsing into the tactical track of either power? It was an irregularity since the majority of the structural theories, especially neo-realism would anticipate small states not to possess extensive power as well as persuade on their own in their association with authoritative states. It would be replied that the restricted rivalry betwixt China and India in an epoch of strengthened economic globalization had offered opportunities to small states to increase their returns as of the '2' devoid of disturbing their affinity with either in a larger way. The controlled competition and economic interdependence betwixt China and India had been enabled by this short-term bargaining window. It also warned that the smaller states might be demanded to make preferences similar to support either one, especially by providing military bases and naval facilities since the Chinese as well as Indian initiatives in the Indo-Pacific clash. If it happened, this growth would severely impact the smaller state's bargaining capacity.

In finding a specific kind of violence, diverse notions, namely PV, Collective Violence (CV), armed conflict, civil war, insurgencies etc., were wielded. Around the globe, the kinds of violence have been varying. Frequently, PV or CV wielded vice-versa. Regarding the description of PV and CV, experts of political theory usually convey an absence of accord.

It is CV that fixes itself as an agent of control or an agent of opposition to a certain collection of ideas. Institutions, namely a modern nation-state and non-governmental actors in the modern period, are conflicting over several problems like individuality formation and are utilizing strength to accomplish their political goals. The SA Region had a struggling culture of violence toward women since the ancient period. Often, this engendered more casualties when compared to war and other types of violence that are usually endowed with greater focus by rulers and humanitarian organizations. For example, India recorded over forty thousand dowry-associated homicides, which is far more than 10 times the whole deaths in the Kashmir conflict, the Naxalite clash, as well as the Northeast India sectarian violence amid that period, encompassing both genders. In Nepal and Bangladesh, current reports from the Asia Foundation-bolstered violence inspection programs exhibited that the primary or 2nd foremost reason for planned slayings in both countries, far ahead of socio- political or ethnic along with religious violence, is GBV. Thus, reflecting and examining the base cause for the unregulated incidence of this conflict against a specific gender in the SA region was the goal. Owing to the current amendments in the laws against VAW, enhancement of the socio-political position of women, women's contribution to the labor force with the stable GDP growth rate, yet, encompassing the rise in the number of crimes done against women, Bangladesh would be the chief concentration.

Terrorism and civil war had been inspected by the existing literature separately on intrastate conflict. Nevertheless, with respect to intensity, terrorism along with civil war was perhaps the parts of a range of intrastate conflicts. The size of the support base along with state strength was the '2' factors that play vital functions in rebels' DM calculus. If the rebel groups had little bolstered amongst their audience and the state is powerful, terrorism is optimal as a stratagem of the feeble. Conversely, if these kinds of groups had a larger support base and the state was weak, guerrilla warfare would be a perfect strategy. The theoretical dispute was tested from 1970–2007 on a dataset of Myanmar together with '6' nations in South Asia.

2.9 SEXUAL VIOLENCE AGAINST WOMEN

The women's personalities have been molded, and their social status is ascertained by the incorporation of Buddhist, Confucian, Hindu, Islamic, along with Christian cultures in SA nations. The extensive incidence of VAW is engendered by rigid cultures along with patriarchal attitudes that diminish the women's role. In the family structure, man is the undeniable ruler, and the activities inside the family are viewed as private, which permits violence to happen. Wife-battering and sexual assault are the customary types of violence, and in these nations, women are also vulnerable to dowry offenses, namely bride burning, abduction for prostitution, along with "honor killings". Bias against women is allowed together with deterred reporting of violent acts by laws. To resolve these, Local laws should be changed, and help from the UN and the international community should be given.

The concentration was on SA women's activism along with its effect on assortment and social growth in SA societies in east London. The experience of the Newham Asian Women's Project (NAWP) was illustrated, which was intent on protecting SJ for women along with children escaping Domestic Violence (DV). The anxieties betwixt the global phenomenon of VAW and female's particular incidents of violence in diverse cultural backgrounds were scrutinized. There was similar stress betwixt universal replies to violence as a HR offense and more culturally sited methods. To authorize women and guide the organization's strategy, this work highlighted the manner wherein NAWP's task handles gender, race, along with class-centered inequality, utilizing participatory methodologies. Activism appears out of their daily resistances to domination, which were centered on notions of community along with family for SA women in Newham.

Krook (2017) evinced the VAW in politics. As women have turned out to be more politically engaged, the physical attacks, threats, along with harassment intended for (a) female politicians, (b) activists, as well as voters have expanded. Frequently overlooked as the "cost of doing politics," such acts engender a severe hazard to democracy and raise questions regarding the advancement that had been made globally toward integrating women as whole political actors. This work plotted the outlines of this happening and propounded evolving solutions by deriving from a different gamut of quantitative and qualitative data and academic research on gender and PV.

As per the study, cultural, environmental, educational, and gender problems obstructed the women's active involvement in politics. Augmenting the number of women, who partake in national politics, was one of the work's aim. To persuade more women to follow and acknowledge education, enlightenment campaigns at every level must be introduced. Hence, extra women would partake in politics. All kinds of discrimination against women must be criminalized, as per the adepts. It was essential to enhance their position and involvement in the entire progress to integrate women into global economies. Instead of concentrating only on women's problems, the GAD method suggested a greater emphasis be placed on gender relations (Dubey & Singh, 2022), and a few elucidations portray this violence as chiefly gender-enthused: female politicians were targeted since they were female. In addition, from a few perspectives, violence was a daily political approach targeting men and women as the same. Only a few were known regarding the level to which as well as how the candidate's sex builds this kind of violence as there was a deficiency in a huge scale, methodical contrasts of men's as well as women's insight to election violence. (Bjarnegard et al., 2020) dealt with the research gap by utilizing original study data on 197 men along with women political candidates in the 2018 Sri Lankan local elections. Since Sri Lanka was a PC nation where PV had been widespread, as well as the number of women candidates had augmented quickly owing to GQ adoption, it was an appropriate case for investigation. It discovered greater similarities in men's along with women's exposure to violence, which recommended that violence at times was a part of a greater political practice. Yet, the type of threats that females were exposed to was of a more sexual nature than men. The requirement for gender-sensitive investigations of election violence was evinced.

Sanín (2020) illustrated the function of diverse actors in the process of norm espousal and alteration at the domestic, regional, and international levels. Legal frameworks criminalizing VAWIP were concentrated. In 2012, the only country in the globe to illegalize "PV and harassment against women" was Bolivia. These bills were developed with respect to the outcome of '3' processes: activism at the local level utilized international norms to propound a pioneering solution to an issue, women politicians and "femocrats" functioned within the state apparatus to conquer resistance, and international actors functioned to promote relationship amongst activists and politicians. Here, for WPR, international norms had been converted with significant inferences.

Fulu & Miedema (2015) propounded to insert a global level to the prevailing ecological system methodology that was made famous by Lori Heise in 1998 to discover the associations of global processes along with VAW's experiences. To evaluate how globalized notions, ED and incorporation, dutiful fundamentalisms, along with global cultural exchange, as elements of a greater globalization process, had influenced men and women's experiences and viewpoints of VAW, data from the Maldives and Cambodia were utilized.

Agbalajobi & Agunbiade (2016) explicated the theoretical methodology that merges the pluralist and psychological theories, particularly Ted Gurr's theory of comparative deficiency in the investigation of the violence. The origin of the endless cycle of violence during and after elections and factors that frequently continued the violence was scrutinized. This work debates that EV acts as an obstacle to WPP with pertinent information on EV and women's participation in electoral. The EV's magnitude and how it impacted women in Nigeria were emphasized and recommended a procedure that could be wielded to safeguard women as candidates and voters. Since most post- electoral violent actions were urged by frustrated citizens with regard to the election results, this work suggested that the electoral body in Nigeria required ameliorating on possessing a free and fair election. During and after elections amongst citizens, vigilance and mutual aid must be the motto.

2.10 GENDER EQUALITY AND WOMEN EMPOWERMENT: CONCEPT, RELATIONSHIP AND UNDERSTANDING

Multi-dimensional social process that aids people in acquiring authority over their own lives can be considered the definition of empowerment. It is a process that encourages power in people to utilize in their own lives, their communities, along with their society by reacting on problems they describe as vital (Czuba, 1999). However, "women's capability to make premeditated life choices in which that capability had been formerly rejected them" was termed WE (Kabeer, 2001). Hence, in the processes of managing the advantages of women at individual, family, community, along with wider scales, empowerment was regarded as core (Malhotra et al., 2009). The act of increasing the position of women via (a) literacy, (b) education, (c) training, along with growing awareness was entailed (Alvarez, 2013). So, WE were all about enriching their skills. International gender norms encompassing female's equal involvement in politics were protected by the international 'women's bill of rights' (CEDAW). But, both in theory and practice, WE was considered controversial and were presumed to be superior mothers, workers, along with citizens (Cornwall & Anyidoho, 2010).

Simply, a social concept that attributes varied qualities along with rights to women and men heedless of individual capabilities or aspirations is called Gender. It implies recognition of masculinity with features of strength and militarism and of femininity with susceptibility, nurturing, and peace. The gender dichotomies feminist theorists were only reproduced that have aimed to unfasten determining men with masculinity, aggression, and a tendency for violence and women with femininity, susceptibility, and victimhood (Collins, 2019). A circumstance in which "... all human beings were free to expand their individual capabilities and make decisions devoid of the restrictions lay down by severe gender functions; that the diverse ambitions and requirements of women and men were regarded, valued and preferred equally" is termed GE (Holzner et al., 2010).

The rights, duties, along with chances of individuals should not be reliant on whether they were born male or female (Warth & Koparanova, 2012). The absence of discrimination based on one's gender was the final objective. At last, WE had a crucial role (Alvarez, 2013), hence, the study would discuss GE and WE concurrently.

Simultaneously, devoid of WE and GE, the SD was not feasible to accomplish. Thus, GE was not a HR problem along with a prerequisite for and indicator of SD (Alvarez, 2013). SD can't be accomplished since gender disparity is widespread across the cultures of the globe and devoid of severe steps to address it (Stevens, 2010). Moreover, accomplishing GE is supreme by developing along with sustainable world along with enriching women's functions in maintaining their households and communities, according to UN Women (2014). Thus, GE would hinder the development and progress of a nation if it was not accomplished. Stevens stressed that "an increasing number of studies denoted that GIs were extorting greater economic costs along with causing social inequities along with environmental deprivation across the world" (Stevens, 2010). Any expansion proposal has to employ and guarantee that men as well as women contribute as well as gain equally from it (Ministry of Agriculture and Rural Development (MARD), 2008).

Although the study concentrated on social aspect of sustainability, other aspects of SD can't be neglected. As per (Hartmut Bossel, 1999), "SD of human society had environmental, material, ecological, social, economic, legal, cultural, political along with psychological dimensions that needed focus". Thus, it was vital to remember the whole aspects of development as only a cooperative and incorporated endeavor would aid in producing the desired outcome to obtain sustainability and GE.

One of the UN's reports talked about the requirement of empowering women. As per this, on account of unequal economic opportunities, women comprise 70% of the world's poor, and it was also that ED's accomplishment is reliant on the full utilization of skills and qualifications of women (OECD, 2008). Furthermore, at the place of work, all women experience discrimination and are also employed in unpaid, tedious household work. Hence, to reduce poverty and endorse ED, it was suggested to pay for women's domestic work (OECD, 2008). Women were understated around the world relating to PP (OECD, 2008) for example, the entire PP by women remains miserable, although South Asia asserted a few of the most influential women leaders of the globe (Omvedt, 2005). The female's involvement in all phases of the government was not strange in South Asia, provided the long record of women's political activism, their contribution in anti- colonial struggles, along with the sturdy impact of the WMs. Yet, in spite of the positive activities in most SA nations, the total number of females in national parliaments in South Asia was less than the average 20% worldwide (Shaheed, 2003). Women always comprised below 10% of members in the parliament whilst elections happened regularly in India and Sri Lanka. People in authority enter politics within extremely patriarchal structures of the society and operate within very same restrictions under the control of men (Gebru & Demeke, 2014). In entire phases of government, they had no equivalent authority in leadership and DM (MARD, 2008). Women's participation in local political, administrative, along with development leadership and DM was insignificant, and this caused females to observe politics as an arena wholly kept for men (Women, 2014). With respect to increasing responsibility and transparency, decreasing corruption, along with safeguarding the interest of society's marginalized sections, active contribution of women in DM positions would aid in promoting the overall quality of governance, and without women accomplishing SD is not possible (OECD, 2008). Hence, there is a requirement for sound gender- sensitive policies for empowering women.

Social development along with social transformation as an element of SD was other chief features of sustainability, which was impossible devoid of women's contribution (Women, 2014). There was a requirement to empower women via education that could further aid in accomplishing other objectives of SD associated with GE and women's health to accomplish social development. A vital need for a sustainable world is accomplishing GE and perceiving the HR, dignity, along with abilities of different groups of women (UN, 1992).

For accomplishing environmental sustainability, the function of women can't be evaded as Principle twenty of the Rio declaration obviously mentioned that "women have an imperative role in environmental management along with progress". Thus, to accomplish SD, women's complete involvement is necessary (Baker, 2006; UN, 1992). Owing to the nature of the domestic tasks, namely fetching water, gathering wood, cooking, washing, etc., women were considered the priceless source of knowledge along with proficiency on environmental fortification problems and were more preoccupied than men with the issue of environment along with climatic variation (OECD, 2008). Women's potential in acquiring SD converts them into agents of change, as per Baker (Finnemore & Sikkink, 2001).

Chukwurah, et al., (2020) evinced the assessment of WPP as well as representation in Nigeria in relation to determining the level of their participation and finding factors that affect the extent of their commitment to politics. The research was against the background of global anxiety for GE as well as women's participation. It deployed content investigation in scrutinizing data sourced majorly as of secondary sources of data production by adopting liberal feminism as its methodology of investigation. The degree of women's participation together with representation in Nigeria was extremely less, and advocates for pressing action. Moreover, it adopted inter-alia that in Nigeria, factors like (a) culture, (b) media depiction, (c) belief, finance, as well as politics nature play a crucial function in the degree to which women partake in politics in Nigeria. It was deduced that the government, via diverse agencies like National Orientation Agency (NOA) together with the mass media, must espouse plans for reorientation of the public as culture was not static. Moreover, to radically decrease the election's negative nature in the nation, suitable laws must be enforced and severely enacted to facilitate equal rights for all without every kind of harassment and threats.

2.10.1 WOMEN'S EMPOWERMENT STRATEGIES ACCORDING TO THE POLITICAL PERSPECTIVE

Currently, there is a great expansion in women's exposure to political power along with their authority on policies. But, even though PE studies on women's roles are ongoing, females are proportional to males in their influence as well as practice of political legitimacy. A stupendous policy mechanism to augment WPP at the national level is the Indian government's national program of the 'PRIs act of 1992. 50% reservation seats for women were proffered by this act; therefore, women were able to achieve power in the political arena. There is a larger likelihood for women to be elected in the political field via this policy; therefore, it processes a greater function in welfare processes in their corresponding administrative localities than ever. The PRI policy's significance on the PE of women in the Panchayat was inspected by (Varghese, 2019). It performed empirical research by amassing PD as of elected female representatives in the '1' district of Kerala to discover the effect of the policy. The importance of augmenting women's PE together with their position in Kerala society was evaluated in the outcomes.

Dahlum et al., (2022) analyzed whether and how women's PE focuses on technological transformation and the major driver of long-standing ED. Descriptive representation, civil liberties protection, along with civil society involvement were the '3' aspects of empowerment that progressed technological transformation along with ED via (a) augmenting the number and inconsistency of novel notions initiated in the economy (b) ameliorating the assortment of highly effective notions. Diverse inferences were drawn from data as of 182 nations and 221 years. Women's PE was positively associated with successive economic growth. This association continued with diverse model specifications and when diverse probable confounders were described. Even though it was not sturdy as an aggregated concept, the '3' sub-elements of empowerment were independently associated with growth. Throughout diverse contexts, the association was maintained; however, it was explicit for "Non-Western" nations and in early periods. It was as well identified that female's PE improves technological transformation.

Dauletova et al., (2022) attempted to scrutinize the causes behind the women's constant political disempowerment in the Middle East along with North African via the view of public opinion. 288 surveys were done with '2' groups of participants- undergraduate along with postgraduate students majoring in Political Science (PS) together with a set of Omani citizens without political education. The effect of formal (government-driven) along with informal (socio-cultural) factors engendered the low degree of PE in Omani women, which was verified by the outcomes. It was perceived that respondents who specialized in PS evinced a low level of gender favoritism analogized to citizens without education in PS by inspecting public opinion formed toward women's PE. If arbitrated by the political awareness variable, the work exhibited that gender bias was neutralized. A rise in the degree of political insight amongst citizens ought to be regarded as a positive interference required for varying public opinion supporting the PE of women, as per the outcomes.

(Akselet al., 2017) put forward a conceptualization of women's PE along with offered a summary of the creation of the catalog as well as operationalization of its '3' sub-dimensions: (a) women's civil liberties, (b) civil society involvement, along with (c) PP. The V-Dem index permitted highly accurate measurement as well as is better in temporal range and exposure of nations of the Global South when analogized to other indices gauging, WE, namely (a) the GDI, (b) the GEM, (c) the GII, along with (d) the CIRI data on HR. The advantages of the new index along with its sub- dimensions via many empirical depictions were evinced in this study.

Alexander et al., (2016) questioned 'women's PE, deeming its description, dimension, and purpose. Initially, academics and practitioners had not expressed an apparent description of women's PE. A novel description that conceptualizes women's PE as a transformative process was suggested to bridge the gap. Next, the prevailing social science literature on female's PE was surveyed. To create a wider image of women's PE and construct gauges, the study should be expanded.

2.11 PROBLEMS AND PROSPECTS OF WOMEN EMPOWERMENT

Khan (2014) concentrated on the nature of socio-political factors for WPP in the context of Azad Jammu and Kashmir (AJK). The hindrances to women's efficient PP were gauged from '3' diverse perspectives: a) structural b) political and c) ideological and psychological factors. In describing the PE's abstract in a specific social context, the core notion of the study is that numerous factors were vital. To fulfill the study's goals, a quantitative technique was utilized. From '3' diverse political parties in AJK, data were amassed from 150 women. On account of the interlinked and indivisible structural, political, and ideological factors, it recommended that women's involvement as well as access to proper political processes were limited.

Saher et al., (2014) evinced that long-standing influences of women's representation were highly significant than temporary gauges in comprehending GGs in different political activities. Also, the outcomes exhibited that the findings of earlier work on WPR together with political behavior might not exceed the US case when WPR was gauged by the incidence of women politicians in a cabinet. At last, the kind of political actions matters when examining the impact of women's representation was evinced.

Arif et al., (2019) concentrated on women's Economic, Social and Cultural (ESC) rights in AJK. Regarding '3' ESC rights like education, employment, and health, the chief HR problems were debated. AJK might increasingly understand its women population and its ESC rights via legal along with policy gauges, for the accomplishment of its state-like national and international HR responsibilities. Initially, the chief HR of women in the AJK, cogitate law as well as policy problems was reviewed. The major focus stayed on equality and non-discrimination whilst examining the '3' rights. For examining pertinent laws and policies, an analytical technique was espoused. Nevertheless, deficiencies in the pertinent laws as well as policies relevant to the '3' rights were indicated.

Abbas et al., (2021) offered valuable perceptions into WE and its assorted determinants in Pakistan. From a large, generalizable body of data, the outcomes were derived that constantly forecasted an important relationship betwixt the investigated demographic, economic, domestic, and information-exposure factors along with WE. The findings suggested the significance of enacting policies to limit girl-child marriages that greatly impact girls' RH along with social welfare. There was a requirement to lessen the feminized poverty in Pakistan via targeted activities, especially in rural regions, in which females' access to information, employment, and inheritance was mostly refused. For improving the women's socio-economic condition and attaining growth on the national level, female's education along with employment were the domains found as necessitating gender-centered equal chances initiatives via a policy. As a result, to ameliorate women's access to employment along with educational opportunities, more efforts were needed. To modify community norms along with values that discriminate against women, a pressing demand to utilize mass communication and education campaigns was needed.

Shukurana & Adamu (2017) attempted to find the possibilities and difficulties of WE in small businesses. By accomplishing diverse empowerment factors accessible to them as well as how entrepreneurship was efficient in their position as a woman, this could be attained. It wielded a quantitative methodology that utilizes the inquiry method to amass data as of target respondents (Businesswomen in Damaturu LG, Yobe state of Nigeria). Utilizing the Statistical Package for Social Sciences (SPSS), Regression analysis was deployed in the 50 questionnaires that were amassed. For assisting the businesses, women entrepreneurs were not conscious of government programs, and they were an absence of bolster from financial organizations since their bolster was majorly as of informal sources. Since most of the women work day and night without taking any leave, entrepreneurship damages women's personal lives; however, the happy announcement was that a large percentage of the respondents stated to vote often denoting a kind of empowerment as it permitted them to possess their say in national development. Thus, to aid the women accomplishing their full potential, it suggested government assistance in the type of finance, awareness programs, infrastructural expansion, enhanced protection for businesses, as well as facilitating the environment.

Srivastava (2021) highlighted the opportunities and difficulties of WE in India. The liberation of women as of the brutal clutches of (i) social-economic, (ii) political, caste, together with gender- centered discrimination was termed WE. Via many parameters, such as the women's participation in family DM rights, freedom of thought, financial authority, GE, PP, media exposure, access to education, etc., they could scrutinize their status. GI was stern concern and was the existing chiefly in the society. The SW had also varied by forwarding them from the '4' boundaries of the home to the working place with varying circumstances. For educating and strengthening their situation in society, more work had to be performed. The study concentrated on the secondary source of data. Proposals and efforts taken by the government were also highlighted. The action that was taken and is to be taken to boost their status was also concentrated.

Prathiba (2017) tried to scrutinize the condition of WE in India and emphasize the problems and difficulties of WE. Nowadays, one of the most vital concerns of the 21st century was the empowerment of women. The SW had been varying slowly and steadily since the early 20th century (national movement). Despite several endeavors made by the government, the women of India were comparatively disempowered and were kept lower than that of men. With respect to access to education and employment, GG prevailed. With respect to age, education, and employment status, the household DM power and freedom of movement of women differ noticeably. It was discovered that unequal gender norm's acceptance still existed in society. When analogized to urban women, rural women were more vulnerable to DV. It was deduced that access to education and employment was only the facilitating factor to empower, the accomplishment of objectives; yet, it was reliant deeply on the people's attitude towards GE.

Manjunatha (2016) evinced that the GE cannot be accomplished devoid of men's roles in it. Also, given that woman fight not to take precedence over them yet to be their equals in every aspect of life. Nobody can impart empowerment to women, devoid of women's individual or collective endeavors and capability to recognize their own welfare. Unless they accompany and aid to self- empower themselves/other women, WE will not be feasible. Further, they would live in a highly developed and educated society. Women would obtain the right to talk, obtain a proper education, possess a fixed income, would not become victims of early child marriage or DV, and didn't have to face and stand the boulevard harassment. Also, their daughters empowered if they were empowered (Thompson, 2005). Thus, also, women's problems must absolutely acquire focus from men.

Farzana et al., (2018) inspected the important points of WE difficulties via investigating earlier study literature and reviewed the reports to create a theoretical plan WE model (Bhat, 2015). The most difficult step and overcoming the obstacles in a woman's life that might improve women's quality to shape her life and society were WE. This model was a multidimensional process that would facilitate women to improve their self-reliance, individuality, along with supremacy at all levels of life. A systematic literature appraisal of qualitative literature was done (Ghatak, 2016). For achieving positive impacts on sustainable global development, the research evinced women's significant role in socio-ED.

Niyonkuru & Barrett (2021) discovered how prevailing gender associations at the family level in rural Rwanda inspire, endorse/obstruct robust involvement in WEE initiatives and investigated the plans utilized by rural women entailed in WEE to challenge power associations at the family level (Paul, 2019). SJ and transformative methodology were wielded by deploying interpretive and qualitative techniques. 126 women and 48 men entailed in this study (Rati & Ferdush, 2021). To scrutinize the amassed information, thematic analysis was wielded. Then, '3' major themes were found: (a) cultural norms, expectations, along with women's involvement; (b) women's voice as well as agency as of their participation in economic activities; (c) women's diverse generations who utilize diverse adaptive strategy and plans to handle unfavorable gender power associations. The study exhibited that they must deal with cultural and structural norms that strengthen GI in the domestic and community spheres (Ghatak, 2016). Regarding gender power relations in rural households along with communities, WEE initiatives and offering economic opportunities for women (men) should also tackle detrimental SJ problems and impact women's contribution to such initiatives and bolster a transformative environment.

Girls and women were of equal status with men as well as were regarded as an economic asset in tribal society. When analogized to non-tribal women, women in the tribal community relish greater (Niaz, 2003). In each decision in the household and society, tribal women shared the economic burden and participated evenly. When analogized to the counterparts, tribal women were more empowered. Tribal women were still poor in education and a decent standard of living from a materialistic development opinion. To discover the difficulties encountered by tribal women and to illustrate the plans that they could deem for addressing difficulties, (Binjha, 2020) centered on the secondary sources of data amassed as of diverse sources. The reason for the tribal wo men's disempowerment, namely low literacy rate, lack of education and wisdom regarding the latest technology, lack of property rights, skill and training, lack of PP, and male authority over resources along with reproductive rights, were discovered (Gill & Rehman et al., 2004). For empowering women, the Government (Central and State) have undertaken several programs. Empowerment of women in India implies several things, as per (Mittal & Dutta, 2019). -

- It implies identifying women's contribution to women's knowledge
- It implies assisting women fight their own fears along with feelings of insufficiency and weakness
- It implies women ameliorating their self-esteem along with self-dignity
- It states female regulating their own bodies
- It implies women turning out to be economically self-governing as well as independent.
- It implies females regulating resources, namely land along with property
- It implies decreasing female's trouble of work, particularly inside the home.

2.12 CHALLENGES TO WOMEN PARTICIPATION

Violence, prejudice, and illiteracy are the cultural and societal obstacles that have a considerable effect on female's political involvement. WPP is impeded by the hazard of violence, according to Martha Nussbaum. Education and marriage are the main factors in relation to sexual assault. Sexual abuse against women is also common. Factors like early marriage and domestic abuse, and low literacy rates affect the economic chances for women in India. 24% of Indian males had committed Sexual Violence (SV) at some point in their lives, 21% had compelled partners to engage in sexual contact with them, and 38% of men confessed to physically assaulting their relationships, as per a 2011 study. Accordingly, several people presumed that domestic VAW is usual. Martha Nussbaum stated that several women had a restricted capability to partake in numerous social and political ties and to convey frankly and be identified by society at huge as decorous beings whose worth was equivalent to that of others.

Kassa (2015) put forward that diverse casual factors like (i) economic, (ii) religious, (iii) social, along with (iv) cultural factors contributed to women's deprived PP. PP permitted females to manage their fundamental problems and requirements in their community as well as guaranteed the honesty, real fight against rent-seeking, responsibility, political dedication, PL, as well as political receptiveness of the customary national, regional, district, as well as local levels. However, when analogized to their colleagues at all tiers of government, they were deficient in accessing political DM. Hence, women's equal contribution in DM as well as politics was not merely a need for straightforward justice or democracy, however, an essential prerequisite for women's interests to be considered.

Tipu (2012) explicated the issue of only possessing females on councils didn't automatically signify that the interests of females in the community had been expressed. Development interventions along with planning sustainable outcomes would not arrive without women's requirements together with interests being considered, devoid of the chance for them to partake in and affect DM. Nevertheless, an imperative step in altering the male-headed political program was possessing women in these leadership roles. In any case, they would have the chance to attend the meetings, communicate with officials, and partake in significant discussions. It as well guaranteed their budge across the social hierarchy. To eliminate hindrances that engender women's backwardness, strong steps were essential. To ensure women's rights, appropriate gauges were needed. To make women know about their privileges, awareness was required. The justice and knowledge regarding women's power, and the capability needed to comprehend community people, were required by the administrative requirements.

Mlambo & Kapingura (2019) recognized the factors affecting WPP in the SADC. The data was withdrawn as of the 30% average woman contribution rate was still only halfway to the target of 50% WPR needed by the Protocol on GAD of 2008. A balance was offered by full along with equal involvement of women as well as men in political DM that highly reflects the society's composition and might enrich the legality of political processes by constructing them more democratic along with receptive to the concerns and viewpoints of the entire sections of society. The outcomes displayed that labor contribution, operation of government, political culture, and the entire PP had a positive association with women PP centered on the combined OLS along with GMM dynamic panel of Blundell along with Blond (1998) on fourteen SADC nations over the time 2010–2017. Civil liberties, HDI, electoral process, along with pluralism had a negative association with WPP. To guarantee that they energetically entailed and employed more women in their political structures, the research suggested the engagement of political players, particularly political parties.

2.12.1 DISCRIMINATION

Nipu (2021) attempted to examine the circumstances of WPP regarding Power Distance Orientation (PDO) as of the Union Parishad (UP) viewpoint, which was regarded as the most famous democratic LG institution at the grassroots level in Bangladesh. The major channel for women's invisibility in the public field and the political domain was the innate social circumstances of women's subordination as well as reliance on male along with the reception of female members that authority would be unevenly dispensed betwixt male and female members. Purposeful endeavors for assessing the level of PDO amongst women members reserved seats) of UPs of Bangladesh as well as investigating the effect of PDO of women on the DM process and typical activities of UP were done. By means of a few mechanisms of quantitative techniques that had been deployed in the restricted form to simply scrutinize the data, this research was conducted that was a qualitative study. A total of 21 women (reserved seat) members of '9' UPs of Southern Bangladesh had been chosen as respondents.

Galligan (2020) examined WPR as Northern Ireland (NI) MP in the House of Commons since 1953. The political along with cultural positions prevalent at the creation of NI in the earlier twentieth century resonate via the generations and persist in reporting women's political under- representation. A historical context for women's political along with public involvement as of the 1950s was offered that emphasized the gendered political culture wherein this engagement occurred. The extra freezing impact of the ethnic national disagreement on women's civic as well as political participation as of the 1970s–1990s was scrutinized. The period subsequent to the 1998 Good Friday/Belfast agreement was concentrated and explained the level of women's candidacies in general elections with respect to women's Westminster contributions. Their contribution to parliamentary voting and a few of the problems to which they had contributed was emphasized. The effect of a conservative, gendered political culture on the problems that had employed women MPs as of NI was exhibited. It was deduced that NI's authorizing of male dominance persisted in framing the political plans and jobs of women MPs.

Clavero & Galligan (2005) illustrated WPR in Central along with Eastern Europe in the 15 years following the collapse of the Berlin Wall as well as the espousal of liberal democratic political systems. The deep-rooted GSs that describe women chiefly as wives along with mothers, with electoral politics viewed as a suitable activity for men, but less so for women, were emphasized. The paths wherein traditional perspectives on gender roles obstruct the supply of as well as demand for women in the politics of Central and Eastern Europe were inspected. Furthermore, how the internalization of customary gender criteria impacts women's parliamentary behavior as some champion women's rights in the legislatures were debated. The links betwixt women MPs and women's organizations were feeble and fragmented, was found, which made coalition-building around schedules for women's rights challenging.

Pokharel (2008) evinced the insight of women in discrimination in diverse aspects of a male- headed society. Grounded on the sample survey, this work was developed as a descriptive study. It was discovered that discrimination against women in diverse aspects prevailed. At the societal and household levels, women were conscious of discrimination. When weighed against the family level, more discrimination was observed at the societal level. More discrimination could be observed in mobility, property, occupation, and education for married women. Likewise, in mobility and manner of behaving, unmarried women observed more discrimination. Gender and customary practices were considered the main factors accountable for discrimination.

Suleman et al., (2021) ascertained factors contributing to gender discrimination in Malaysia. Particularly, the areas in Malaysian where the GG had been on the elevation were evaluated. 50% of the populace was women in Malaysia. However, they were disfavored against and not regarded in the DM processes. For instances, in (a) the education field, (b) leadership, (c) politics, (d) the corporate environment, as well as (e) entrepreneurship with women have taken offstage. The entire model was modeled to estrange women from being counted. Malaysia was called a multi-cultural country and affluent in traditions with about 30 ethnic groups. Because of these cultural thoughts, there was a fall in the SW. The work was grounded on readings as of a book on women, politics, along with transformation in society. Lenore Manderson (1980) attempted to exhibit how she was enthused to know more regarding the Malay women following statements by a British journalist as well as other European visitors. Furthermore, the outstanding characteristic of women in Malaysia trying to battle for their survival in society via (a) rallies, (b) demonstrating, as well as (c) creating national movements amid the late 40s along with post-world war II were explored. The functions that Malay women performed in the public as well as the prejudice, inequality in rights, along with problems they experienced in the community were elucidated.

Abdi (2021) intended for scrutinizing profoundly the difficulties Somaliland's women were encountering in political contribution along with the existing chances. The PD that had been amassed via questionnaires was wielded. The most of respondents considerably agreed with the presence of difficulties against female's PP in Somaliland, causing a mean index of 3.68. '4' diverse complexities were displayed, and they were political, cultural, religious, and socio-economic difficulties. In contrast, in engaging in politics, most respondents considerably agreed that females in Somaliland had diverse opportunities, with a mean index of 3.71. According to the research, one of the chances for women to contend in politics was GQ, the espousal of gender policies and laws, and encouraging female's socioeconomic position. For encouraging and empowering WPP, the research suggested that the government along with all concerned organizations must shift rapidly to espouse policies along with laws to stimulate and authorize female's contribution in politics.

2.12.2 ILLITERACY

Stromquist (1991) surveyed the accessible proof of the educational SW and policies ratified by states worldwide concerning education and gender. Illiteracy and higher education were the '2' extremes of the educational field that were concentrated to identify not only state behaviors toward women but as well the relations betwixt gender and class. Irrespective of the kind of governance as well as approach to economic production, the states employ in activities that either resume to allocate domestic obligations to women or leave undisturbed social representations of female's 'appropriate role' in society. When resources from lower-class women were extracted, though these representations were handled via ideological forces, they had an obvious material base and were bolstered by an implied alliance of men along with women of upper and middle classes that allowed wealthier women to transmit a few advantages with men.

Israr & Naz (2021) concentrated on the effect of education on WPP. For data gathering, a sample of 320 women local body councilors were chosen via the proportional allocation technique in '7' districts of Khyber Pakhtunkhwa, Pakistan. For data gathering, a questionnaire was wielded, and data investigation was performed via SPSS 20 Chi-square ($\chi 2$) Test for univariate and bivariate analyses, respectively, at a 0.05 confidence level. The outcomes displayed that due to the mass illiteracy constraints on women to household chores, their interest in public spheres and economic opportunities were reduced, and augmented their dependency. Likewise, the deficiency in awareness concerning their constitutional and Islamic rights was engendered by illiteracy, which in turn developed the complexity of accessing mass media. Also, women's access to partake in civic activities and to operate a public office was restricted by the socio-cultural and religious commitments that existed in Pashtun society. Education was vital at the primary and higher scale to elevate women's position. The function of mass media and religious scholars in identifying the function of women in society was suggested in this research. To effectively furnish women to partake in the political process of the Islamic Democratic System, the government should propagate appropriate policies.

Katiyar (2016) evinced the rate of literacy is 73%, as per 2011 Census of India. In this, it could be observed that the rate of literacy for men was 80.9%; for women, it was 64.6 %. This implied that of the nation's populace, one-fourth were still illiterate. Moreover, when weighed against more than one-third of women, almost one-fifth of males were illiterate. The greater concern was the slow rate of growth of women literacy analogized to male literacy. A considerable number of illiterate females in society and an alarming issue for the entire expansion efforts prevailed in spite of the several endeavors carried out at national along with global levels. Since female literacy was a force multiplier for social progress, it was significant. The growth of an individual, society, along with the country was delayed by illiteracy. A vital role in decreasing GI has been played by literacy. Mapping and examining GI in literacy across the states along with Union Territories (UTs) of India was the objective of the work. It also denoted the future prospects of levels of female literacy.

2.13 OVERCOMING BARRIERS TO PARTICIPATION

The main attention of women's groups is prejudice and abuse against Indian women. Concerns about DV and SV have weakened the empowerment that is tied to family support and a higher social status in the family. Women are disheartened from working for public office and even voting owing to socio-economic problems encompassing poverty and illiteracy. If one doesn't comprehend Panchayat Raj legislation, working for public office could be a risk. The ways wherein Indian women should be empowered are renegotiating gender conventions, the gender split in the workforce, and dealing with prejudicial attitudes. Women who have the bolster of their families are more possibly to acquire entailed in politics. The Indian government has dealt with WE by incorporating all women's programs under the National Mission for WE (NMEW). As mentioned in NMEW's mission, the organization targets to "improve the EE of girls as well as women via skill-development, microcredit, vocational training, along with entrepreneurship." PM Atal Behari Vajpayee signed it and it was made into law in 2001. In the policy, Women's progress, development, and empowerment" are highlighted. Decreasing the disparity betwixt men and women and the VAW is the goal of this policy. The UN has endorsed Indian WE amongst its several initiations.

Prodip (2021) investigated the cultural hindrances that female members in reserved seats tackle regarding their PE at the local council level in the Gram Panchayat in India along with the UP in Bangladesh. Betwixt July 2018 and February 2019, PD was amassed as of West Bengal in India together with Rajshahi in Bangladesh. From country to country, the outcomes were mixed and assorted considerably. For Indian women, patriarchal behaviors were less dominant in the place of work, while the main difficulties for Bangladeshi women arrived from their male coworkers. A considerable kind of male domination in India was Proxy representation, whilst this was not a severe problem in Bangladesh. But, the intervention of politicians was the other type of male domination that limited female as of efficient involvement in local councils in India along with Bangladesh. For regulating women in politics in Bangladesh, Harassment was widely utilized, while this was less wielded in India. Religion was no more a primary obstacle to WPP in either nation. For constructing an environment, women members in both nations must battle against patriarchal behavior along with male domination, in which they could speak regarding women's interests in the DM process.

Sultan (2018) offered a comprehensive investigation of women's experience in LG along with their capability in implementing political agency to discuss local-level politics and diverse obstacles. There was a lack of subtle along with context-based scholarship on what were the diverse pathways via which females earn access to political power at the local level as well as what improved women's political group (being effectual representatives) in spite of the worth of literature on the effect of quotas along with direct elections on female's representation at the local level along with diverse program assessment research. Addressing this gap was the aim o f this work. The outcomes displayed that the quality along with processes of female's involvement in the local-level bodies had altered their consciousness and understanding regarding political as well as community interactions and their rights together with entitlements had augmented, and they were progressively independent actors in their own right.

Islam & Islam (2012) inspected the current situation of women's PE in the lower level of a LG institution, the UP in Bangladesh. (1) Conceptualizing the extent of the task of the elected members, (2) discovering the hindrances to women's contribution to local politics, and (3) detecting the issue encountered by female members in doing their activities were the goals. A qualitative technique was deployed. Very gradually, women members in UP were being empowered, as per outcomes. Women's representation in the DM process had not yet been guaranteed even though quotas had augmented the total number of women in political fields. Women encountered many social-cultural along with religious challenges that obstructed their contribution and are still deeply deserted by their male counterparts. UP female members were not able to do their duties and implement their power in an effective way owing to illiteracy and lack of experience. Only a couple of years, women were greatly considered for caring for and rearing a family and domestic chores. Nevertheless, they are presently resolving social issues in their locality. It was anticipated that LG would offer women as of the most marginalized communities the opportunity to employ politically to vote, lobby, as well as work for elections.

Mahamud (2021) intended for understanding the real political situation of women's contribution in the local politics of Bangladesh. The work defined social hindrances that had exhibited difficulties for women partaking in the political arena along with emphasizing the historical development and present circumstances. In fact, PP surrounded women's roles as a voter, an organizer, and a candidate. A few efficient recommendations were supported by scrutinizing this element for the inclusive political contribution of women in the forthcoming days. At the local level administration of Sylhet &Rajshahi districts of Bangladesh, the study was performed. For data collection, a study technique was espoused. It found a strong correlation betwixt study outcomes and WPP. A few extensive suggestions for women's contribution to local-level politics of Bangladesh were emphasized.

Palladino (2020) employed several of the prevailing theories on GQs to prevailing quotas in SEA and particularly evaluated the irregularity of Thailand. The findings of this research implied more intricate socio-cultural forces whilst Thailand persists to drop back from other SEA. The outcomes recommended that the efficiency of GQs was greatly reliant on the context of every country separately, and the results were reliable with prevailing theories of women's representation in global legislatures. To comprehend both women's roles in government and the obstacles in executing institutional variations for quality, the research embraced crucial inferences.

Chapter - 3

Methodology

3.1 INTRODUCTION

In the sphere of political and public life, this methodology emphasizes and synthesizes information on the problem of discrimination against women in law as well as practice. With respect to the status as full and equal citizens in diverse political systems and with various national, regional, and global contexts, it evaluates problems of women's equality and empowerment. Regarding representation, participation, and impacting the agenda, it discovers new developments and trends in WPP.

Across the globe, political parties encounter an emergency in public confidence. Several citizens observe them as unreachable and insensitive to their concerns (Aggestam et al., 2018). Particular challenges are caused by parties for women, who encounter formal together with informal obstacles to partaking, encompassing nomination processes, violence, along with parties with hypermasculine cultures. A potential chance to crush these paradigms is expressed by the creation of new parties amid durations of political transition. To a comprehensive type of politics, transitions can be the beginning to convert the extensive political, legal, and social obstacles. In these moments of flux, women and other marginalized groups are pushing for higher political representation in party structures can be facilitated by the creation of new party branches and rules, along with the bargaining of wide-ranging institutional methods.

The '2' crucial theories of IR are Feminism and Social Constructivism (SC). For appending to the discussion that has been chief in IR, both theories are developed. (Guyo, 2017) emphasize neglected aspects of neo-liberalism and realism regarding feminism and SC. There are cases when these theories might be deficient in the real-world application; nevertheless, if utilized as applications to how we view the globe, both theories provide a guarantee.

The single theory of IRs that constantly concentrates on women is Feminism. In explicating betwixt what it means to be a feminist, there are '4'dominant kinds of feminism (Muzaffar et al., 2017). Overall, feminism is devoted to the liberation of women. To combat politics' theories that don't encompass women or their rights as a vital aspect of IR, feminism was launched. Amid the 1980s, feminist international theories emerged as of a disciplinary disappointment with the traditional and powerful theories and techniques.

Liberal feminist IR, critical feminist IR, Postcolonial feminist IR, along with post-structural feminist IR is the '4' feminist international theories (Gender and Land Rights Database, 1978). Functioning in the present system and moving a few of the authority that has conventionally been possessed by men over to women were concentrated by Liberal feminist IR. Women possessing companies, being elected together with evolving those that as well utilize authority in the present system are regarded by liberal feminists. Liberal feminists criticized the critical feminists as, "Critical IR feminists, employing socialist principles, and pay specific focus to the uneven distribution of global capital accretion". The impacts of colonialism together with imperialism are still very real in the contemporary world for postcolonial feminists (Dhungel, 2004). These feminists "aim to place historical knowledge of outlines of colonialism as well as post-colonialism as bisecting with (a) economic, (b) social, and (c) political domination and modification, emphasizing the essence of notions of gender together with women to colonial rules and their ongoing impacts". From the work of Judith Butler, Poststructuralist feminism extracts heavily and debates that "sex is not the base or origin of gender but is itself a consequence". Post structural feminism is concentrated on the language along with observed ideas of gender.

In the worldwide North and South, women encounter very real complexities. Feminists are mainly focused on women and don't waiver in their interests distinct from other theories of IR. Irrespective of the country, feminism introduces its values to the life and political condition of every woman. This has engendered problems when the global south and developing countries are handling far diverse problems since several women in the global south are crucial to Western feminists for attempting to force their ideas and notions of women's rights. The method of IR in SC, Feminist Constructivism are concentrated on in this chapter and explicated the theory of IR to '3' countries in SAARC (India, Bangladesh, and Sri Lanka)

3.2 ASSESSMENT OF SAARC'S GENDER FRAMEWORK

In Dhaka Declaration on 8 December 1985, the SAARC, a regional and geopolitical organization was created to improve regional solidarity, economic prosperity, and political stability amongst the Member States (MS) of South Asia (Rahman et al., 2012). The MS of SAARC are (i) Afghanistan, (ii) Bangladesh, (iii) Bhutan, (iv) India, (v) Maldives, (vi) Nepal, (vii) Pakistan, as well as (vii) Sri Lanka. Kathmandu, Nepal is the headquarters of the SAARC.

The fortification of affirmed policies inside MS along with follow-up assessment is amongst the major difficulties encountered by SAARC in several regions, as well as its incompetence regarding GE is one of the most prominent instances owing to the absence of modalities and mechanisms. The execution of efficient mechanisms is made very complex by the principle of the accord, provided that not the entire SAARC MS follows the problem of GE with an equivalent volume of energy. Still, the Maldives presently prohibits women as of holding the office of President together with Vice President. Furthermore, Pakistan as well as Bangladesh has merely approved CEDAW with reservations. As per a review on GE published by UNDP, in Sri Lanka, 52% of the nation's formal laws are either completely non-compliant or only partly accordant with the CEDAW benchmarks. Sri Lankan Government (Parsuraman & Somaiya, 2016) discarded a Women's Rights Bill since it was observed as endorsing 'Western values that oppose regional culture together with traditions. With respect to international standards on GE, the complexities faced by MS are reflected at the SAARC level. Following only some meetings, endeavours to develop a feasible working group on women's problems have been rejected. This was the event with the SAARC Autonomous Advocacy Group of Prominent Women Personalities, which was summoned in 2004 (UN 2021) to confer its terms of reference but deserted devoid of any further meetings. For incorporating women's problems into regular SAARC operations, the currently developed Gender Policy Advocacy Group (GPAG) might be a highly feasible choice. How thriving the Group will be, but stays to be seen. The position of gender specialist to offer a recommendation to the SAARC Director of Social Affairs is developed by SAARC; however, this post is yet to be permanently filled, as well as a temporary gender specialist was employed via UN Women amid the growth process of the terms of consideration for the GPAG.

3.2.1 RECOMMENDATIONS

If SAARC prefers to take a robust standpoint on enforcing WPP and GE inside its MS, the deficiency of policy implementation mechanisms as well as the recent non-committal place it accepts on these problems is one of the most vital challenges that SAARC should handle. A huge volume of resources is needed, which is presently assessed at 10-20% of South Asia's GDP until 2030 is a technical hindrance to the complete execution of the SDG Agenda along with Goal 5 in specific. A challenge is created for the national governments by areas with less tax-to-GDP ratios to increase these essential funds; however, this could partially be handled by SAARC via augmented regional cooperation. Access to low-cost capital for SA firms could be developed by cross-border listings along with the progress of regional bond markets. Moreover, it has been earlier suggested that the SAARC Development Fund be converted into a SA Development Bank to superior fund projects associated with Agenda 2030 (Rahman, 2014).

As an association, SAARC is as well required to become attentive of the regions where national politics as well as the mentioned significance of 'sovereignty' and 'culture' obstruct the efficient execution of devised policy goals, and to discover the tools to operate towards these goals via a bottom-up method that endures the political party leader's interests and the outcomes of interstate conflict. It is also critical that all initiatives introduced by the organization are fine-tuned to these actualities prior to being executed, deeming the greatly diverse socio-economic together with political actualities inside and amongst the SAARC MS.

Only to be rejected afterward or stall in expansion, working groups and projects were frequently established with determined policy objectives in the past. SAARC requires processes that will be constantly inspected, advanced together with enhanced for a prolonged duration. A chance to act as only such a coordinating body for these mechanisms is provided by the Women's Policy Advocacy Group. Nevertheless, the proposed '3'-year action plan must be sanctioned immediately by the SAARC MS to achieve. Thus, apparent time limits, goals, along with indicators for every MS, and approvals for the members that violate the communally approved policies, which are all encompassed in the execution charter, must be created.

Furthermore, to achieve the objectives devised in the '3'-year action plan, MS must agree to mutually bolster each other. For example, those MS that are more progressed on specific the problems handled in the plan must utilize their resources along with experience to advantage the entire area. India's financial statement on bolstering humanitarian programs in the SAARC region is an instance of such support. It is decisive that the GPAG serves as an independent together with powerful approach with considerable effect concerning the progression of women's problems in the area even after the end of the action plan in the long term. Group meeting yearly once is the present aim. Meetings must be conducted biannually to augment its effect and the stability of its projects. Furthermore, it is significant that as of South Asia along with the international community, the Group constructs sustainable collaborations with the governments of the SAARC MS, together with civil society organizations and gender adepts. Also, SAARC must invest in a gender central point everlastingly designated by the Secretariat. Presently, the Director for Social Development chiefly handles gender problems. Nevertheless, inside SAARC government structures, women's development must be provided a highly major status. A vital breakthrough for SAARC in recognizing the significance of women's affairs is designating somebody whose work concentrates completely on gender problems.

3.2.2 MOST SIGNIFICANT CHANGES MADE IN THE LIVES OF WOMEN BENEFICIARIES

Regarding enhancements in their economic status, the majority of the surveyed organizations elucidate modifications in the lives of women beneficiaries. The recognition of economic advancement as a 'significant' transformation caused by their work is to be anticipated because livelihood is a vital field of work for several in the sample (Women for Politics, 2021). The domain of ameliorated awareness, augmented voice, and the agency is another group of considerable transformations in the lives of women beneficiaries. At the local levels (community-centered organizations of women) and higher levels of networking amongst women, organizations regard women's contribution in unanimity groups as a significant transformation in the lives of women beneficiaries. They view women as more conscious of their rights, more confident, and more negotiating power to fight for their rights and oppose breaches. Women's participation in local governance institutions and as leaders is another Area of Change (AoC) viewed. For these types of transformations, training offered by these organizations for constructing confidence and leadership skills amongst women members has been rewarded. However, another AoC that is viewed by surveyed organizations is the augmented access to services for women, enabled by the work of these organizations: access to services in the field of education. Figure 3.1 powers, namely safety nets and support services like legal aid.

Figure 3.1: Significant Changes in Lives of Women

In Bangladesh, the area of justice for women is broadly debated, with firms split over their perspective on extra-legal arbitrations via the approach of 'shalish' or village courts. Whilst a few donors and firms are functioning to ameliorate this practice to develop it gender responsive and rights-centered, several challenges its legitimacy and fear that it causes restraint of justice. Arbitration via the village courts system has engendered settlements instead of 43 convictions and penalties in several cases associated with rape or VAW.

3.3 REDUCING THE GAP IN UNDERSTANDING THREE COUNTRIES (INDIA, SRILANKA, AND BANGLADESH) GENDER GAP

The whole global gender index as well as the 15 most heavily populated countries in the globe are catalogued in the alphabetical arrangement as per the report of the ten best performers listed in rank order (Children with Disabilities are Just Like Other Children, 2022). On the whole, they are abode to about 2.5 billion women, which is 65% of the world's women populace.

With respect to PE, the growth towards gender parity is highly advanced. On this aspect, Bangladesh ranks 7th worldwide, since 54.6% of this GG have been closed till now. Remarkably, Bangladesh is the nation in which a woman has been in a head-of-state position for the most prolonged period (twenty-seven years) over the past 50 years (ranking 1st). For entailing women at the entire level of political life, even more, should be carried out. Presently, just 20.9% of parliamentarians along with 7.7% of ministers are women. Furthermore, in tertiary education, there exist gaps in enrolment (17% women vs 24% men); a few women still don't have equal rights to (a) justice, (b) inheritance, (c) right to use land along with (d) non-land assets, (e) divorce. Frequently, women are exposed to violence: 45.2% of women of ages 15–19 have been married as children, along with 53.3% of women have undergone harassment in their life. A particular observance of health signifies that a wider change is needed to accomplish superior security and health status for women even though GGs in Health and Survival (96.2%) as gauged by sex ratio at birth together with LE are comparatively small.

Worldwide, India ranks 140th, i.e., it has closed 62.5% of its GG so far. When analogized to the earlier edition, this gap is 4.2% points greater than logged, and it explicates why India has dropped twenty-eight places in the ranking (Deka, 2019). The majority of the drop has happened on the PE sub-index, in which India has regressed 13.5 % points to attain a level of gap closed so far of only 27.6%. A considerable reduction in the share of women amongst ministers is the major change that occurred in 2021, i.e., it has been halved as of 23.1% in 2019 to 9.1% in 2021. Also, at 14.4%, the contribution of women in parliament stays dormant and 15.5 is the share of the last fifty years where a woman has been the leader of state. Although to a lower degree, a reduction happened on the EP together with Opportunity sub-index. India's GG in this range broadens by 3% this year, causing a 32.6% gap closed so far. A reduction in women's labor force contribution rate, which dropped as of 24.8% to 22.3%, is one of the factors of this decline. Also, the women's share in specialized and technical roles reduced further to 29.2%. Just 14.6% of senior and managerial posts are possessed by women, which are less, as well as there are just 8.9% of organizations with Women's top managers. Moreover, women's anticipated earned income is just 1/5th of men's, which places India amongst the bottom ten worldwide on this gauge. In Health and Survival sub- index statistics also, the bias against women is replicated. India ranks amongst the bottom 5 nations in this sub-index with 93.7% of this gap stopped so far. Greater occurrence of gender-centered sex-selective practices is the reason for broad sex ratio at birth gaps. Also, above '1' in '4' woman has encountered close violence in her life. In contrast, with equality accomplished in (i) primary, (ii) secondary, along with (iii) tertiary education, 96.2% of the EA sub-index GG has been stopped. However, regarding literacy, GGs continue: when contrasted against 17.6% of men, 1/3rd of women are illiterate (34.2%).

In the global rankings for gender parity, Sri Lanka has declined. According to a WEF report, in the GGG Report 2020, which took the data from 2018, Sri Lanka was ranked 102 out of 153 nations with an index score of 0.680, down from the rank of 100 in 2019 report. But, in the 2020 rankings, Sri Lanka had slightly enhanced its score by 0.004 points, signifying that nations which were ranked lesser than Sri Lanka had reduced their GG quicker. Across the globe, Sri Lanka was amongst the top 20 nations in 2006, when the nation had a greater score. The scoring is centered on a technique in which where 0.00 indicates imparity along with 1.00 indicates parity. In South Asia, Sri Lanka was ranked after Bangladesh together with Nepal.

3.4 WOMEN IN LEADERSHIP AND DECISION MAKING

Women in leadership and DM, women's EE, VAW, and girls, in addition to women's health problems are the chief priorities to be emphasized in the action plan. The action plan has been created. From March 2017, it was waiting for consent to be executed by the SAARC MS and the SAARCGCPAG. Countries will be inquired to support their national gender improvement plans with the objectives proposed in the action plan once it is sanctioned.

- The following are a few of the action points, which have already been announced by the SAARC Secretary General, Arjun Bahadur Thapa, and are encompassed in the plan even though the manuscript of the '3'-year action plan is not openly accessible.
- Concerning the PP of women in the area, constitution of discourse as well as meetings with diverse political parties and parliamentarians;
- For women in the SAARC area (for example: at the SA University), performing systematic and institutionalized leadership skills training;
- Presentation of publications and reports on techniques and tools along with instances of fair practices as of the arena on women's leadership and PP, encompassing mechanisms together with acceptable practices that encourage women's function in DM;
- For building and executing awareness creation, work with activists and adepts; advocacy programs for the general public, party leaders, and parliamentarians to construct their involvement in comprehensive women's representation and make a decision to guarantee that a minimum of 1/3rd of the entire parliamentary seats are assigned to women;

- To motivate women to partake politically together with augment their representation in political parties as well as DM bodies at every level, build/modify rules on leadership and capacity expansion;
- To fight VAW in politics, the initiation of a SAARC region-level campaign;
- Compilation of information together with data to create a proof-centered campaign (through social as well as traditional media) on the problems associated with the PP of women, for comprehensive representation in politics, along with to guarantee women's reasonable access to the political field.

Table 3.1 depicts the comparison of '3' countries with respect to WPP centered on the current elections of every country.

Table 3.1: Comparison of WPP based on Quota Type

Country	Total seats	Total women	% Women	Election year	Quota type
Bangladesh	350	73	21	2018	Reserved Seats
India	540	78	14	2019	No legislated
Sri-Lanka	225	12	5	2020	No legislated

At the sub-national level, Sri Lanka (Democratic Socialist Republic of Sri Lanka) has a unicameral parliament with legislated quotas. Women hold 12 of 225 (5%) seats in Parliament. For the single/lower house as well as at the sub-national level, Bangladesh (People's Republic of Bangladesh) has a unicameral parliament with legislated quotas. Women held 73 of 350 (21%) seats in the Jatiya Sangsad / Parliament. At the sub-national level, India (Republic of India) possesses a bicameral parliament with legislated quotas. Women hold 78 of 540 (14%) seats in the Lok Sabha / House of the People.

For guaranteeing the quota's execution, the ECB is needed, but no mechanism presently exists to scrutinize or persuade progress toward the 33% objective. So, to initiate the execution of this law, political parties have been extremely slow; not only is it uncertain that the objective will be accomplished by 2020, yet constant compliance by the ruling government could engender legislative modification in the nick of time. As same as the reserved seat systems, it is also feasible that the quota will be filled numerically but devoid of important representation for women. The ECB has not evidently outlined the process for evaluating compliance in 2020 although the law needs the ECB to hold back registration for non-compliant parties.

3.5 INTERNATIONAL NORMS OF WOMEN IN POLITICAL PARTICIPATION

Worldwide, a basic constituent of transparent as well as accountable governance, SD together with social cohesion is the notion of GE. In a sequence of international conventions and declarations, this principle has been implanted, starting with CEDAW espoused by the UNGA in 1979. In 1995, the UN espoused the Beijing Declaration and Platform for Action, which encompassed a particular goal regarding 'Women in power and DM'. Governments restated their adherence to the objectives of the 1995 FWC on Women in Beijing at a special session of the GA in 2000. Furthermore, a resolution on Women, Peace along with Security was passed by UN Security Council. Amid this discussion, UN Secretary-General Kofi Annan mentioned that 'peace is indistinguishably connected with equality betwixt women and men … supporting and endorsing peace along with security needs equal participation in DM'. Promoting GE and empowering women is Goal 3 of the UN MDGs, which is accepted in 2010. It stated that 'women are gradually mounting to political authority, but chiefly when motivated by quotas together with other special efforts. Even though quotas remain controversial in a few parts of the globe, they remain chief to the development of a basic element of democracy —gender parity in political representation as per the IPU Secretary- General.

3.5.1 FAST-TRACKING GENDER EQUALITY

Growth in augmenting the number of women in national parliaments has been sluggish, while there is a usually rising trend as of data amassed by the IPU since 1997. The global average for women in parliament was 11.7% in January 1997. It has augmented to 20.9%, yet is still far short of the 'decisive minority' of 30% regarded vital for women to impact DM by July 2013, a few 15 years afterward. The UN MDG of GE is probably to take another half a century to accomplish at the present rate. The regional averages for women in nationwide parliaments centered on the IPU's survey of 188 nations are portrayed in table 3.2.

In the countries wherein quotas, whether legislated or voluntary, are in utilization, the largest boosts in women's parliamentary representation have happened. Out of ten countries, 9 of them with the highest augment in women MPs (in lower houses) had espoused an electoral quota, whilst 7 of the 9 lower houses where the number of women MPs reduced had no quota system. Women won 24% of parliamentary seats in nations with legislated quotas together with 12% of seats where no quotas were utilized out of 48 countries where elections were held. Temporary special measures, namely quotas, are required to 'initiate' WPR, especially in nations where women have conventionally been under-represented in the national legislatures as per Article 4 of CEDAW. The convention states that such gauges are aimed to be temporary, concluding 'when the goals of parity of opportunity along with treatment has been accomplished. Actually, this means until women have acquired adequate skills and acknowledgment to employ on an equivalent base to men, they obtain an initial bolster to join political life.

Table 3.2: Regional Averages of Women in National Parliaments in 2013

Region	Single House or Lower House %	Upper House or Senate %	Both Houses combined %
Nordic countries	42.0	---	---
Americas	24.8	25.0	24.9
Europe— Organization for Security and Co- operation in Europe (OSCE) member countries encompassing Nordic countries	24.5	22.6	24.1
Europe—OSCE member countries exclusive of Nordic countries	22.8	22.6	22.8
Sub-Saharan Africa	21.1	18.8	21.7
Asia	19.1	13.8	18.5
Arab States	17.8	7.6	15.9
Pacific (encompassing Australia)	13.1	39.8	15.9

Since the FWC on Women in Beijing in 1995 (20 years before), women's representation in parliament has augmented by 10% points as of 15% to 25% as per IPU. At such a pace, accomplishing gender parity might take 50 years (until 2070). SDG 5.5 dedicates the government to accomplish "complete together with efficient contribution as well as equal chances for leadership at every level of DM in political life" for women by 2030 as of table 3.3.

Table 3.3: Women's Political Participation in Global

Region	Sub-region	Lower Chamber and Unicameral	Upper chamber	All Chambers
Americas		**32%**	**33%**	**32%**
	Caribbean South	41%	32%	40%
	North America	36%	42%	37%
	Central America	28%	36%	29%
	South America	26%	27%	26%

	South America	26%	27%	26%
Europe		**31%**	**30%**	**30%**
	Nordic Countries	45%	0%	45%
	Western Europe	35%	32%	34%
	Southern Europe	28%	37%	31%
	Central and Eastern Europe	25%	19%	24%
Global		**26%**	**25%**	**26%**
Africa		**25%**	**20%**	**24%**
	Horn	33%	30%	33%
	East Africa	33%	29%	32%
	Southern Africa	28%	29%	29%
	Central Africa	19%	20%	19%
	North Africa	24%	11%	21%
	West Africa	16%	12%	16%
Asia		**21%**	**17%**	**20%**
	Central Asia	26%	22%	25%
	East Asia	22%	23%	22%
	South East Asia	21%	13%	20%
	South Asia	17%	19%	18%
Pacific		**18%**	**45%**	**21%**
	Australia and New Zealand	39%	51%	42%
	Pacific Islands	6%	8%	6%
Middle East		**17%**	**13%**	**16%**

The whole global averages cover vital regional and sub-regional differences as of the aforementioned table. For instance, in parliament, women's representation in the Americas is at 32% (40% in the Caribbean) as well as in Europe at 30% (45% in the Nordic nations). Africa is just a little low than the global average with 25% of women in the lower houses as well as 24% overall. However, varying as of 33% in the Horn of Africa to 16% in West Africa, there exist considerable regional differences. Certainly, 180 in the global ranking, with 6% female in parliament, women's representation in parliament in Africa varies from the finest performer Rwanda (61% females in parliament - view Annex 4) to Nigeria regarding IPU ranking. The Barometer comprises a wealth of investigation together with perceptions to aid the meaning of this intricate tapestry by exploiting a blend of quantitative along with qualitative techniques, encompassing 60 case researches from 40 of Africa's 54 countries.

3.6 SDGS AND GENDER EQUALITY

The international community consented in 2015 on 17 SDGs to follow over the next 15 years directed by the UN. The UNICEF's work on GE is reasserted and revitalized by the SDGs, particularly regarding the rights and empowerment of adolescent girls.

The requirements and rights of girls are summarized in

Goal 5: GE and WE and cut across the 2030 Agenda for SD.

Other SDG targets as well as indicators that vibrate with UNICEF's gender work are:

Goal 3: Good Health and Well-being - decrease maternal mortality, stop avertable fatalities of newborns as well as children below 5, guarantee access to sexual along with RH and terminate (1) HIV, (2) AIDS as well as other diseases.

Goal 4: Quality Education - from pre-primary to tertiary levels, universalize access to quality education, with a particular decree to rectify social inequalities that disable access to educational chances. To develop efficient learning environments, eradicate gender disparities at every level, and ensure education amenities are gender-sensitive. The equal right of girls to quality education is core to the SD agenda as of GA resolution 70/138.

3.7 CULTURAL, TRADITIONAL AND RELIGIOUS BARRIERS TO WOMEN POLITICAL PARTICIPATION (WPP) IN THREE COUNTRIES

Numerous factors persist in challenging WPP in spite of proof of why it is decisive to have women in DM. It can be categorized into '2': The 1st is the deep-rooted systemic "informal factors", namely tradition, culture, custom, socialization, and GS which in their most intense state are articulated as gender violence. All night suddenly, these age-old patriarchal norms will not be eliminated. They will give rise to the steady "1 step forwards, 2 steps backwards" syndrome.

Primary to the constraints that women encounter is a deep-rooted patriarchal structure where family regulates and DM powers are in the hands of men. Particularly with respect to women's functions and conditions in society, conventional beliefs and cultural attitudes stay robust, especially in rural regions. Still, conventional functions and the labor division are apparently gendered. It is highly complex for women to depart their customary household functions for more public functions outside the house because of the social norms. Naturally, Women's gender individuality is still chiefly envisaged as domestic and persists in obstructing women's entry into formal politics.

Why the idea of Political Feminism? Is it not the specific nature of feminism per se to form part of the Polis - the body of citizens - a compilation of diverse interests aiming for the betterment of all? Doesn't feminism symbolize only one of the several groups and activities in the political dialogue that comprises our democracies? The political party's struggles are not concentrated by a feminist conversation, yet it definitely holds the argument's plurality, notions, and primary visions on how to construct a real and pre-eminent society.

A process in which women take charge of their lives: (a) materializing their own plans, (b) acquiring skills, (c) constructing self-confidence, (d) solving issues, along with creating self- sufficiency is called WE. Just the individual can authorize herself or himself to make choices or to speak out; no one can empower another. Via the combined endeavors of the WM, institutions inside the State as well as civil society are bolstering processes that can look after women's self- empowerment. The women's rights movement of the last quarter of the 20thcentury can be understood from this viewpoint.

3.7.1 INDIAN SOCIAL CONSTRUCTIVISM AND FEMINISM

Women possess chiefly remained inert receivers of teachings along with passionate practitioners of religious ceremonies when analogized to men who are dominant as receivers, translators, and propagators of divine messages. Perspectives created around patriarchal understandings of religious faith have delineated and formed the social as well as cultural backgrounds of Indian women bringing about their deprivation of rights together with 2nd-class position.

3.7.1.1 VIOLENCE AGAINST WOMEN

An alarming problem in India is VAW, the marginalized sections of society, along with minorities. In the family, violence is widespread as well as extends to a woman's circle of recognized persons, even those she is educated to respect and divulge in, like spiritual leaders as well as in public areas.

The painful miseries in the lives of nuns coming as of patriarchal mindsets are illustrated by Cyrilla Chakkalakal, a Franciscan Sister of

St. Mary of the Holy Angels. She narrated by mentioning the murder of '2' sisters as of her congregation in 1990, how the character defamation of the sisters in the media turned limelight to the sexuality of the sisters along with derogated as of who or why of the murders. Also, the Catholic community's leaders failed to support them. Their apathy as well as silence was hurting. Whether they were repressed by other powers? The grief that the congregation experienced has simply diminished gradually.

Furthermore, religious systems possess a pessimistic effect on victims of sexual abuse. Women were elucidated as wrongdoers, exploiters, and enchantresses by women internalizing scriptural rendition. This gives way to their silence on abuse. Viewing the priest on behalf of God blends chaos and regret. Consequently, the psychotic and religious effect of abuse perpetrated by the clergy is massive on women sufferers.

Women from marginalized sections like Dalit as well as tribal, industrial workers and agricultural laborers, and deprived women in urban and rural regions - have rallied against VAW in the society and family, harassment of female-headed families, mass rapes of tribal as well as Dalit women, dowry slayings, DV and alcoholism, and offenses for the sake of honor. The members of the novel independent women's groups deem in fighting against all kinds of sexual domination as well as consider women as a subjugated sex. According to them, similar to casteism along with communalism, one of the most efficient weapons utilized by the ruling class to segregate people is sexism. Thus, they reckon on battling against the caste structure, spiritual prejudice, and sexism, concurrently. In the Dalit or outcast community, the women's bodies are viewed as "available", and they are depicted as characterless; hence they are used for sex. Cruelties against Dalit women are very evident together with executed with total immunity. Their social condition's internalization induces them to be voiceless. In every religious set encompassing Christians, the outlook of the cast supports culture. Nevertheless, recently, Dalits have acquired knowledge of their condition and value. They cover 17% of the Indian populace; hence, with diverse political publicity stunts, politicians frequently try to get in touch with them, which engender dividing the community. From a Dalit viewpoint, Shyamla, a Dalit woman, propounded the enunciation of feminism.

In India, VAW has its foundation in cultural behaviors toward men's dominance, and in the family, it cuts through the entire religious and caste clusters. It will be awful to describe the stories of VAW in the family. It is always a surprise how women persist in living and looking after their children and household. The stories are the same, i.e., hitting, smothering, gagging (also amid pregnancy), sexual and emotional violence, and violence performed on the girl children. However, women possess access to legal aid to take legal action against DV with the presence of a powerful WM that assisted in bringing transformations in the law.

3.7.1.2 SEXUALITY AND THE POLITICS OF GENDER

The politics of representation is at work largely by casting humans in a gendered mould in every mainstream religion and culture according to Kochurani Abraham, a feminist theologian. For masculinity, the illustration keeps men at a benefit, whilst women are delineated as feeble, sensitive, along with reliant, are more deprived. Paradoxically, although Pope Francis speaks about escalating the women's roles, he is too trapped in the harmonizing gendered attitude. Abraham viewed that his otherwise advanced letters mention gendered functions for women, ignoring qualities, namely intellectual group, theological proficiency, managerial capabilities, together with leadership skills.

As authority is hegemonic as well as specifies violence to govern, overpower and implement a system of rule, there is a requirement to crash gender dual folds. Huge VAW and LGBTIQ persons are done by the gendering of body and sexuality. Men are regarded as the norm, as well as scriptures are utilized to delineate women as faulty, wicked, and requiring to be regulated, even by utilizing violence. Certified doctrines of religions exclude LGBTIQ persons and their subjectivities. In India, the problem of LGBTIQ persons is still emerging. An individual who planned to speak to us regarding this subject didn't come, yet they are encompassed in the program for change.

Fr. Shaji George Kochuthara of the Carmelites of Mary Immaculate stated that whilst affirming women's equality, church education endorses the idea of complementarily designating specified functions to women as well as men, with women normally in inactive and subservient roles. Procreation is the core of the marriage affiliation and the leader in theological principles regarding sexuality. (a) Love, (b) equality, (c) respect, along with mutuality that bring about reinforcement of the marriage association are neglected. He stated that this engendered the active/passive concept that allows violence, namely marital rape, yet as well emotional, psychological, along with financial brutality that secretly regulates women's sexuality. Kochuthara inferred that on the problems of DV and dowry, church leadership sustains to be silent; however, it underlined a morality that denounces abortion together with contraceptives as well as promotes loyalty in marriage and parenthood regardless of the occasion.

Gender justice is influenced for political benefits in India. A debate over a Uniform Civil Code to split people on religion along with gender is constructed by the government. The government is fuelling Muslim women to rise against polygamy as well as the triple talaq as it is followed in India (in which the man tells "talaq" 3 times to divorce his wife). However, it was found by the women's rights lawyer Flavia Agnes, who has engaged in many cases of Muslim women's divorce in court that Muslim law can certainly provide justice to women, particularly to get alimony for them, whilst women in other customs persist in the struggle for those rights. In Muslim custom, 2nd wives possess entire rights, whilst in other customs, they have no rights. When analogized to other traditions, polygamy is highly widespread in Islam. She highlighted, "We require equality of rights and not equality of the law."

3.7.2 BANGLADESH SOCIAL CONSTRUCTIVISM AND FEMINISM

A lesser status of women as well as a violation of fundamental HR, and a blockage to the accomplishments of the goals of women's parity, progress, together with peace are encompassed as discrimination against women. In Bangladesh, discrimination against women evolved as one of the most visible as well as expressed social problems in the last '2' decades, and it led to women's subjection. The fundamental doctrine of the Bangladeshi social system is men's domination as well as women's subordination. The (i) social, (ii) political, (iii) economic, (iv) religious, as well as (v) cultural differences betwixt men and women are composed of all kinds of discrimination, and it initiated men's dominant society. It as well removes women's equality with men, creates women's submissiveness along with devises a social structure that generates women's subordination.

3.7.2.1 CULTURAL HURDLES

The research was (Deka, 2019) carried out on 19 UPs from diverse socio-cultural zones of Bangladesh, and the main complexities concerning domination, patriarchy, and hegemony were discovered. The central obstacles to women's PP are the patriarchal behaviors and the absence of social reception. Pessimistic community mindsets to political and community movements, more subordinate social endorsement as peoples' representatives, less liberty of movement, less access to the public arena, social responsibilities, absence of security, limitations in entailing standard outdoor actions, unequal power associations, strict labour division, opposing social values regarding women, absence of social mobility, patriarchal cultural backgrounds, stringent gender uniqueness of women, absence of confidence owing to social delinquency, and negative social standards were the cultural obstacles for the WPP in the local governance of Bangladesh.

3.7.2.2 FAMILY RESTRICTIONS

It was found that the main obstacle for women to PP in the local governance in Bangladesh is family limitations. The woman's function as a caregiver of the family and simultaneously a representative to the UPs constructs large conflict that negatively affects their active PP. A significant role is played by the age of an individual in her active contribution to different socio- political actions. When analogized to young people, aged women enjoy more liberty in social mobility. Partaking in activities, namely PP, attending social meetings, along with volunteering in diverse social events have been discovered to be positively correlated with productive aging. Ubiquitous violence in the country's electoral process affects the women in Bangladesh as voters, candidates, political party allies, and activists to discover the impact of EVs on women's significant involvement.

3.7.2.3 POLITICAL VIOLENCE AGAINST WOMEN

Women's PP is hindered by Bangladesh's widespread intense political culture. Women are scared of becoming targets of political attacks and clashes. Moreover, they also frighten their families restricting their involvement in the political field. Most of the EV undergone by women is psychological (that is, oppression as well as harassment). Also, inside the house, several women are victims of EV, chiefly psychological violence. Via harassment and attack on women candidates, political activists, and voters, SV (as a kind of EV) has been undergone. A few women are perpetrators of EV. They are utilizing oppression to restrict voter alternatives inside the household. They are maligning other candidates in the public arena. As WPP augments, this phenomenon also augments; offenders of such violence may view engagement in such strategies as essential to guarantee a "seat at the table". To discourage WPP, retaining entry to financial aid generally and exclusively to partake in politics is utilized.

3.7.3 SRI LANKA SOCIAL CONSTRUCTIVISM AND FEMINISM

To handle these obstacles, women's rights activists have pressed for an electoral GQ. Until now, only at the regional level, their demands have been fulfilled. Sri Lanka initiated its 1st quota for women in LG, which demands that 25 % of elected legislators in LG must be women because of the 2016 electoral amendment (Jackson, 2010). The gauge has augmented women's representation in LG as of 2% in 1989 to 24 % in 2018 even though not every local council has obeyed the quota need. Throughout the nation, 1,926 Women local councilors are working in LG. Advocating the same electoral reforms at the national level is the aim of the Women Parliamentarian Conclave, which was established by women politicians in 2020. Until now, proponents' reform recommendations have not been achieved, and a measure to execute a 25 % GQ for women in provincial councils has been delayed. To recruit more women, the local quota law has pressurized parties; since women elected via proportional representation lists are treated by men leaders as 2nd-class politicians, it has also weakened their political effect.

Projects 'rarely surpassed the recognition of differences in work carried out by men and women to really executing programs for modification in gender relations' is one of the most perceived issues. Frequently, NGOs try to compromise by encompassing gender considerations in situations of humanitarian crisis where survival is considered the most significant objective. Nevertheless, gender considerations merely entail "appending on" women beneficiaries or women's viewpoints to prevailing methods of intervention in most of these cases. Certainly, the event of humanitarian crisis aid debated in this is diverse to that of long-term development projects; yet, Rathgeber's investigation of feminist development practices emphasize precisely a similar eventuation.

3.7.3.1 POLITICAL CULTURE

A marginalized factor that is profoundly embedded in well-established behaviors, societal institutions, as well as market forces in Sri Lanka are gender sensitivity. When analogized to men, women who partake in politics encounter more abuse, criticism, and violence. To address the prevailing hegemony of the political arena, the constitutional provisions for equality of treatment along with the regulations of non-discrimination are insufficient.

Also, the present political culture was utilizing and maltreating women as underprivileged communities, and it seems as a 'filthy political culture'. At provincial and local levels, (a) EV, (b) the approach of surprising elections, (c) disappointment with the political process, (d) discriminations against ethnic minorities, and (e) sexual abuse of women are the chief features of this dirty political culture. For instance, a contentious speech against former President Mrs. Bandaranaike Kumaratunga was said by Minister S.B. Dissanayake, members of the Sri Lanka Freedom Party that he will make her naked and indicted before the public if he were in authority subsequent to the general election. However, he is functioning as a cabinet minister of the current coalition government in spite of the press release against his remark neither any political party nor ruling government didn't take any measure against his undesirable political perspective. Likewise, several women candidates, who rebel and confront this man-dominated political structure, are continually excluded and insulted. Regarding women candidates exhibiting poor sexist behaviors and devaluing language about their sexuality and personal life, the proof can be viewed from social media. Simultaneously, women from the Islamic are not really welcomed in PL, as well as they have to address cultural as well as PV if they desire to partake in politics.

3.7.3.2 VIOLENCE AGAINST WOMEN IN SRI-LANKA

In Sri Lanka, VAW is widespread with Intimate Partner Violence (IPV) (physical as well as sexual) being the most executed act. IPV incidence varies as of 20 to 72%, with current research recommending that 25–35% of women have undergone partner violence amid their life span as per a current scoping study on IPV. To reduce VAW, Sri Lanka has a reasonably well-built underlying legal as well as policy structure and also possesses approved many international treaties (for example: CEDAW along with Convention on the Rights of the Child), which have pertinence for VAW. Currently, a supportive regulatory structure and service response is created by the health domain to deal with VAW. In spite of these, the partner violence's issue sustained greatly underreported by women. In Sri Lanka, research on men's behavior and VAW discovered that just 32% of Women undergoing violence and who required medical assistance had reported the violence, as well as just 10% had reported their families regarding the violence and the distress they have undergone.

3.7.3.3 BARRIERS OF FINANCE TO WOMEN ENTER INTO POLITICS SRI-LANKA

One more obstacle is finance. Standing for an election has turned out to be an extremely expensive venture owing to the patronage-centered politics of most Sri Lankan political parties. For organizing and combining their electoral foundation, candidates have to campaign across a broad geographical region and utilize their own resources. Frequently, women are discouraged from contesting for political office since women tend to possess low access to independent wealth and political donor networks. 16 Furthermore, intensive inter- and intra-party rivals and violence in electoral politics operate against women aspiring to evolve into political leaders, primarily as there are some bolster services or responsibility means for women aimed at PV or sexual harassment.

This project funded by the German Federal Foreign Office is executed by Democracy Reporting International in partnership with the Rural Women's Front to avert EV in Sri Lanka by extending core electoral reform problems and fortifying the reliability of the public dialogue (2019-2021). Averting EV is the chief goal of this project and it has a robust capacity building and greater knowledge element concentrated on women in politics. Such as the training of a trainers' Programme on women in politics, launching district-level groups of women political representatives, performing public discussions on electoral reforms, and augmenting the efficacy of women politicians' commitment to socio-political problems are carried out by the project. Moreover, bolster for local institutions for workshops on typical media communication for women political representatives from LG bodies are encompassed in it. As well, interviews of important women political figures are utilized for awareness boosting on the radio, and it has headed an awareness-raising campaign that utilizes animated videos that are centered on the actual experiences of Sri Lankan women in politics.

3.8 EDUCATION EMPOWERMENT

An important area of emphasis is education. Still, girls make up a maximum percentage of out-of- school children than boys even though the globe is advancing in accomplishing gender parity in education. In developing countries, around one-quarter of girls don't attend school. Usually, families will emphasize education for their sons when they have restricted means and can't pay off expenses like (i) school fees, (ii) uniforms, as well as (iii) collections for each of their children. For the purposes of domestic chores, fetching water, and childcare, the families may depend on girls' labor. Nevertheless, in developing countries, prioritizing girls' education offers possibly the single maximum payoffs. An educated girl is more potentially put off marriage, elevate a smaller family, have fitter children, along with send her own children to school. More chances are present for women to earn an income together with partake in political activities, and she is less feasibly to become prey to HIV. Table 3.4

Table 3.4: Theoretical Methodology of Reducing Gender Disparities in Educational Outcomes

GE Dimension	Sample GE Indicators
Human Capital	• Scores on literacy as well as numeracy tests and other national evaluations, by sex, ethnicity, as well as location (rural or urban) • Number of men as well as Women students gaining as of novel or ameliorated educational services
Economic Empowerment	• By subject field, number and percentage of extra women as well as men finishing a technical, vocational, or other tertiary criteria • Number and percentage of women as well as men bestowed a tertiary scholarship • Number and percentage of women and men scholarship beneficiaries who graduate as well as are engaged in their field of proficiency • Number as well as percentage of men and Women principals
Voice and Rights	• Proof that legislation as well as rules forbid bias in educational bodies (for example: subject alternatives, technical as well as vocational courses and apprenticeships, pregnancy, parenthood, as well as disability) • Number of educational organizations with strategies as well as approaches for addressing SH and GBV, and discrimination
Gender Capacity Building	• Proof that education policy along with plans comprise GE goals and actions to deal with obstacles to reasonable education results • Proof that school prospectus endorse equality betwixt women and men, girls and boys

3.9 MODEL SPECIFICATION

Here, for the purpose of amassing data to answer particular research questions, an analytical study design was employed in research design. To collect and gather data and information needed, this research utilized online sources as a tool since the information required can be easily and rapidly amassed from the internet.

Centered on WPP problems, GE, and WE in '3' countries like Bangladesh, India, and Sri Lanka, data was collected grounded on Women's Representation and Participation in Politics. In chapter 6, the data were tabulated and scrutinized, and it was created as per the online data.

By making WE for the aforementioned dimensions, an attempt has been made to gauge women's PP and GE in this research.

Figure 3.2: Relationship between Sustainable Development Goals and Women Political Empowerment

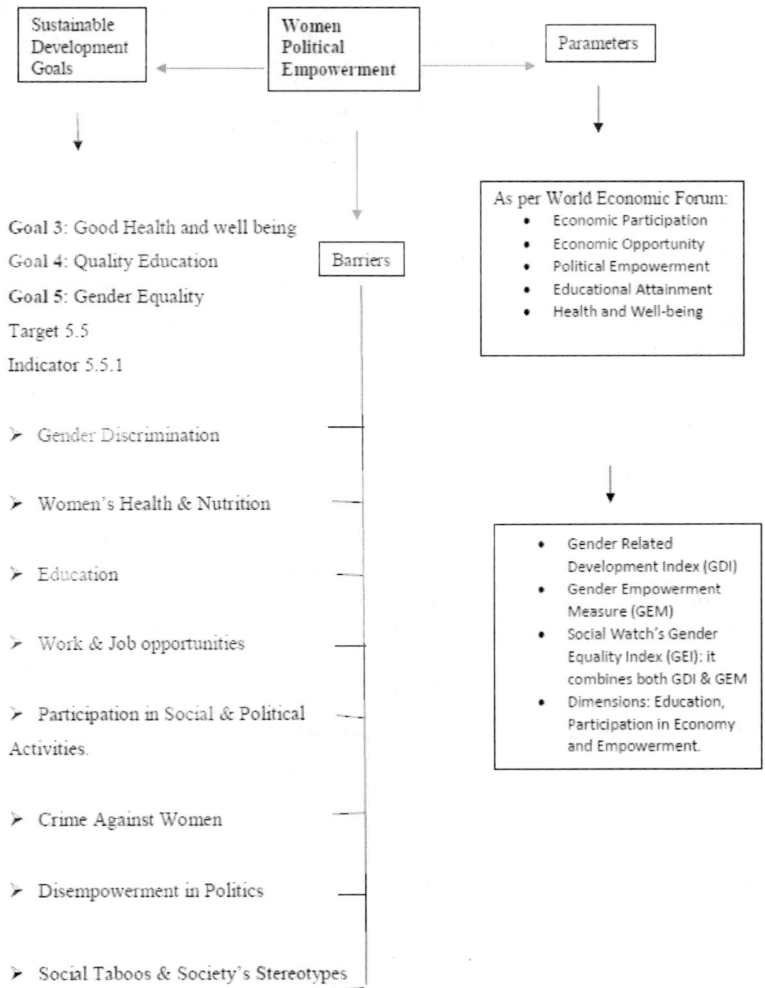

The present study shows the relationship between the SDGs and Women Political Empowerment and various barriers which are responsible for low representation and participation of the study as shown in the figure 3.2. The focus of the study is on Goal 5 that is Gender Equality further focusing on the Target 5.5 of the Goal 5 and the indicator 5.5.1.

Target 5 of Goal 5 talks about ensuring full participation of females in leadership and decision- making by 2030. Whereas, indicator 5.5.1 give emphasis on proportion of seats held by women in national parliaments and local governments.

At the same time, the correlation between various goals is highlighted. As the concept of sustainability is multi-dimensional, similarly, Goal 5 of the SDGs is directly related with Goal 3 and Goal 4 as shown through the literature. Goal 3 of SDGs ensure healthy lives for females and Goal 4 emphasis on the quality education of the women.

Apart from the above correlation, various barriers of women political empowerment that hampers the representation and participation of women are listed through the literature available in India, Bangladesh and Sri Lanka. The common barriers in three south Asian countries include discrimination based on gender, less emphasis on women's health and nutrition, lack of education, less work and job opportunities for females, less participation in social and political activities, crime against women, disempowerment of females in politics, and various social taboos and the stereotype nature of the society.

There are various parameters which are used for this study. Firstly, parameters given by World Economic Forum (WEF) are used to study the current condition of women. The parameters given by WEF includes economic participation, economic opportunity, political empowerment, educational attainment and the health and well-being of the women. Also, various others parameters are given by the UN which includes GDI and GEM. Later, Social Watch's Gender Equality Index combined the GDI and GEM to study various dimensions of the women which including education, participation in economy and empowerment of women.

In order to find out the correlation between various parameters of women empowerment given by WEF and in the SDGs, the data is run through SmartPLS which clearly highlighted the direct and indirect relationship between economic participation of women, economic opportunities, political empowerment, education and health as shown in the figure 3.3.

Keeping political empowerment as the main parameter of the study, the result is as follows. Political empowerment of women is directly related to the economic opportunities which is further directly related with the economic participation of the women. Whereas, there is an indirect relationship between political empowerment of women and their education and health. And there is no direct relationship between political empowerment and economic participation of women. Also, there is no relationship between the health and education of the females. But good health and well-being of the females does make a positive impact on their economic opportunities For the purpose of seeking holistic picture of the topic, the study is based on secondary data collected from various sources such as Annual Reports of the UN, State Publications of the Directorate of Economics and Statistics of different states of the three countries (India, Bangladesh and Sri Lanka), Economic and Political Weekly and Research papers available online. Major data based on the political status of women is collected through Inter- Parliamentary Union, which is an international organization of national democracies. The data collected was calculated on linear and exponential basis. A linear regression model is predicated on the following four premises: Linearity, Homoscedasticity, Independent of one another and Normality through EViews Software. And further the Exploratory factor analysis is conducted through SmartPLS in order to find out the relationship between various parameters of the study.

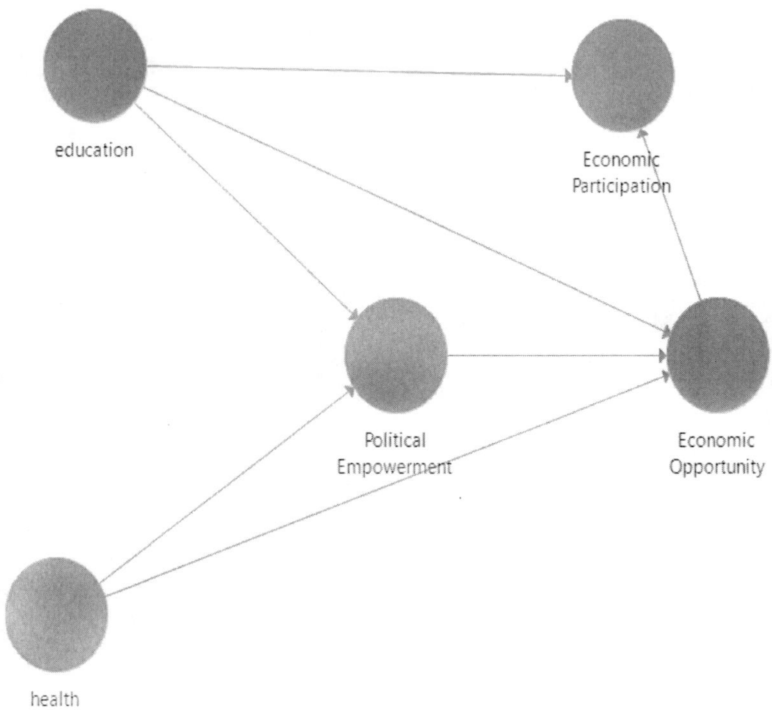

Figure 3.3: Relationship between factors given by WEF and SDGs.

Chapter - 4

India

4.1 INTRODUCTION

Men as well as women are not identical and are equal in status. Being complementary to each other, they are an incomparable pair; also, they help one another. So that, without the presence of each other, they cannot be perceived. Thus, as of these concepts, an essential consequence is followed that would imbalance their status in which the equal ruin of both is involved. Globally, in many countries, democracy, which is more popular along with the most debated topic, has become an objective nowadays (Acharya, 2019). It is also the state's concept in which without discrimination, the higher values of freedom along with rights to everyone are provided; moreover, it denotes equality amongst everyone. In life's DM walk, towards equality together with the entire individual's representation, democracy endeavours. The concept's growing popularity along with the democratic practice is only made by this. Factually, "the rule of the father" is the patriarchy's meaning. Formerly, grounded on the authority of households' men heads, for defining the social organizations, the term was wielded (Non-standard employment around the world, 2016). The political system, which was ruled by men was defined by the term. Here, women had inferior social along with political status, including basic rights. Here, to the man, the patriarchal social order authority is assigned where the responsibility for the family is taken by the man. Thus, in contrast to the women, the man is considered stronger.

Mahatma Gandhi's words echo such non-detachable men as well as women's presence. Worldwide, it is not a novel concept that played a patriarchal nature's role (Mosse, 2018). Globally, the patriarchal structure of a society, state, along with ruling structure, there are many examples. As of the society's formation, the workplace is considered the man's domain;

also, weak along with less skilled is considered the woman. Women are meant to be in the social traditions along with the hard rules in the house boundaries though women have symbolized in society's various regions. Representation, which comes next to WE, is the subsequent phase for their participation even for others. All over the world, WE are a problem along with discussion nowadays that is the front topic in numerous formal as well as –informal campaigns. When women's rights are secured, WE are probable in figure 4.1.

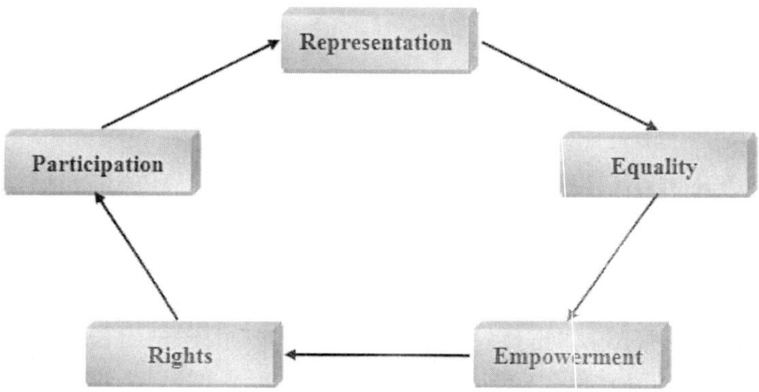

Figure 4.1: Areas of Development in Women Politics

4.1.1 WOMEN EMPOWERMENT OF POLITICAL REPRESENTATION IN SOUTH ASIA

Generally, a person or group's action where with the other's support, they speak or act is named representation (Singh, 2013).Expressly, in any region, the particular group's action is indirectly represented by a person; for example, women representing their gender (Mulky, 2013). In society, women have not attained any vital position even though they establish half of the entire population. The thought is that the workplace considers the man's domain; also, the woman is thought to live in margin everywhere (Times of India 2019) (Kundu and Mohanan). The equality consolidation is interpreted as the representation. Enabling women to achieve access along with control of material intellectual together with human resources is termed empowerment. It is the redeployment of power in which the patriarchal notions together with the men dominance is challenged.

4.2 INDIA

Worldwide, the most populous country is India, which has 1.29 billion people and 66% of them exit in rural regions. Several developmental tasks like insufficient infrastructure that includes energy as well as water, lack of connectivity, along with inadequate sustainable livelihoods are faced by rural India (Bajpai, 2015). For private companies along with consumers, distribution in rural markets is tedious. Detecting prevailing networks or creating novel ones are tough for companies in fragmented along with disorganized distribution channels. The distribution cost along with the after-sales service can be increased owing to the huge geographies that have broadly dispersed populations as well as inexistent transportation (Bajpai, 2015). Moreover, to work in management, sales, marketing, or technical, specifically in remote regions, ready access does not exist for skilled individuals. Some local distribution agents are there in the villages who deliver the products. Reaching brick as well as mortar shops takes a long time along with additional cost, which leads to offering a limited range of related products frequently. These mostly affect women as they are impacted via mobility along with time constraints. Like, the time is increased when there is inadequate energy that women should do their household responsibilities, which consequently lowers their opportunities to participate in social events. Owing to kerosene oil as well as other fuel-centric lighting sources, women are exposed to health issues. Also, certain constraints towards participating in social events are faced by women in rural India. In rural India, only 5.6 % of women have a consistent salary; also, they are employed in low-skill as well as low- productivity occupations with low or no pay (President, 2011).

In India, with the welfare strategies for HD, every Five-year plan was drafted after the independence. However, for the first time in Indian planning history, the 6th five-year plan (1980-85) comprised a chapter on women as well as Development. For women's development along with WE, it comprehended a multi-pronged strategy. 'Despite development measures along with constitutional legal guarantees, women have lagged behind in almost the sectors' was the report admitted by the sixth plan. Moreover, in the seventh plan (1985-90), the concept of WE as a Development Strategy was accepted by the Indian government. Further, the five-year plan has WE as its overall plan objectives. The Indian Government declared 2001 as the "WE Year".

To all citizens, the Constitution of India guarantees equal justice on social, economic, along with political grounds. The equal rights for men as well as women are stated by Article 14. It also states equal opportunities on social, economic, along with political grounds.

In the spheres of sex, caste, race, religion, et cetera, discrimination against any citizen is prohibited by Article 15. In women's favour, Article

15 (3) authorizes the State to make affirmative discrimination. Likewise, related to public appointments, equal opportunities are provided for all citizens.

Towards securing the rights of all citizens, men as well as women, the right to means of livelihood, the state can direct the policies says Article 39(a). Meanwhile, equal pay for equal work is ensured by Article 39(c). For guaranteeing just along with humane conditions of work as well as maternity relief, to make provision, the state can be directed says Article 42. Significantly, on every citizen, fundamental duties are imposed by the constitution via Article 51A(e) that is, to give up the practices offensive to women's dignity.

But, under the Indian Constitution, the question is whether the women gain the benefits provided for them. Unfortunately, the answer is not promising. Thus, in the constitution, for attaining the goals, there is a long way to move.

4.2.1 HISTORICAL BACKGROUND OF WOMEN EMPOWERMENT IN INDIA

Over the prior few millenniums, SW has been exposed to numerous changes in India. To men, women had more than equal status in the early Vedic age. Various names of woman sages along with seers are mentioned in Rigveda as well as Upanishads, especially Gargi and Maitrey (Sharma, 2015). But, at approximately as of 500B.C, the SW degraded with the Mughal's invasion; then, by European invaders. Jainism, Pandit Rama Bai, Ishwarchandra Vidyasagar, Guru Nanak, Raja ram Mohan Rai, along with several others did reformatory movements in the SW. The British also upgraded the SW in India like 'Abolition of Sati Pratha', 'Widow Remarriage Act, 1856', et cetera.

After the Independence, the actual change took place. Equality for women is ensured by the Indian constitution. Article 15(1) is an example of which women's rights are ensured (Shakti, 2017). During the late 1970s, feminism started rising up in India. For WE, numerous social active groups along with NGOs are working. India is the first country before the USA along with a few other European countries to have the voting right for women, which is a huge asset.

Globally, India has the biggest democracy. Also, many other prior colonies, noted that the democratic political systems failed and except for the period betwixt 1975 and 1977 when PM, Indira Gandhi declared an "emergency" and suspended the Constitution, numerous good commentators have told that India must have remained a democracy.

The Congress party came to an end by the late 1980s after a long period of Indian political dominance. In the 1984 General Election, with a devastating victory, Rajiv Gandhi won the election. However, he failed to renew the party's organization following her assassination. In his period, the government had wandered. The government become embroiled owing to the corruption at the uppermost level; specifically, in the "Bofors affair" where insurgencies had collected in Punjab as well as Assam and then in Kashmir. Then, all over the country, violence along with instability appeared in an "advanced" state (Gujarat) or a "backward" state (Bihar).

After that, in December 1992, the Indian polity's fabric was torn when the movement of Hindu cultural nationalism's supporters spurred; however, the Bharatiya Janata Party, which aroused at that time the opposition to the Congress degraded an old mosque in Ayodhya. After that, a huge political instability was faced by the Indians in the 1990s.

In the period of 10 years, '5' general elections occurred. They are in 1989, 1991, 1996, 1998, along with 1999 respectively. Meanwhile, in the former 40 years, only '8' such elections were conducted. Also, for the first time, minority governments were experienced in the country that is, starting with

V.P Singh's government in below table 4.1. But this is the decade where regarding economic policy, India changed. In 1991, this started to be instituted in moderate liberalization showed in given figure 4.2.

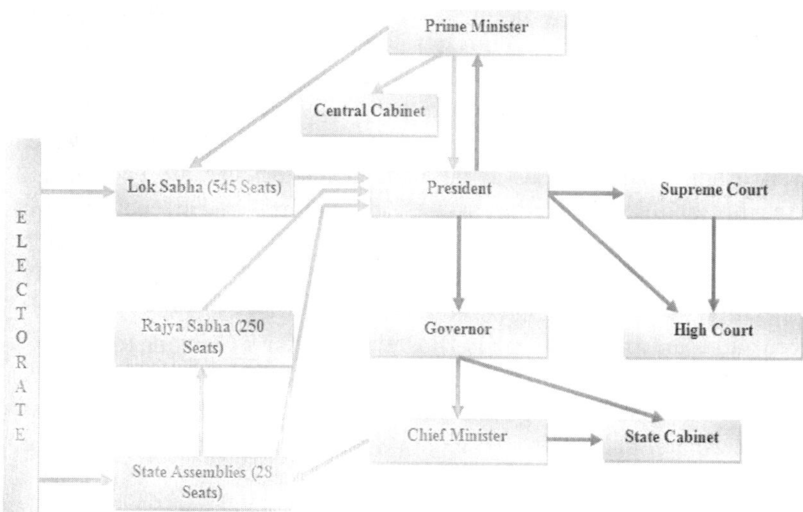

Figure 4.2: India's Institutional Arrangement

Table 4.1: Separation and Division of Powers in India (Jakub Zajaczkowski et al; 2015)

Levels of Government	Powers		
	Executive	Legislative	Judicial
National	President-in-Council	Parliament	Supreme Court
Regional	Governor-in-Council	Assembly	High Court
Local	District Magistrate	Zilla Parishad	District Court

4.2.2 FACTORS AFFECTING THE POSITION OF WOMEN IN INDIA

The woman's condition did not remain the same that is, economically, politically, along with socially, as of the ancient to the modern age; also, it changed with time. In India, since the SW experienced numerous ups as well as downs, it has been a cheered one. However, women were worshipped as goddesses in the Vedic period. Men were largely dominated in Indian society. In society, via the ages, most women adopt their position as a fair description. Amongst them, to enhance the expansion opportunities, remedies were made since the country got independence. A mode of thinking along with writing about Indian history as a challenge betwixt the British Raj and Indian nationalism is referred to as Imperialism-nationalism. Indian history's colonial, as well as indigenous side, has an idea to embed within the imperialism-nationalism frame. Here, during British rule in India, the events, phenomena, along with processes that happened are seen, thought about, and written. Prior to a century, the schools like nationalist, postcolonial, Cambridge, Imperial, along with subaltern emerged. In the last 1980s, various issues related to theory along with methodology with scholarship initiating the imperialist-nationalist historiography, which every single student learns at the undergraduate level, are encountered (Anagol, 2008). Since India, as well as Pakistan, got independence in 1947, the nation's birth has preoccupied historians owing to the nationalist perception along with the several movements' descriptions. A novel generation of feminist aroused in the 1970s as well as 1980s. They have been interested in either way: (1) The Indian women's changing role, which was Gandhi's impact (2) what women aided in Gandhian- led movements. By scholarship considering the nationalist movement's gendered creations, passive women who followed Gandhi in a credulous way have been altered. Also, in the resistance struggles, considering the women's voices. By a unique formulation, bringing the women to the public in India, Gandhi played a role, which was termed Gandhian Feminism where the women along with the scholars as of the social sciences entered brave novel India in the 1970s as well as 1980s. When wielded in the modern Indian women, the word 'feminism' or 'feminist' has seen numerous hesitancy that was the scholarship's consistent with the inconsistencies. However, regarding equality, equal rights and opportunities, along with justice, women are facing numerous challenges.

(a) **Child Marriage**: When a girl marries certainly beneath the age of 18 years. It is referred to as child marriage. In India, mostly in rural areas, still child marriage happens although maximum nations have declared the legal minimum age as 18 for marriage.

(b) **Education:** Improving the academic skills as well as capabilities amongst individuals along with producing awareness regarding several areas are education's major objectives. Girls are not encouraged in education in several rural regions. Instead, they were taught to do household activities. However, changes have appeared in the perspective that girls should have their education nowadays. Thus, in higher education, girls, as well as women, are being enrolled; also, they are getting bachelor's, master's, along with doctoral degrees.

(c) **Empowerment Opportunities:** In India, the EOs amongst women relies on numerous factors like socio-economic background, educational qualifications, class, geographical location, age, ethnicity, along with caste. At the local, state, along with national levels, the policies on WE remain. GBV, economic opportunities, HC, PP, along with education are the fields where women attain Eos. Within rural regions, the EOs amongst women is not considered.

(d) **Crime against Women:** Crime against women has been occurring all over the country. To several criminals along with violent acts, girls, as well as women, are exposed. Within and outside the house, this occurs. Verbal abuse, trafficking, rape, physical abuse, sexual harassment, murder, along with acid attacks is the various criminal acts.

(e) **Political Participation of Women:** For GE along with democracy, the basic requirement is the women's PP. In the DM processes, the women's direct involvement is enabled here; also, it is observed as the source to promote women's accountability in an enhanced way. In the DM positions, with the growing number of women, the PP of women starts.

(f) **Domestic violence:** According to the Women and Child Development (WCD) officials, the utmost 70% of Indian women are affected by DV, which is an endemic along with common diseases that are done by the relative, husband, or other family members. Like boys, girls have no property rights (Bharatiya Stree Shakthi 2017).

4.2.3 POLITICAL VALUES

For soft power, India has enormous resources owing to its, multi-cultural, multi-ethnic, along with open society, and democratic, federal, together with a secular state. For numerous internally divided countries, India can be a model as it is a tolerant country, which was created on the concept of 'unity in diversity (Henry & Adams, 2018). For the democracy's promotion, a robust argument is provided by the democratic scheme's endurance in an illiterate, poor, along with hugely diverse society. It was only the cold war's end even though India got independence in 1947, which has been democratic. Also, the ideological confrontation's consequent replacement betwixt communism and capitalism via the race betwixt authoritarianism and democracy provided importance to India's democratic credentials. Thus, for democratic promotion, in the west, many believed that India will become an ally significantly in worldwide efforts. A modest approach was adopted by India rather than aligning with the west, which leads to their disappointment. In foreign relations, specifically, with a democratic partner like Japan, the EU, along with the US, the value along with the political utility is recognized by India. However, exporting its model to other countries is reluctant. Instead of active outside pressure, democracy in other states is supported via its own power. This was preferred by India. In September 2011, in a speech at UNGA, PM Manmohan Singh said that 'A democratic, plural and secular India can contribute to tolerance along with peaceful co-existence among nations' (ministry of external affairs, 2011) (Mittal & Singh, 2020). But, he warned, 'the rule of law's observance is as significant as it is within countries; also, via military force, societies cannot be reordered as of outside. In all countries for choosing their destiny along with deciding their future, people have the right. Regarding democratic promotion, the dissimilarity betwixt India and Western democracies is real; also, it is grounded on ideological differences as well as historical legacy. It comes as of India's colonial past along with the Non-Aligned Movement's principles like state sovereignty as well as territorial integrity, non-intervention as well as non-interference. In Western-led international efforts for promoting democracy, a vital role is not played excluding some instances when India elongated negligible bolster for electoral processes or training to parliamentarians. Democracy cannot be enforced as of outside was India's thought in which it stood consistent.

4.2.4 STATUS OF WOMEN IN INDIA

In India, the Hindu SW has been altered from time to time. During different historical phases, it has gone thru various changes. Traditionally, in India, women in their lives have passed thru '2' stages. They are (1) the subjugation period and (2) the liberation period. Women are devastated as well as oppressed at times. Simultaneously, they are also denoted as the home's deity. From time to time, SW along with positions has been changing as of the Vedic period till now. Thus, for evaluating the women's real position, analyzing the Hindu women in several phases is essential.

Towards Equality: Committee on the SW in India's report published in 1974 provides a vantage point to have a parallax view of the WM in India, Indian democracy along with the modern nation's buildings. The Planning Commission as of its inception concentrated on a very limited notion of women's development, which was confined to education, social welfare, along with health (Hasan, 1974). "Up to the Fourth Plan, the priorities' order has been education, health, and finally other welfare aspects as it was commonly assumed that all other programs will profit women indirectly, if not directly". Neither the Report nor the subsequent models of development need to prioritize the notion of women's earning capacity come to the fore. The conceptualization of the development strategy is not affected by this attitude of the state. Nonetheless, the attention of the women's organization is diverted as of its focus on the women's active contribution in the economic arena to women's position as a mere beneficiary of the ED outcomes. This attitude is not only inherent within the state policies but also it is entrenched within the socio-cultural along with the conventional framework. This views women's economic role as an extension of women's domestic role as the caregiver and homemaker (Report, 1978).

For the women in India, in the paradigm of planning, a major change was brought by the report. For the Indian planning exercise, it was the starting phase that executed very five years for recognizing women as an agency regarding an economic being that contributes to the nation's welfare together with growth. Numerous concerns towards equality highlighted hindered the overall women's development in India; also, the 'disconnect' betwixt the Indian planning exercise and the 'women's question in India' is forwarded that are voiced via various WM's strands.

In the methodology to women's problems as of welfare to progress, it has been a marked shift as of the 5th Five Year Plan (1974-78). In defining SW, the WE is considered the major issue nowadays. In 1990, the Act of Parliament set up the National Commission for Women (NCW) for securing the rights along with women's legal entitlements (Issues related to WE in India).

4.2.5 STEPS UNDERTAKEN IN INDIA FOR WOMEN EMPOWERMENT

In Indian society, the Constitution framers were more conscious of the declining issue or declined SW. Thus, in its Directive principles, Fundamental duties, along with the preamble, the GE principle to be treasured in the Indian constitution are ensured by them. In India, to ensure the GE, several articles in the former paragraph are indented. Furthermore, the states are empowered by the constitution for adopting positive measures in favour of women. When Mrs. Indira Gandhi was the PM, the actual motivation of this movement was achieved; also, a system named Indira Mahila Yojna was launched. Moreover, the women's upliftment problems were considered the primary aim and were incorporated by the UNDP. For WE, several schemes like Indira Gandhi Priydarshni Vivah Shoguns Yojna, Rashtriya Mahila Kosh, self-help groups at panchayat levels, Mahila Samridhi Yojna, Kishori Shakti Yojna, Dhanlakhsmi, SABLA scheme, et cetera, were launched. In the WE's direction, the National Women's Commission, as well as the State Women's Commissions' establishment, were significant milestones in India.

To accelerate the WE's pace, a significant step taken by the government was the national policy for the WE (2001). For the entire women's development, the policy was indented to ensure WE via positive economic along with social policies. Thus, the complete potential can be realized. In participation as well as DM in social, HC, nation's political along with economic life, together with quality education, equal access was assured to women by the policy. Also, to eradicate discrimination against women, it aims at strengthening the legal system. With civil society specifically, women's organizations, strengthening partnerships are visualized by the policy. For WE, several measures are also taken by the states.

4.2.5.1 SIXTH FIVE-YEAR PLAN PARADIGM

In the 6th plan (1980-85), the change in the approach as of 'welfare' to 'development' of women took place. Consequently, on the '3' core sectors like employment, education, and health, a special thrust was made by the multi-disciplinary approach that was adopted by the plan. For welfare, instead of considering passive subjects, women are considered active partners. Moreover, via creating livelihood opportunities along with providing enhanced access to assets, the concentration was more on lowering women's poverty. At this time, under the HRD's ministry, a distinct department for WCD was created. Also, a national committee on women was formed under the PM. For protecting women against atrocities, discrimination, violence, along with exploitation, various legislative measures were formed; also, for securing the women's interest as well as providing welfare, amendments were created to the prevailing legislations.

4.2.5.2 FORMATION OF WOMEN AND DEVELOPMENT DEPARTMENT IN MHRD

In 1985, to provide the essential impetus to the holistic progress of women as well as children, the MHRD Department of WCD was formed as a Ministry of Human Resource Development. Plans, programs, along with policies are formulated by the department after the women as well as children's advancement as a nodal agency in its ability. Also, the legislation affecting the women as well as children area is enacted. Moreover, in WCD, the governmental along with NGO's efforts are guided as well as coordinated. Also, several innovative programs are implemented by the department. In the areas like welfare together with support services, training and capacity building, awareness generation and gender sensitization, along with employment and income generation, these programs are held. The major aim of these programs is to make women independent as well as self-reliant; also, children growing up in a healthy secure environment are ensured.

4.2.5.3 NATIONAL PERSPECTIVE PLAN FOR WOMEN

In 1977-78, on women's employment, the working group was appointed by the Government as an exercise for the 6th plan. Also, as an exercise's part, two other critical reports on village-level organizations as well as women's participation in agriculture along with rural development were created. This Plan was undoubtedly influenced by the CSWI Report of 1975.

4.2.5.4 INDIA RATIFIED THE CEDAW CONVENTION

The most comprehensive treaty of Women's HR is the CEDAW. With several reservations, on July 39, 1980, India signed CEDAW; also, it was authorized on July 9, 1993. The Optional Protocol to CEDAW was not yet ratified. Amongst current achievements in the Convention's implementation was established in March 1997 and was represented by the representative of a parliamentary committee on WE. Also, in rural regions as well as the municipalities, the constitutional amendments' passage as 33.33% seats for women in the PRIs at the LSG level. Also, in late 1999, a bill was introduced that will reserve not less than 1/3rd of the total number of seats filled by direct elections in the Lok Sabha as well as the State Legislative Assemblies for women.

4.2.5.5 FORMATION OF NATIONAL COMMISSION FOR WOMEN

The NCW was constituted as a statutory body by the NCW Act, 1990 (Act No. 20 of 1990 of the GoI). With Mrs. Jayanti Patnaik as the Chairperson, the 1st commission was established on 31st January 1992. With Dr. Mohini Giri as the Chairperson, the 2nd commission was established in July 1995. With Mrs. Vibha Parthasarathy as the Chairperson, the 3rd commission was established in January 1999. With the chairperson Dr. Poornima Advani, the 4th commission was set up in January 2002. With Dr. Girija Vyas as the Chairperson, the 5th commission was created in February 2005. With Mrs. Mamta Sharma as the Chairperson, in August 2011, the 6th commission was set up. With Ms. Lalitha Kumaramanglam as Chairperson, the 7th commission was constituted on 2014.

4.2.5.6 CONSTITUTIONAL AMENDMENT FOR RESERVATION OF SEATS FOR WOMEN IN PRIS

The '3-tier' system of PRIs was recommended by the commission in 1994. They are (1) village council (gram panchayat) as the village level basic unit (2) Block (block is the larger subunit of a district) council (or panchayat samiti) at the Block level (3) district council (or the Zilla Parishad) at the district level. In India, the PRIs introduction was taken as a significant political initiative.

4.2.5.7 COMMITMENT TO MDGS-GOAL 3

The Millennium Declaration was espoused by 189 UN MS in 2000 that filters the major goals as well as agreed upon at the international conferences along with world summits during the 1990s. For providing a set of benchmarks that computes the progress toward global poverty eradication, '8' MDGs were sketched by the UN system as of the declaration drawing. One target on education along with extra indicators on women's employment as well as political representation was included in the MDG

3 for promoting GE along with WE. The GE is interpreted by the MDG 3 narrowly. Also, there is an increasing appreciation that the targets together with indicators that frame the objective on GE and WE are inadequate. The corresponding targets' absence on these problems means that they received lower attention; also, they are less prioritized while the MS's commitment to track these WEs' elements is acceptable.

4.2.5.8 WOMEN EMPOWERMENT POLICY

The National Policy on WE adopted in 2001says that all kinds of VAW, physical as well as mental, whether at domestic or societal levels, comprising those emerging as of customs, traditions, or accepted practices shall be addressed efficiently to eliminate its incidence. To prevent violence like SH at the workplace as well as customs like dowry, institutions as well as schemes will be formed; also, to take effective action against the perpetrators as well as the victims' rehabilitation. Bringing advancement, development, along with WE is the aim of this policy.

4.2.5.9 ADOPTION OF GENDER BUDGET

In 2005, by including a separate statement on spending programs, India formally adopted Gender Budgeting (GB), which profits women. The process of conceiving, approving, utilizing, auditing, and analyzing the budget in a gender-sensitive manner, thereby giving priority to GE is termed GB.

(1) The IMF economists show that an important impact was held on enrolment ratio in schools by spending on infrastructures like free bicycles, and safe toilets for school-going girls.

(2) On public goods like drinking water, village panchayats controlled by women spend more that are nearer to the women's concerns than men.

(3) Through Mahila e-haat, stand up India, et cetera, women entrepreneurship has been encouraged. It has been estimated that equal EP of women can increase GDP by 1.4% per year.

(4) Focus on education and health of girls via *beti bachao, beti padhao, Sabla Scheme*, *Surakshit Matritva Yojana*, et cetera, to enhance human resources.

(5) Free LPG connections and subsidies in the name of women are also a step to empower them.

But GB is not likely to resolve the huge issue of GIs.

- In the labor force, India has a very low level of Women participation, when enhancing the economy, the employment rare case goes down; also, the reason is social norms.
- Rights of women like freedom of movement, financial rights, freedom to work et cetera, are protected by the constitution but restricted by social or religious norms.
- Creating awareness about schemes available for women is also significant.
- Safety is a perennial issue and requires a change of attitude towards women.

When it comes to GE India is still a laggard; also, it requires a change of mindset.

4.2.5.10 ADOPTION OF SDGS-GOAL 5

For the UN SD Summit, 193 UN MS gathered in September 2015. Also, the novel global plan of action named, "Transforming Our World", the agenda for SD, 2030, was adopted. The universal goals for the 2030 Agenda are 17 Goals as well as 169 targets. Meanwhile, over the next 15 years, ensuring that no one is left behind, it aimed at protecting the planet, fighting inequalities as well as augmenting the country's productive capability, eradicating poverty, increasing social inclusion, restraining climatic variations together with safeguarding the environment, along with enhancing everyone's lives. GE is an HR; also, to lower poverty as well as advance development, it is a precondition. Worldwide, UNICEF works; thus, the same opportunities, resources, protections, along with rights can be enjoyed by boys as well as girls. For ensuring the children grow, learn, along with the thriving, the gender outcomes are embedded. Adolescent girls' empowerment, and data analysis, along with data assessment to aid governments to find barriers to GE are focused on.

4.2.6 ENTRY POINTS FOR WOMEN IN POLITICS

Five distinct entry points for women in politics have been identified by various studies that are widespread in India and prominent in SA countries. For women, dynastic is the first point of admission, which means women originated from families with political history. For example, Sonia Gandhi entered politics following the death of Rajiv Gandhi, a member of the illustrious Gandhi dynasty. Marital status is another point of entry for women. Women enter politics by marriage to politicians like

Hema Gemang, Maneka Gandhi, Rabri Devi, and so on. The third point of entrance is education. In the lives of female politicians, education is extremely important. Given the nature of Indian politics, for females, it is tedious to get admission through college education, given the majority of India's female population is uneducated. The women who entered politics through education are Sushma Swaraj, Bijoya Chakravarty, and Jaskaur Meena. The celebrity level is the fourth entry point. For example, actresses like Jayaprada and Hema Malini use their stardom to make their political debuts. Lastly, women become activists in politics. Their educational level makes a little impact here. Many female politicians like Mamta Bannerji, Mayawati, and Uma Bharti, rose through the ranks through activism (Palley, 2009).

4.2.7 WOMEN REPRESENTATION IN INDIAN POLITICS

A pre-requisite to GE's realization is gender parity along with PP. Also, via Constitutional amendments, it ensured 33% reservation for women. Yet, it is 50% in a few states. But, in the 'natural transition' as of the Panchayats to the State Assemblies together with the Parliament, the women's representation is dismal.

Betwixt the PP's level and the women's participation enlargement, there is an upturned relationship that is, when the participation level increases, the number of women at the maximum levels of participation decreases. However, politics as well as political parties are still men. Beyond voting, there is a vast gap betwixt the men and women since the PP's history amongst women displays. As campaigners, a few women's visibility exists, yet some women became contestants. In contrast to the men, the proportion of women who contest is still low. Generally, women do not have the winning capability; thus, are considered denied tickets. Politically, during the electoral process, women are hardly pursued as they do not create a significant constituency. A women's wing is contained by every single political party; however, it is mere tokenism. At the lowermost level, women are engaged in political parties. During elections, for campaigning amongst women voters, soft roles are given to them.

545 members in the lower house, as well as 250 members in the upper house, are comprised by India's bicameral legislature. In both houses, women mostly belong to the middle class and are educated (Bruggemann, 2018). Also, via the caste quota, a few women enter. Irrespective of these lower numbers, Jayalalitha (Tamil Nadu's CM), Vasundhara Raje Sindhiya (Rajasthan's CM), Sonia Gandhi (President of former ruling Congress party), Mamta Banerjee (West Bengal's former CM), along with Mayawati

(UP's former CM) are several women who reached the political power in the mainstream. In post-independence India, for women who are attempting to attain political representation along with the place in the power structure, Indira Gandhi has been the archetype in table 4.2.

Table 4.2: Women Representation in Lok Sabha in India (Rai, 2017)

Year	Total Members	Total Women Members	% of Women Members out of total
1952	499	24	4.81
1957	500	24	4.8
1962	503	36	7.2
1967	523	32	6.1
1971	521	27	5.2
1977	544	21	3.9
1980	544	32	5.9
1984	544	45	8.3
1989	517	28	5.4
1991	544	42	7.7
1996	544	41	7.5
1998	543	44	8.1
1999	543	52	9.6
2004	545	52	9.5
2009	545	59	10.8
2014	543	65	12.5
2019	543	78	14.39

4.2.8 WOMEN IN CONTEMPORARY INDIA

India has a dismal record on women's representation, ranking 140 out of 156 countries, according to the WEF's GGG Index 2021. The most notable reduction is in the sub-index of PE where India ranks 51, dropping as of 18 last year (Venkiteswaran, 2021).

In Kerala, women were only able to occupy 9% seats, 7.8% in Assam, roughly 11% in Tamil Nadu, Puducherry, along with West Bengal in the most recent 2021 rolling elections in '4' state assemblies as well as one union territory (Betigeri, 2021).

However, Lok Sabha elections set new records as there were 78 elected women in Lok Sabha and 25 women MPs in Rajya Sabha for the 1st time in Independent India's history. Also, women's membership in the Lok Sabha has been gradually increasing since 1957 as seen in the chart below. Only 3% of seats were won by women in the 2nd Lok Sabha Election. Nevertheless, this figure increased to 14.6 percent with 716 female candidates running in the 2nd Lok Sabha Election. The election years were divided into three distinct stages to compare the percentage of male Lok Sabha MPs to female Lok Sabha MPs in table 4.3.

Table 4.3: Percentage of Men and Women in Elections (Poojari&, 2021)

Election Years	Percentage of men MPs in Lok Sabha	Percentage of women MPs in Rajya Sabha
Phase I (1952-1977)	95%	5%
Phase II (1977-2002)	93%	7%
Phase III (2002 onwards)	90%	10%

Moreover, India's status regarding women's representation in legislative bodies has deteriorated in recent years. For example, India was ranked 95 in January 1998, 144th in February 2008, and 148th in January 2021 (Poojari, 2021). But, one pattern that should be noted is that women candidates were younger and more educated than men in general Lok Sabha elections. Also, most people had a bachelor's degree, along with 37.8% had a graduate degree, according to Paul as well as Vivekananda's research (Samuel & Vivekananda, 2004).

Key Recommendations

- In the Parliament, Local bodies, Ministerial levels, State Legislative Assemblies, along with all government's all decision making bodies, at least 50% reservation of seats should be ensured.
- Particularly, in general as well as in elections, to combat political criminalization, effective steps should be taken by the state.
- State funding of elections is required.

The SW has altered as of several periods in Indian society. In the early period, equal status had been enjoyed by Indian women in every field. Regarding "Ardhangini", the same education, as well as significance, was received by women that is, half body (to her husband). The SW decreased gradually in the medieval age; also, it was considered inferior to men. In society, child marriages, purdah, restrictions on widow marriage, along with sati entered are the causes of the injustice toward women. However, the SW has changed in modern India. Politically, socially, legally, economically, along with educationally, the SW becomes equal to the men recently. Moreover, these causes are eradicated by social reformers like Dayanand

Saraswati, Swami Vivekanand, Raja Ram Mohan Roy, etcetera, as well as the British government. Thus, Indian women are marching towards liberty as well as equality recently via several social legislation means. The foundation for women's arising was prepared by the social reform movement as of the mid-nineteenth century that resulted in the eradication of child marriage, women infanticide, Sati, widow's plight, polygamy, et cetera. However, the opposition was there by the Orthodox who delineated it as an assault on religion.

4.3 SDG GOALS BY INDIA

To frame the stages that should be taken to achieve this tripartite vision of how resources must be wielded for forming low-impact, durable, prosperous, along with inclusive societies, the comprehensive, inclusive effort was represented by the SDG. For India, regarding its poor infrastructure, rampant poverty, weak socio-economic indicators, along with large population, the SDGs can ensure sustainable along with inclusive economic growth. In ensuring the planet along with the people's prosperity, India has a significant stake as well as responsibility as it has 1/6th global population. 10 national-wide indicators have been recognized for computing India's performance towards good health as well as Well-Being that enclose 8 out of 13 SDG targets for 2030. At the sub-national level, these are selected grounded on the data availability; they also ensure comparability across States as well as UTs.

Goal 3: "Good Health and Well-being"

Neonatal, slashing maternal, along with under-5 mortality rates are enclosed in the third SDG to ensure good health as well as well-being. The major communicable epidemics elimination along with tropical diseases eradication as well as non-communicable diseases (NCDs) reduction is involved here. Moreover, road deaths, deaths as of air as well as water pollution, along with substance abuse prevention are also included here. Universal health coverage that comprises vaccines, affordable medicine, together with RH services must be attained to form a system that can accomplish all this. Thus, via implementing health risk reduction and management strategies, expanding ODA to the health sector, along with increasing health financing, recruitment and training, can be done.

For Goal 3, the index score for states ranges betwixt 59 and 86; then, for UTs, it ranges betwixt 68 and 90. Amongst the states as well as UTs, the highest performers are Gujarat as well as Delhi correspondingly. In the Front Runners' category, the entire states as well as UTs captured a position. In the Aspirants' category with a score lesser than 50, no state or UT was there. With the Affordable health insurance scheme's provision under PM-Jay, a lowered infant, as well as MMR, associated that resulted in better. But, in this parameter, a huge issue is the larger gap betwixt performing and non-performing states.

Goal 4: "Quality education"

11 national-wide indicators are recognized for computing India's performance towards the Goal of Quality Education. Under this goal, 6 out of 10 SDG targets for 2030. At the sub-national level, grounded on the data availability, these indicators are selected for ensuring comparability across States as well as UTs. For Goal 4, the index score for states ranges betwixt 29 and 80; then, for UTs, it ranges betwixt 49 and 79. Amongst the states as well as UTs, the highest performers are Kerala as well as Chandigarh correspondingly. In the Front Runners' category, 5 states, as well as 3 UTs, captured a position with a score that ranges betwixt 65 and 99. In the Aspirants' category with a score lesser than 50, 9 states, as well as 2 UTs, were there.

Gender discrimination, enrollment being a focal point rather than learning, poor teacher-student ratio, high dropout rates, along with absenteeism are a few challenges to this goal. But, via the programs like "Samagra Shiksha Abhiyan", which has amalgamated '3' programs, such as Teacher's education, Rashtriya Madhyamik Shiksha Abhiyan, along with Sarv- Shiksha Abhiyan, the government aids in the enhancement of quality education. In the education field, for promoting gender parity, Beti Padhao (the flagship scheme of Beti-Bachao), is forming an environment.

Goal 5: "Gender Equality"

In a particular aspect, to enhance innovative strategies as well as policy formulation, vital progress has been shown by India. In development, joining the north-south gap is one of the main targets. Since the northeastern states have rich resources along with human capital, their poor performance is the main paradox. Still, few citizens are not able to afford '2' meal per day is the fact. Thus, for ensuring the right to food, antipoverty programs are accelerated.

For the country, the main region to focus on is gender disparity. Conventionally, with women's less participation every day in the DM process, Indian society is considered to be patriarchal. The basic HR is winding up the entire discrimination against women; also, for SD, it is a prerequisite. Mostly, women are homemakers, which are regarded as a noneconomic activity. Still, incidents like Women's feticides, sexual harassment, rape, along with dowry exist. As of the horrible labor workforce participation rate of 32%, these are evident.

Eradicating the violence, trafficking, along with sexual exploitation of women is Goal 5's aim. With an emphasis on the full as well as effective participation along with equal opportunities for leadership in DM in political, economic, along with public life for women, this goal's vital component is to recognize along with the value of unpaid care as well as domestic work. 9 national-wide indicators are recognized for computing India's performance towards the Goal of GE. Under this goal, 5 out of 9 SDG targets for 2030.At the sub-national level, grounded on the data availability, these indicators are selected for ensuring comparability across States as well as UTs. For Goal 5, the index score for states ranges betwixt 25 and 64; then, for UTs, it ranges betwixt 33 and 68.Amongst the states as well as UTs, the highest performers are Chandigarh as well as Andaman and Nicobar Islands correspondingly. In the Front Runners' category, no state as well as 2 UTs captured a position with a score that ranges betwixt 65 and 99. In the Aspirants' category with a score lesser than 50, 14 states, as well as 3 UTs, were there.

In SDGs, various challenges are faced by India. Poor infrastructure is one of the major challenges that affect development. Still, the financial markets are not developed vibrantly; specifically, the debt market that borrows for infrastructure is tedious; also, it depends on the banking sector solely. The credit crunch is given to the private sector by the Indian banking sector, which was affected by the NPA crisis. India lagged behind owing to the research as well as developments' poor levels along with inadequate innovation. Poor access to sanitation, primary HC, along with education is regarding poverty higher level. Also, it leads to slower SDGs indicators progress.

But, with the government investing in programs like *Sukanya Samriddhi, Beti-Bachao Beti- Padhao, Pradhan Mantri Ujjwala Yojana*, et cetera, the enhancement in the index is a relief.

Chapter - 5

Srilanka and Bangladesh

5.1 PREFACE

The act of a person or group, which speaks or acts for or in bear of another person or group, is termed representation (Singh, 2013). As women are indicating their gender in a few areas, representation of any person in any area fits in to the actions of the anxious cluster circuitously. In the social phase (Equality Rights), women have still not gained any significant position even though they comprise half of the total population. Always, the work place is under the leadership of men; whereas, the woman is regarded to live all over either at home or outside. The representation might be built as the equality's consolidation mean. A procedure, which permits women to attain entrance to control of material intellectual, along with human resources, is termed empowerment. The power redeployment, which defies the patriarchal ideology as well as men's dominance, is called empowerment.

5.2 SRILANKA

In Sri Lanka, there is huge VAW. Recently, such violence hugely caused grave and brutal nature and the extent of harm and trauma to women. Rape, cyber violence, and DV are on the increase within the family unit and in the community at large, which was revealed by the reported incidents of sexual and GBV against women (Mel & Pathmala, 2009). VAW or the threat of violence is means of maintaining and re-enforcing women's subordination. GBV is influenced and re- enforced by previous patriarchal norms, GS, and individual negative attitudes. For the current status quo, unequal power relations, a lack of awareness, insensitivities, and negative attitudinal perceptions of law enforcement authorities are the key contributors. From reporting such violence or even seeking medical, psycho-social, or legal assistance, those factors prevent several victims. In front of the law, men together with women are equal; in addition, the Constitution of Sri Lanka does not permit discrimination based on sex. Constitutional and other mechanisms, which detect the rights of women and mechanisms for redresses are offered by the domestic legal framework while those rights are violated (Chandrika, 2019). Nevertheless, when considering the daily reports of various violence forms committed against women as well as girls, questions arise about the actual implementation of these non-discriminatory provisions.

For several international treaties that govern the rights of women, Sri Lanka is a signatory. For guaranteeing substantive equality and all individuals could admission competent, impartial judicial together with adjudicatory mechanisms equally without discrimination, that call for states to take measures. Women's access to justice is to the realization of all rights, which was determined by the CEDAW. Sri Lanka has failed even though it is a signatory to that convention; for example, to fully comply with the obligations contained therein. To women victim-survivors of sexual and GBV, counselling and legal services were offered by Women in Need (WIN) Sri Lanka (Rocha et al., 2018). Many social, cultural, and economic barriers prevent women victim-survivors from disclosing the abuse they face or seeking assistance and justice. Instead of formal legal redress mechanisms that are just viewed as a final resort, traditional and informal mechanisms of redress are intended by victim-survivors of GBV. Victim survivors are caused to lose faith in seeking formal legal redress by the institutional barriers including long delays in completing cases, lack of adequate courts, lack of adequate legal aid services, and lack of empathy by those administrating formal justice.

The work's body impact openly on the democracy theme is slightly thin in Sri Lanka's PS. The significant research effort made openly in democracy studies is the studies on the 'State of Democracy along with Human Security' done by the Social Scientists' Association (SSA) in 2004-2005.

(1) Level of legal, electoral and parliamentary practices; (2) counter-state mobilization, armed rebellion together with counter-insurgency war are the '2' places taken by the politics in Sri Lanka from the early 1970s. As characterized by a relatively modern democracy's long institutional history, electoral participation's high level, political party system's penetration into every society corner, the regular as well as peaceable change of regimes by elections, Institutions of parliamentary democracy has taken definite roots in the Sri Lankan society. Nevertheless, twin counter-state insurgencies

are generated by Sri Lanka; 1st in the majority Sinhalese society together with the 2nd in the minority Tamil society. From the 1970s, a meticulous co-existence betwixt '2' apparently contradictory, parliamentary democracy, along with anti-state rebellions was demonstrated by the concentration of the civil war process. In addressing the substantial social as well as ethnic grievances, Sri Lanka's democracy has had key constraints. However, that systemic issue didn't predicate any key democracy reform endeavour. The task of interpreting along with understanding Sri Lanka's contemporary political together with social alter is exploring that 'democracy problematic'.

5.2.1 FORMAL JUSTICE SYSTEM FOR WOMEN IN SRI LANKA

Before women and girl victim-survivors of Sexual and GBV (SGBV) in Sri Lanka make the decision to seek legal redress for their grievances (WIN 2019), they face many challenges. The below points have been compiled via the countless cases that come to WIN each year and help understand the challenges and issues faced by these victims.

- DV cases that showed severe forms of physical harassment, inhuman treatment, emotional violence, and SV caused by husbands towards the victims are the most observed cases.
- Most of the abuser's husbands were alcohol addicts.
- SV also included marital rape, but that they have no way of getting redress, legal or otherwise, especially as marital rape is not recognized as a criminal offence in Sri Lanka, which was started by many victims who approached WIN for services.
- In Jaffna and Mullaitivu, it was found that severe forms of DV are experienced by women for long periods. Notably, such violence was committed not only by the husbands but also by close relatives in the Jaffna and Mullaitivu districts (in the North along with East of Sri Lanka, Women's Access to Justice 2016).
- With increasing cases of rape, incest and illegal abortions being reported to WIN. 6, pregnancies in unmarried women and teenage pregnancies are common in Jaffna and Mullaitivu. Whilst all people in the Northern and Eastern, prevalence of SGBV against women and girls in the North along with East has a close link to the civil war which lasted for three decades.

5.2.2 WOMEN EMPOWERMENT AND REPRESENTATION IN SRI-LANKA

The right to equality that ensures equal treatment together with protection of the law together with prohibitions beside discrimination on sex is one among the basic rights set out in Sri Lanka's Constitution. For the development of women, special provisions are permitted by the constitution. The main policy document, which highlights rights in a gamut of areas together with the commitments for securing these rights is the Women's Charter adopted in 1993. The charter highlights rights to education; training, ED; benefits, HC; nutrition, fortification as of social discrimination, along with protection against GBV moreover of political as well as civil rights. With the input of government together with nongovernment actors, a National Plan of Action depicting the effect of the Women's Charter was presented. Recently, that plan has been updated; however, approved along with posted as an official document. For the Protection along with Promotion of HR, National Action Plan 2011-2016 is the rights document. Participation; earnings, deployment; working circumstances, VAW, political image, discriminatory laws removal, along with effectual re-incorporation of women affected by conflict are the '8' sections that tackle with rights of women.

5.2.3 REPRESENTATION OF SRI-LANKA WOMEN IN POLITICS

A multi-religious country with varied legal systems pertinent to diverse communities is Sri Lanka. Nevertheless, negative and positive effects on social transformation are included in the (1) centuries of Western colonial rule, (2) visionary education, together with (3) health policies. Even though not destroying discrimination beside Sri Lanka women centered on their sex below various traditional practices such as (A) life cycle ceremony, (B) son liking, (C) premature marriage, (D) dowry, (E) caste discrimination depicting a hierarchy in social status is an opposition, Buddhism's Liberal values have had a positive impact in undermining.

While Sirimavo Bandaranaike became the world's 1st Women PM, Sri Lanka made history in 1960. In SEA, Sri Lanka still has the least Women leaders in spite of achievements toward women's PE (Bruggemann, 2018).

At national and local levels, Women's representation in politics sustains low. For women in politics, just 13 from 225 members (5.8%) of Sri Lanka's national parliaments were women in 2017 ranking the country 179 from 190. Before elections in February 2018, women made up a meager 2% of LG posts (What requires to change for the 5% of Women in Politics along with the 52% populace of women in Sri Lanka –I).

In addressing the under-depiction of women, the "Local Authorities Elections Act No. 1" was passed by Sri Lanka in 2016. In 2018, that act took effect with the local elections; in addition, on every local council, an obligatory quota of 25% of Women officials was presented (IPU, 2008). The count of women in management roles maximized as of 89 to 2,300 with the quota in place. The First woman mayor, Rosy Senanayake was in the 2018 elections of Sri Lanka.

In Sri Lanka, an augment in Women's political engagement along with more progress toward GE were caused by those outcomes. The initial step to Women citizens' integration into all government levels is electing more women; keeping those women in offices is the main issue.

At the local along with national levels, strides in Women's representation were caused by the effective application of GQ globally. To the United States, Sri Lanka had considerable weight. China's influence has grown-up, particularly in the economic sector under Chinese President Xi Jinping's Belt together with Road Initiative. The program amounts to (i) a debt trap for vulnerable countries, (ii) fueling corruption as well as (iii) autocratic behavior in struggling democracies that is expounded by the critics of China's Belt together with Road Initiative. Nevertheless, proactive steps should be done to further Women's representation in Sri Lankan politics for developing the function of its democracy. Sri Lanka's freshly applied GQ is a significant way towards gender parity in government I table 5.1.

Table 5.1: Percentage of Women Elected to the National Legislature in Sri Lanka

Year	Total Members	Total Women Members	% of Women Members out of total
1947	101	3	2.9
1952	101	2	1.9
1956	101	4	3.9
1960 (mar)	157	3	2.9
1960 (July)	157	3	2.9
1965	157	6	5.9
1970	157	6	3.8
1977	168	11	6.5
1989	225	13	5.7
1994	225	12	5.3
2000	225	9	4
2001	225	10	4.4
2004	225	13	5.7
2010	225	13	5.7

2015	225	13	5.7
2020	225	12	5.3

Source: Inter-Parliamentary Union, Sri Lanka

Equal status was offered to women in every walk of life since Sri Lanka was alert on parity as a Buddhist nation. It seems to be very disappointing in the parliamentary input status of Sri Lankan women; while, as per the World Bank report 2011, the literacy ratio is quite satisfactory. Ever in the post-1947, women candidates have not been above 15 that are hugely traumatic. In the 1977 general election, among 168 total members, the most women participation ever was 6.5%. Out of 225 members, it has improved itself up to 13 women in the 2010 elections, which is a complete marginal development. In SA countries, which prevent the Women society as of the vigilant participatory actions together with equal standards, GI is effectual. A few important roles played by women in Sri Lanka are Otara Gunewardene, Founder of ODEL; Renuka Fernando, the Chief Executive of NTB; Smadani Kiriwandeniya, chairperson of Sanasa Development Bank; Varuni Fernando, Co-Founder of TRIAD. The women are in empowering status, which is an enhanced symbol of SA augmentation in this country.

5.2.4 WOMEN DEMOCRACY NETWORK IN SRI-LANKA

For improving the freshly elected local councilwomen's dynamic leadership skills, the Women's Democracy Network (WDN) joined with IRI together with the Federation of Sri Lankan LG Authorities (FSLGA) in May. For emerging as effectual along with permanent leaders in their communities, WDN supports Women candidates and elected officials via training, which equips them with the tools.

Raising a plan, constructing a coalition, along with liaising with constituents is the '3' areas in which the WDN's training in Sri Lanka is targeted. In the Sri Lankan context, an indication of a councilor's roles along with responsibilities was offered by the local trainers (Nazneen, 2004). Gathering on communication together with working across party lines were encompassed in the 2-day training. For maximizing their cooperation along with practicing verbal as well as non- verbal communication, participants engaged in interactive activities. For documenting the required work, they do the communities, action plans were created by the participants at the last of the 2nd day.

Re-writing the false narrative, which women can't govern, is exhibited by the application of the 25 percent quota (Rameez, 2018). However, it takes empowered women heads to modify perceptions. For empowering that women are facing along with other efforts that surpassed those barriers, WDN had politically active young women entrepreneurs together with businesswomen for knowing more regarding obstacles in Sri Lanka. By exhibiting their effect on those elected positions, the public view is dependent on women in GQs. for the future enforcement of the GQ; the 2,300 local councilwomen are responsible along with its introduction at the national level. For assisting those women to achieve their target, WBN is deployed.

To erode and close, archaic stereotypes about women's inability to govern and the gap toward equal rights will continue with more Women's voices at play. Mobilizing and supporting Women candidates is the next step along with empowering these holding offices.

Key points about GE and women's position in Sri Lanka

- On various key genders, Sri Lanka has made worthy progress.
- Complacency, which prevents recognition of continuing GIs, was fostered by it.
- In political structures, women are very poorly depicted.
- In public service's senior levels, women are poorly represented.
- Women are overrepresented in agriculture along with as unpaid family workers in the labour force.
- Women's skills are underused, which was depicted by Women's law workforce participation and greater unemployment levels.
- Against women, there is a high commonness together with tolerance of violence.
- Huge components of the migrant stream are encompassed by Women; however, at the low skill and wage levels.

5.2.5 STRATEGIES ADOPTED BY WOMEN'S ORGANIZATIONS

For women in 1970s, the under representation of women in political institutions was recognized as a key problem. For handling those problems, initiatives were undertaken by the women's organizations. Recently, on those problems, a minimum twenty national level organizations along with various other organizations at the district level have worked (WE 2006). (1) Activists, (2) academics, (3) government officials; (4) political party representatives are grouped together in various national-level seminars and conferences. For learning from other countries' experiences, individual women activists had the chance of taking part in international conferences.

Owing to the bolster of donor organizations like (1) CIDA, (2) FES, (3) NORAD, (4) Ford Foundation, together with the (5) UNDP, that activity was possible. Regarding augmenting women's representation in Sri Lanka, very little progress has been made rather than those efforts. For maximizing women's participation along with representation in political institutions, '8' main strategies deployed by women's organizations were detected.

- Research/publications
- Training together with capacity building for PL
- Awareness raising
- Advocacy meant for a quota
- Experiments with independent lists
- Interventions at the level of political culture
- Networking
- International advocacy previous to the CEDAW Committee

5.2.6 GENDER QUOTAS' ROLE IN INCREASING WOMEN'S POLITICAL REPRESENTATION

By electing Sirimavo Bandaranaike as 1ST PM globally, Sri Lanka made history in 1960. By becoming the country's first Women president, her daughter Chandrika Kumaratunga broke the glass in 1994 (Abidi, 2013).

In Sri Lanka, WPR is low in spite of those historical Women politicians. Country's 225 members merely 5 % (12) are women since Sri Lanka ranks the poorest performing countries in international comparisons, which gauge WPR (Towards broad democracy by bolstering female politicians). Women are in the position of the minister just in one government. In WPR, Sri Lanka pauses after other SA countries. For instance, 32.7 representatives in Representatives' the Lower House along with 37.9 in the Representatives' Upper House Are Women in Nepal.

As a result of the 2016 amendment, local level improvements have been made; thus, for women to go into Sri Lankan LG in 2018, GQ was presented. At the LG, 25 percent of elected legislators should be Women. WPR at the LG was not above 2 %, which was exhibited by the quota's effects for WPR. In the 2018 elections, over 2,000 women were elected to the local councils as a result of the GQ. Hence, WPR has hugely maximized as of the previous 82. The enhancement of representative democracy was fulfilled by GQs.

5.2.7 TOWARDS A MORE INCLUSIVE SRI LANKA BY INCREASING WOMEN'S POLITICAL INFLUENCE

In maximizing women's political ownership, GQs have a significant role; however, for participation, equal opportunities are not ensured by just them. In the Sri Lankan LG, the augmentation of Women politicians hasn't directly translated into equal shares of political power. To the women's PP, social and cultural barriers continue to pose various issues (Chowdhury, 2009).

In Sri Lanka, Demo Finland is initiating a project with the local One-Text Initiative (OTI) at the start of 2021 whereby offering training and networking opportunities, those challenges were tackled along with support for women's contribution at the regional level. For a similar purpose, a multi-party of 40 Women politicians was launched during the pilot project 2019–2020. For more inclusive and equal political participation, conditions are engendered.

5.3 SDG GOALS BY SRILANKA

For supporting the more coherent implementation of the country's SD agenda, Sri Lanka has given precedence to the SDGs in its key enhancement agenda together with attempting to attain them by working for the fulfillment of the common requirements along with developing the people's living standards, gradually alleviating poverty, eradicating every discrimination along with inequalities as well as establishing a society grounded on social justice along with human security base on serious SDG interactions with the progress of the SDGs in 2015 by the UN Development Programme (UNDP).

Goal 3: "Ensure healthy lives and promote well-being for all at all ages"

By warranting safe hospitals together with enhanced community participation in health emergency management, mortality and morbidity are indented to be minimized by Sri Lanka's Strategic Plan meant for Health Sector Emergency/ Disaster Preparedness. 74.3 (72 for men, 78 for Women), 98 percent, and 10 per 1,000 live births are the LE at birth, literacy for the 15 to 24, and infant mortality. At 19.6 %, ranking 128 from 130 countries, Sri Lanka is the highest wasting prevalence rates, which was reported by the 2017 Global Nutrition Report; in addition, one among the few countries with higher wasting rates than stunting, depiction of the longer-term impacts of poor nutrition on Sri Lanka's individual development. For men's LE at 71.7 years in 2021, critical problems around men's health together with the physical risks are reflected in projections when weighed against 81.7 for women. After the tsunami in 2004, the prevention of disease outbreaks was guaranteed by the robust public health network in Sri Lanka. Recently, the country hasn't had any huge disease outbursts following disasters and emergencies. A flood and landslide disaster were had in Sri Lanka that caused over 100 deaths along with the displacement of over 400,000 people in May 2016. The rapid, effective, public health response was linked by the Ministry of Health. By training the HC staff together with provision of medical supplies as well as specialist equipment (WPP), Sri Lanka is escalation disaster preparedness regarding Chemical, Biological, Radio; Nuclear (CBRN).

Goal 4: "Ensure inclusive and equitable quality education and promote lifelong learning opportunities for all"

By offering comprehensive, public-funded primary and secondary education, more Sri Lankans SDG 4 at every level with higher rates of school enrolment successive post-independence governments' commitment product. To be universal at the primary together with near-universal at the low-secondary, 30 Completion has expanded in the post-conflict period. In 2019, nearly 25,000 students graduated from tertiary studies nearly double of 2010. In enrolment as well as completion of primary along with 13 secondary educations, 31 Sri Lanka has as well always keep gender parity. With a Gross Enrolment Ratio (GER) of 26.7, Women have constantly had a higher enrolment in tertiary education as opposed to men at 16.6 in 2020. 32 Nevertheless, for future transformational skills, earlier childhood education along with guaranteeing relevance together with quality of learning sustain under-developed. 33 For peace and social cohesion, applying an incorporated trilingual education system is significant. With English as a 'link' language, the Sinhala; Tamil languages are recognized as official and national languages by Sri Lanka. 34 To reinstate English as a medium of instruction as well as the teaching of 2nd national languages as a way to eradicate language discrimination along with endorse social unity, A 10 Year Plan for a Trilingual Sri Lanka (2012-2021). 35, 36 Nevertheless, implementation has fallen short of its ambition.

Goal 5: "Achieve gender equality and empower all women and girls"

Even the ability to practice these rights is constrained by outdated legislation; basic rights and nondiscrimination based on sex were warranted by Sri Lanka's Constitution. Posturing social constrains on the preferences women make together with interpreting them more susceptible to gendered violence; across national systems, institutional cultures, together with socio-economic structures that dynamic nature is reflected. In spite of sustained ED; moreover, increases in human capital amongst women, large along with persistent disparities in deployment result remain betwixt men and women.

Sri Lanka hasn't offered sufficient priority to this feature owing to the exam-oriented education system. In policy documents, gender, HR, CRC, inclusion, and equality are available; however, they are not in practice. Within education officials and teachers, there is a large gap in the above specific areas. For integrating (a) key sustainable lifestyles, (b) HR, (c) GE, (d) endorsement of a culture of peace as well as nonviolence, (e) global citizenship; (f) admiration of cultural diversity into the curriculum, there are huge efforts taken.

On the notion of mother, the Sri Lankan family culture usually depends on. Sri Lankan women didn't get the chance to connect with education or occupation initially. The complete accountability is grounded on the family. They attained a choice to enhance their abilities after the introduction of the free education system. Women's participation in management-level employment is greatly influenced. Since it is tedious to confirm that the public along with the private sector society is 100% away as of gender discrimination, in Sri Lankan job culture, they are still struggling to receive equal opportunities. Since there was men dominant community system previously, cultural influences are one among the great reasons. In job culture, the men domination pattern is still present; in addition, for women to work independently together with obtain equal opportunities, the opportunity is made less. The Women's LFP rate has lagged far behind that of men, a fact which points to a few cultural as well as structural obstacles to their entry into the productive regular labor force despite steadily declining unemployment.

In the societal framework, the GG & discrimination still remain, which is one among the key issues. Thus, community awareness & policy development is necessary. For Sri Lanka, financing the SDG remains a huge issue. Thus, it is complex to enhance investments. The sustainability is directly impacted since a weak institutional capacity is generated in Sri Lanka. Amongst relent stakeholders& building capacity of relevant institutions, it is necessary to construct awareness. Under policy changes & resource mobilization, it is not just significant to have interventions but also capacity building. For developing a social protection floor (1.7%), Quality education (1.6%), ESCAP (Economic & Social Commission for the Asia

Pacific) recommends that Sri Lanka requires a yearly extra investment of 4.4% (Akhtar, 2015). Those are significant to minimize the GG and maximize the live hood of women & girls. To implement SDG 5, not just the cultural along with economic obstacles, but as well the extremely dishonest, violent along with polluted country's political environment are impacted. Thus, securing a perfect political culture with apt representatives who are having appropriate qualifications along with vision is significant. In 2030, executing SDGs is a tedious task. There is a possibility of implementing SDGs in Sri Lanka if the responsible authorities could determine the vital challenges precisely along with execute the best solution.

5.4 BANGLADESH

The political input that women have made to Bangladesh is not documented by the famous history. In the anti-British political movement, Bangladeshi women participated in the 1930s-1940s. While Bangladesh was a part of Pakistan, women participated in the autonomy and democratic movements in the aftermath of independence in 1947. Women's historical contributions remain largely invisible, even though they performed a considerable role in the liberation resist of Bangladesh in 1971. When Bangladesh was a part of Pakistan, for the 1st time, women exercised their voting rights.

In the 1954 East Pakistan Provincial Assembly Elections, women voted in which just '1' woman was elected in spite of a provision for '10' reserved seats for women. In the 1970 general elections of Pakistan, women exercised their voting rights. The Ministry of Women Affairs was established by the government of Bangladesh to mainstream women into the development process along with promotes GE and WE. One among the few countries, which has established a separate ministry for women, is Bangladesh. In politics, Bangladesh is the poor women's participation level previously.

Merely '2' women were nominated by the chief parties in the 1st common election in 1973 along with both women were overthrown. Until the early 1980s, women's active contribution in politics along with government was strange as well as minimal (Rai, 2017). Huge political parties denied along with discouraged WPP. Women's direct participation was regarded as 'anti-Islamic' by the religion-centric political parties like the Jamat-e-Islami. Thus, the analyst argued that unless Bangladeshi women are brought into political institution, the economic and social WE can't be improved.

People are Bangladesh's key resource. Half of the populace along with work force is women. For guaranteeing a truly democratic along with representative government, women necessarily partake in ample amount in politics along with government; however, it is discouraged, denied, and resisted. Women have lingered outside the play of power politics in Bangladesh, which was pointed out by Choudhury. In the public domain, their profile in the famous fight for democracy, in election campaigns; in community work hasn't elucidated into greater sway. Just a few were able of entering the public DM post.

5.4.1 BANGLADESH GOVERNMENT IN POLITICS

In the history of Bangladesh, the quest for a representative government is a vital feature. For creating a democratic political system, the eastern Bengali peoples' independence struggle against the British, the partition as of India in 1947, along with secession as of Pakistan in 1971 got for Bangladesh people. For independence, guaranteed HR along with political freedoms, the Constitution embodied the democratic yearnings of the long battle since it was initially promulgated in 1972; similar to those prevailing in the British along with US governments. However, events ended those hopes lately. The Constitution was amended by the hero of the 1971 war Sheikh Mujibur Rahman (Mujib) along with assumed dictatorial powers. His successors ruled via autocratic means; most were military men who seized power during several troubles. Thus, with the leader deploying absolute power, consecutive regimes exhibited fascistic systems delineating military interests.

From the late 1980s, the struggle for democracy was present still in Bangladesh. The varied political movements along with interest groups weren't satisfied by the single-party system (1970s-1980s). Opposition parties remained a fundamental force, which commanded large proportion of loyalties even though they depicted contradictory views together with were as reluctant as the ruling regime to split power.

The defunct regimes, along with conservative Islamic parties is representing the Socialist together with communist parties, centrist parties each with an entirely diverse vision of the path but combined in their opposition to President Hussain Muhammad Ershad in the late 1980s --all contended for power. The position is relegated to illegal activities along with demonstrations on campuses as well as in the streets, which brought economic life to idle in urban regions was deployed to take part in parliamentary politics under Ershad, who had detained power in 1982. The regime's hold over Parliament was just strengthened along with permitted the military to persist its sturdy autocratic rule to the opposition's ineffectiveness together with confrontational position.

By a commitment and adherence, the Bangladesh's autocratic military rulers were distinguished by democratic ideals along with Constitution. In the name of the Constitution, Ershad seized power; in addition, for ensuring democratic freedom, by claiming stability to the country, he aspired to legitimize his position. The establishment of local elections, which permitted selecting local representative councils, is one among Ershad's most considerable moves toward democracy. The local elites are permitted to control government patronage by that democratic reform along with made them passive group. However, for democratic rivalry all through the nation, the local councils had emerged as training grounds by the late 1980s for novel political leaders along with forums.

For securing economic assistance from each possible foreign source, Bangladesh has hunted a neutralist policy in IRs continuously. One among the few countries highly with the US along with the Soviet Union with their allies as well as with China, the Islamic.world along with most 3rd World nations in 1988 was Bangladesh. In the UN, the Nonaligned Movement, together with other international groupings, a key role was played by Bangladesh; in addition, for Regional Cooperation that provided propitious economic cooperation, it was the driving force after the organization of the SAA. It was neutral; however, it was forceful on international problems. Strong stands from Dhaka were elicited by the Cambodian, Palestinian, along with South African problems; in addition, since independence, complex bilateral issues with India have raised powerful displays of hostility along with national pride amongst Bangladeshis recently.

5.4.2 WOMEN REPRESENTATION IN POLITICS (BANGLADESH)

During the 1930s and 1940s, women took part extensively in anti-British agitations along with was an active force during the independence struggle. It is indispensable to recognize the women's along with men's participation in DM in various Organizations for appreciating gender problems along with detect the GG and unequal scenario in every institution. In DM institutions, the women's participation is restricted by the ideas grounded on the variation betwixt private and public worlds (Nussbaum et al., 2003). LG remained the exact sphere of men during the British period. Via the accomplishment in 1935 of the GoI Act, entry of women's entry into the political via a broader franchise as well as the contesting of elections on reserved along with general seats were 1st launched as per Forbes (2002). Out of a total of 345 seats, 45 seats were for the WQ, which is experiencing reaching its present level. For women of participating in every public life, the Constitution together with the legal system has ensured equal rights since 1972. A national openness to women's political power was depicted by Hasina and Khaleda Zia who are the prominence of famous opposition party leaders. Nevertheless, in Bangladeshi politics, both were exceptional. They actually governed their positions to family connections and merely later on skill- fully constructed their followings and platforms. In the 1970s and 1980s, there was a rarity of Women candidates for political office. Conservative men labeled the Women's participation as anti-Islamic although the country. While protecting women and assuming their dependence, Secular provisions laws safeguarded their equality of them in Bangladeshi laws.

Only a few women going for office succeeded. For 300 seats, just 17 women were among 2,125 candidates in the 1979 parliamentary elections; no one succeeded along with just 3 polling over 15 percent of the vote. Just '1' woman chairman was returned by the 1973 elections at the union council; in addition, just '4' Women chairmen were returned in the 1977 and 1984 elections. '30' seats were reserved for women in Parliament by leaders running the country, knowing that women undergo disabilities while competing for office beside men. The women's profiles in Bangladesh occupying those seats instanced the women's subordinate positions even those occupying public offices in Bangladesh. '15' women members were housewives formerly; '27' had no legislative experience previously in the 1979 Parliament. 60 percent were less than 30 ages, just 8 percent were 40 ages, along with just 4 percent had college degrees.

For women, the provision for reserved seats was permitted to lapse before the 1988 parliamentary elections. Even though there was other debate meant for political involvement, the women were left practically devoid of representation nationally. '3' women sat on union and sub-district councils in mid-1988. Women were included in municipal councils; however, the law prohibited women as of beyond 10 % of council membership. For discussing women's issues along with mobilization strategies, a few women's groups like Jatiyo Mohila Sangstha have held major conferences (National Organization for Women). Those women's organizations served as training grounds for a novel generation of politically active women even though they were the province of middle-class women.

From 1991 to still, Khaleda Zia and Sheikh Hasina are dominating in the political arena of Bangladesh. They were associated with powerful leaders; however, doesn't make any important enhancements for women. In Bangladesh, Women that don't have families haven't failed to mark in politics. In the political arena, Bangladesh hasn't been insensitive to gender problems. Both women leaders didn't make much development for women in parliament in table 5.2.

Table 5.2: Women's Representation in different Parliaments of Bangladesh (Source: Election Commission of Bangladesh)

No	Year of election	Women elected among all elected MPs (%)	Reserved Seats for Women	Total Women in Parliament
1	1973	0	15	4.8
2	1979	0.7	30	9.7
3	1986	1.7	30	10.6
4	1988	1.3	-	1.3
5	1991	1.7	30	10.6
6	1966	2.3	30	11.2
7	2001	2	45	2
8	2009	5.4	50	20
9	2014	5.5	50	19.1
10	2018	7	50	23

5.4.3 WOMEN'S CONDITION IN BANGLADESH

Bangladesh is characterized as patriarchal in which men control household resources and women's labour, sexuality, and mobility outside the household (Kabir & Haque, 2014). Equal benefits, opportunities, and rights in the family and society, in general, are not endured by women since men and women aren't regarded as equal.

In every state and public life, equal rights for men along with women were guaranteed by the Constitution of Bangladesh [Article 28(2)]. Article 2 (A) confirmed the use of Shariah laws in the personal life sphere by specifying Islam as the state religion. Hence, by the Muslim personal and other general laws, Muslim women's legal status is defined in Bangladesh. Problems like (a) marriage, (b) divorce, (c) maintenance, (d) guardianship of children, along with inheritance are tackled by the Muslim personal laws. The rights under the Constitution, penal codes, the civil together with criminal codes are covered by the general law. Personal laws are frequently discriminatory betwixt men and women as they conform to religious provisions. As legal provisions are in direct contradiction with the personal Muslim laws, still the government is sustaining its reservation to articles 2; 16(1) (c) of the CEDAW. Women of Bangladesh of their equal rights in marriage, its dissolution, and inheritance of properties are deprived by the prevailing reservation on CEDAW. One among the courtiers with the maximal incidents of VAW is Bangladesh. Since January-August 2017, 3,474 women and children have become a victim of GBV as per Bangladesh Mahila Parishad 30 (BMP) (Steps towards Development, 2017). Rather than the enactment of novel laws, the incidents along with kinds of GBV are maximized; various laws like Action Plans (NAPs) and other policies are espoused by the Bangladesh government for combating VAW.31. Similarly, the law enforcement is weak.

5.4.4 SOCIO ECONOMIC DEVELOPMENT AND WOMEN EMPOWERMENT IN BANGLADESH

The women with their EE and contribution should be addressed for minimizing poverty and further a country's ED. The women's capability of attaining their rights and comfort along with minimizing domestic poverty, maximizing productivity effectiveness, and ED is termed WE. When weighed against the economic, political, and social participation of women, nothing is more important for development, as Amartaya Sen a Noble-winning economist has argued. Economies can't reach their full efficacy without women's contribution. Women could aid businesses and markets grow along with contribute more to their families, communities, and nations when they are empowered if they are provided the right skills and opportunities. Either by building women's power or by advancing women economically WE can be achieved.

There is no alternative to WE in establishing equality, development, and peace. Women are the half population of Bangladesh; in addition, recently, their EP has considerably maximized. For guaranteeing women's advancement, National along with international policy strategies was reflected in the policy; thus, they have control over their lives along with has a key role as decision- makers. In 2016-2017, the working women augmented to 18.6 million16.2 million in 2010. As per The GGG Report, among 144 countries, Bangladesh secured the 47th position in 2017; when the other countries of south Asia such as (i) India (108), (ii) Sri Lanka (109), (iii) Nepal (111), (iv) Bhutan (127) and (v) Pakistan (145). In several sectors like reducing infant together with child mortality, poverty reduction, augment in women's entrepreneurship, education, as well as health, Bangladesh's attainment recently has been exemplary.

The obstacle to women's empowerment in Bangladesh includes

- In rural areas, child marriage sustains high; thus, women are underestimated with a dowry to the status of a bonded labourer.
- In Bangladesh, MMR is high in which owing to pregnancy issues

or in childbirth, 12,000 women die every year (although it was very high sooner than).

- In women, Malnutrition is general; in addition, (30%; 37%) of adolescent girls has anaemia as well as iodine deficiency.
- For women SH along with acid attacks, DV is a grave threat; in addition, suicide is common.
- In school, girl attendance is extremely low along with some women receive tertiary education.
- Several women sustain unemployed and those earning wages have extremely little independence in spending it.
- The huge issue is Commercial sexual exploitation.

Novel initiatives are taken in Bangladesh by the government although there are diverse obstacles in the way of WE. In the parliament, there are 50 reserved seats for women via this they are attaining PE. Women can contribute to socio-ED when they are empowered. Corruption, poverty, DV, facilitating national development etc can be eradicated by them. Begum Rokeya Sakhawat Hussain, Sufia Kamal, Jahanara Imam, Birprotik Taramon Bibi, Dr. captain Sitara Begum, Sheikh Hasina, Kaleda Zia, Rowshan Ershad, Shirin Sharmin Chowdhury, Bibi Russel, Nazmun Ara Sultana are the role models of socio-EE in Bangladesh. To raise the heads of women of Bangladesh to the world, Sheikh Hasina, the prime of Bangladesh, has played an extra ordinary role.

5.5 SDG GOALS BY BANGLADESH

In national planning, the SDGs were espoused by Bangladesh being a signatory of Agenda 2030. Various initiatives were brought by the government, which gave a few visible progresses; however, there are a few sectors, which require special attention. There is a high risk in Bangladesh with a continuous effect on life and livelihood since the mixture of lofty disaster events and augmenting human vulnerability results as of (a) demographic pressure, (b) poverty, (b) social disparity, along with coupled with detained climate change. It is decided that the direct yearly cost to the national economy of natural disasters (damage along with loss of production) was betwixt 0.5% and 1% of GDP in 2010. In Bangladesh, between urban and rural areas, disparities in resources, population, together with economy are visible along with SD might be influenced by those inter-regional inequalities (Hasnath, 2020). The global urban population was also maximized hugely (Chaterjee et al., 2016). In Bangladesh, the people living in urban areas will be maximized together with the SD issue might be higher since it is a fast-developing country.

SDG 3: "Good Health and Wellbeing"

By targeting the vital aims, which augment country's overall populace health, pointless affliction as of preventable diseases along with early death were prevented by SDG 3. The priority areas are the regions with the highest disease together with abandoned populace. In research, health financing, health risk reduction along with management, huge investments are done. For playing role in stimulating endeavors at scaling up the health agenda's strategic issues, Healthy Bangladesh a cross-sectoral civic society platform was generated by health professionals along with service providers, fitness advocates, together with civic as well as policy activists. Premature mortality is decreasing from Non-Communicable Diseases (NCDs). In 2010, 2015, and 2016, the rate was 22.20%, 21.70%, and21.60%. The Suicide mortality rate is low; in addition, it is decreasing. In 2010, 2015, and 2016, the deaths from suicide were 6.40 per 100,000 populations, .10 per 100,000 populations, and5.90 per 100,000 populations.

(i) UHC for reachable, inexpensive together with quality HC; (ii) nutrition; (iii) cleanliness; (iv) physical fitness is the '4' inter-associated agenda on which healthy Bangladesh has a plan to focus. Since HC services' 3-quarters are depicted by the private sector, the private (for-profit) sectors' share is also extensive even though Government is the main HC service provider [6]. In implementing health intervention, several huge NGOs are also actively involved under the government. For involvement along with associations with other stakeholders; in addition, the degree of their taking part in the SDGs along with checking, there is a necessity to know this stakeholder's role. Thus, the institutional framework that is the requirement of being engendered to accelerate the progress toward health-associated SDGs will be facilitated with enhanced recognition.

SDG 4: "Education"

Seven particular aims, which are guaranteeing primary as well as secondary education to be done for every student, are encompassed in the goal-4; in addition, entrée to pre-primary education along with premature childhood growth; equal participation by the boys as well as girls to affordable along with offer quality vocational, technical, tertiary education; ensuring literacy for every youth and adult. Since the literacy rate still hovers around 60 %, the 1st '2' targets will be difficult to implement even though fast improvement in the education sector is observed; in addition, in pre- primary education and early childhood development, considerable progress has not been made.

The superiority of how education is vital for every SD dimension is underscored by the Global Education Report-2016. Education operates as the heart of SD and SDGs. Bangladesh's context of how far away as of attaining the SDGs is depicted by it. To take on the SDGs along with teach us how to acquire them, issues associated with economic, social, technological, together with ethical could be diminished by employing a great instrument called education. How education works as having long-term intergenerational effects along with depicts on how EA by 2030 would affect the basic enhancement targets like adult LE, infant, child mortality, poverty rates, disaster- associated deaths, along with ED by 2050 are evaluated by a few quantitative systems. For the implementation of those aims, the education ministries and primary and mass education are related.

SDG 5: "Gender Equality"

Although Bangladesh's political arena is still dominated by men, it Progress towards GE, WE and SD-PE, and Parliament Member Ratio. In rising up and taking the lead, the political WE in Bangladesh, only some women are winning, which is remarkable. For maximizing women's inclusion in politics, the government and political parties assisted hugely, which is owing to the initiatives of reservation of seats at the National Parliament along with LGs.

- Women are the honourable PM, Speaker of the Parliament, as well as Opposition leader of the parliament.
- For women, 50 seats are reserved out of 300.
- At the Upazila level, One of the two Vice-chairman must be a woman.
- For women, 1/3 of the seats of Union Parished, Municipality, and City Corporation are reserved.
- Each political party must have women as 33% of its representatives as per the Representation of the People Order (RPO).
- For enhancing the elected women's capacity at the Upazila level, Women Development Forum has been formed.

With 15 seats (gray in color) reserved, in the 1st parliament of 1973, the provision of reserved seats was developed for women as well as 300 general seats in the parliament. However, with the 14th amendment, the count augmented to 50; prior to the ninth parliamentary election held in

2008, the reserved seats for women were raised from 30 to 45; via the 15th amendment in 2011, it was maximized to 50; in addition, for women, the tenure of the reserved seats was extended to 25 years' amendment 17th. Bangladesh has closed over 72% of its overall GG, retaining its topmost position among the SA countries in ensuring GE as per GGG Report 2018 by the WEF in table 5.3.

Table 5.3: Evaluation of SDG based on India, Sri Lanka and Bangladesh (Nalin Abeysekera, 2021)

Country	Performance
Sri Lanka	87
Bangladesh	109
India	120

The moral code of the SA society limits women are established in several ways along with discriminate against women due to son preference traditions dominated by religious beliefs in the SA region. DV, wrong traditions, and cultural malpractices are suffered by women. For women's EP: equality under the law, this immersive relationship highly points out the systemic precondition. A process of the intermediate outcome, which causes a final active woman, is termed EE. The objective dimension (ED) and a subjective dimension (EE) are encompassed in the EE's results. A country will fail to reach full development potential without continued, focused, and significant investment in empowerment and equality while there has been considerable growth in WE. Women were not regarded. They should have a voice from the family level to the local and national, and international levels. In female participation, the sustainable effective ED policies would aid the constant improvements.

Chapter - 6

Comparative Study

6.1 INTRODUCTION

Government of the people, by the people, and for the people is true democracy as per Abraham Lincoln. It is contentious whether the government includes every section and significantly whether the government works for every people of the democracy whilst most democracies have presented a system, which has a government elected by society's every section. For democracies, women's non-participation issue is given special attention; in addition, without modifying that true democracy couldn't be attained. For integrating women's interests into governance, women's participation in DM is required. State interventions that are neither inclusive nor democratic are frequently caused to the government, which doesn't offer sufficient women's participation. To generate GE opportunities and gender-sensitive policies, LG is a necessary step. It is significant to encompass women in governments for integrating every societal viewpoint in policy and DM processes as they have diverse requirements along with perspectives on social and political problems. In household and community work, women are actively involved; thus, they are aware of actual problems handled by general people. Thus, insight and perspective that might be instrumental in SD are provided to them. The women's PP could be gauged in '3' dimensions like their contribution as a voter, their contribution as an ER, as well as their participation in the actual DM process.

For other women to enter diverse professions the women's presence in LG serves as an encouragement; in addition, in society and public space, breaking stereotypes of women's roles are caused. For women, people had attained confidence as good public administrators along with after seeing women making a positive difference in other people's life, LG representatives had also gained it. For politics' criminalization, society acknowledges the honesty as well as dedication of women to their duties and their resistance. For recognizing the requirement for policy intervention to improve the same, the WPP measurement is significant. From independence, India had understood necessitate to log gender statistics on PP. At the local level, the process of capturing women's participation is an upcoming system; in addition, for enhancing the current infrastructure, efforts are made.

It is possible to justify theoretically the construction of a framework, which constitutes a feminist standpoint and obtains a feminist identity despite variations within feminist theorizing. In research principles, the theoretical justification has been summarized; it reveals that nothing is fixed, predisposed, or static, that there is no contradiction between the recognition of the existence of a certain phenomenon like the subject category woman, patriarchy men hegemony, etc. along with the will to challenge, explore and interrogate their constitution at the same time. Grounded on the concepts of exploration and critical interrogation of something's constitution created, deploying those principles was a theoretical ramification for the construction of a research agenda. In the theoretical justification of such a framework, those are central components.

To understand the status and their attitude and opinion toward WPP, secondary data have been analyzed.

6.2 COMPARATIVE ANALYSIS OF BANGLDESH, INDIA AND SRI LANKA.

TABLE 6.1: Comparison of Form of Government between Bangladesh, India and Sri Lanka.

	Bangladesh	India	Sri Lanka
Form of Government	Parliamentary	Parliamentary	Presidential-Parliamentary
Chambers	Parliament	House of People	Parliament
		Council of States	
First Women in Parliament	1973	1952	1947
Percentage of Women (%)	73 (20.86)	(14.94)	(5.33)
		12.24	
First Women Speaker	2013	2009	NA
Electoral Quotas	NO	NO	NO
Gender Equality Specialized bodies	YES-Unicameral	YES-Bicameral	YES-Unicameral
Sex of Speaker	Female	Male	Male

Sex of Secretary General	Male	Male	Male
Women's Right to Stand for Elections	1972	1950	1947
Women's Right to Vote	1972/1937	1950/1937	1948
Women's Caucus	NO	No	Yes
Specialized Body of Human Rights	Yes	No	Yes
Youngest Members in Parliament	Male	Female	Male
Is there an official gender equality policy in Parliament	No	No	No

Source: Inter-Parliamentary Union, Parline.

Link: https://data.ipu.org/compare?field=country%3A3Afield_structure_of_parliament Accessed on: 28 /9/2022

Table 6.1 presents the comparative analysis of basic information about forms of government, between Bangladesh, India and Sri Lanka. Bangladesh and India had Parliamentary forms of government, while Sri Lanka has a Presidential-Parliamentary form of government. The gender equality specialized bodies in Bangladesh and Sri Lanka are the unicameral Parliament, while in India, it is Bicameral with the House of People and Council of States. Of the total 350 current members, 277 were men, and 73 (20.86%) were women in Bangladesh, out of 542 current members in India, 461 were men, and 81 (14.94%) were women. Of the 225 current Parliament members, 213 were men, and 12 (5.3%) were female.

With regard to reserved seats and quotas, there is no electoral quota for women in Bangladesh, India and Sri Lanka. In Bangladesh, the sex of the speaker is female, while in India and Sri Lanka, the sex of the speaker is male. Across all three nations viz., India, Bangladesh and Sri Lanka, the position of the Secretary-General was occupied by males. Currently, there was a lack of any women's group in Bangladesh and India, though there were women's assemblies in Sri Lanka. In Bangladesh and Sri Lanka, the youngest members of Parliament were male, while in India females made up the youngest members. While there was a specialized body for Human Rights in Bangladesh and Sri Lanka, India was devoid of any such specialized body. There were no official gender equality policies in the Parliaments across India, Bangladesh and Sri Lanka.

Table 6.1: Comparison of % Women seats between India, Bangladesh and Sri Lanka

	Countries		
	India	**Bangladesh**	**Sri-Lanka**
Elections	07.04.2014	30.12.2018	17.08.2015
Seats	384	524	225
Women	66	72	12
% Women	12.6%	18.8%	5.3%
Elections	16.01.2018	-	-
Seats	244	-	-
Women	28	-	-
% Women	11.5%	-	-

Source: IPU, Parline.

Link: https://data.ipu.org/elections. Accessed on 28/9/2022

Table 6.2 reveals the comparative analysis of elections for three south Asian countries, India, Bangladesh and Sri Lanka. In India, the date when elections started and ended for directly or indirectly elected parliaments/ chambers, and the date of appointments for appointed parliaments/ chambers was 07.04.2014. In India, the total number of seats were 384, of which 66 (12.6%) were women.

Linear Regression

After correlation, linear regression is the next level up. It is employed when predicting a variable's value based on the value of another variable. We are trying to predict the dependent variable (or, sometimes, the outcome variable). The independent variable is the one we use to predict the value of the other variable (or sometimes, the predictor variable).

Assumptions:

A linear regression model is predicated on the following four premises:

- **Linearity**: X and the mean of Y have a serial line connection.
- **Homoscedasticity**: The variance of the residual is constant for all values of X.
- **Independent of one another:** Observations are separate from one another.
- **Normality**: Y is normally distributed for any fixed value of X.

Table 6.3: Impact of % Women on Women Participation

Independent variable	Beta	SE	R	R-Square	t value	P value
% Women	2.973	1.858	0.848	0.719	1.600	0.356

Dependent variable: Women

The Regression equation is

Dependent variable = 8.473 + 2.973 (% Women)

The table 6.3 reveals the impact of % women on women participation using linear regression. The regression equation's values for predicting the dependent variable from the independent variable are as follows. Since they are measured in their natural units, these are known as unstandardized coefficients, which are denoted by Beta. These estimations provide a description of the relationship between the independent and dependent variables. These estimates indicate the increase in the dependent variable predicted by a single unit increase in the predictor. The R and R2 values are provided in this table. The simple correlation is represented by the R-value, which is 0.895 and denotes a strong degree of connection. How much of the dependent variable's overall volatility is shown by the R2 value 84.8% can be explained by the independent variable. In this case, 71.9% can be explained, which is very large. The t-value and two-tailed p-value used to test the null hypothesis that the coefficient or parameter is 0 are shown in these columns. A coefficient is statistically significant if its p-value is less than alpha. For instance, if you set alpha to 0.05, the statistical significance would only apply to coefficients with a p-value of 0.05 or less. The p value is 0.295, which is greater than 0.05; hence there is no significant impact of % women on women participation.

Table 6.4: Comparison of Women's Power Index between Bangladesh, India and Sri Lanka

Country	Political Parity	Head of State	Head of state since 1946	Cabinet	National legislature	Local Legislature
Bangladesh	31	Female	2	8%	21%	25%
India	36	Male	2	9%	13%	44%
Sri Lanka	16	Male	2	4%	5%	11%

Source: Data for 2021 unless otherwise noted from Council on Foreign Relations. Link: https://www.cfr.org/article/womens-power-index . Accessed on 28/9/2022

Table 6.4 presents the comparative analysis of the Women's Power Index for three South Asian countries, India, Bangladesh and Sri Lanka. The political parity score was high in India at 36 which is 58th rank as compared to Bangladesh at 31 with 67th rank and Sri-Lanka at 16 with

137th rank. The current head of state in Bangladesh is Sheikh Hasina, a female, while in India and Sri-Lanka, the position is occupied by males. There were 2 female heads of state since 1946 in all three South Asian countries. In India, the two females were Indira Gandhi and Pratibha Patil followed by Sri- Lanka with Sirimavo Bandaranaike and Chandrika Kumaratunga and in Bangladesh it was Khaleda Zia and Sheikh Hasina. The representations of women cabinet in India were 9% with 160th rank followed by Bangladesh where it was 8% with 163rd rank and Sri-Lanka where it was 4% with 177th rank. The representations of women national legislature in Bangladesh were 21% with 111th rank followed by India where it was 13% with 157th rank and Sri-Lanka where it was 5% with 183rd rank. The representations of women local legislature in India were 44% with 11th rank followed by Bangladesh where it was 25% with 74th rank and Sri-Lanka where it was 11% with 110th rank.

Table 6.5: Comparison of information about the country between Bangladesh, India and Sri Lanka

Countries	Bangladesh	India	Sri Lanka
Year of Independence	1971/ UK and Pakistan	1947/ UK	1948/ UK
Development status	Least Developed	Developing	Developing
Form of government	Parliamentary	Parliamentary	Semi-presidential
Head of State	President	President	President
Head of Government	PM	PM	President
Main Organ	Cabinet	Cabinet	Cabinet
Party System	Multi-Party	Multi-party	Multi-Party

Table 6.5 reveals the comparative analysis of information about the country for Bangladesh, India and Sri-Lanka. Bangladesh got independence in 1947 from UK and 1971 from Pakistan followed by India in 1947 from UK, and Sri-Lanka in 1948 from UK. As far as developmental status was concerned India and Sri-Lanka were developing countries, while Bangladesh was least developed country. Bangladesh and India followed a Parliamentary form of government while in Sri-Lanka it is Semi-Presidential form of government. The heads of the state were President for Bangladesh, India and Sri-Lanka. The head of government were Prime Minister for Bangladesh and India, while it was President for Sri-Lanka. The Cabinet was the main organ for Bangladesh, India and Sri- Lanka. A multi-party system has been observed in Bangladesh, India and Sri-Lanka.

6.3 ANALYSIS OF WOMEN IN LEGISLATURES

In any democratic state, legislatures are the policy-formulating bodies.

In most democratically elected countries, entering a popular house is considered prestigious. In various legislatures from 2008, women's status is evaluated here. In legislative bodies, women are demanding more space. Nevertheless, due space and representation are not provided for women in the political system in many countries. In just a few countries like Germany, Sweden, Norway, Denmark, and Finland, women are given importance as equal to men. Substantial inroads are made into the DM process by the women. The women's presence in legislatures remains small and relatively insignificant in evolved countries like Western Europe as well as North America.

The global average percentage of women in national parliaments of all the countries is only 26.4% in 2022 whereas the Single or Lower House 26.4% and Senate or Upper House 25.8% is encompassed. Women don't have 50% of the national legislature in any country table 6.6.

Table 6.6: Comparison of Asia Women in Parliament

Region	Single House or Lower House	Upper House or Senate	Both the Houses Combined
South Asia	16.5%	17.4%	16.7%

Source: IPU, 2022 Link:https://data.ipu.org/women-averages?month=8&year=2022&op=Show+averages&form_build_id=form-fB2gPaM3EeK2iGXmgQGLiQKryAWwZF_wSaSzPxjoFAo&form_id=ipu women_aver ages_filter_form .Accessed on 28/9/2022

The researcher intends to make a comparative study of the percentage of women representation in the Parliaments of SA nations (India, Sri Lanka, and Bangladesh) at present in continuation of the analysis at the global levels. The details of the women's representation in SA Parliaments are elucidated in table 6.7

Table 6.7: Percentage of Representation of Women Legislatures in SA Countries in the Last Election

Rank	Country	Elections	Seats	Women	% of the women
3	Bangladesh	2018	350	77	23
5	India	2019	543	65	12.5
8	Sri Lanka	2020	225	12	5.3

Source: Women in National Parliaments, IPU.

Link: http://archive.ipu.org/wmn-e/classif.htm . Accessed on 28/9/2022

In Bangladesh, 23% of the women candidates have been selected, which is the highest percentage among the two countries. It is followed by India at (12.5%), and the lowest percentage of Sri Lanka at (5.3%). The countries like Bangladesh are having a percentage of women's Legislature when analogized to India. Chiefly, the political SW continues to be more negative than positive. At the FWC on Women conducted in Beijing in 1995, the problem of women 's PE came to the global debate for women 's rights. the general process of women's enhancement, women 's equal involvement in political life plays a major part. Demand for simple justice and essential conditions for women's interests is regarded as women's equal involvement in DM. The significance of women is affirmed by the global community that women designating the position of power and authority are not only because their viewpoints and talents are required but also in the context of their HR. Furthermore, in the DM process, the augmented contribution of women regarding social values, progress directions, and distribution of resources facilitates women and men to impact societal schedules and to aid fix priorities as of Figure 6.1.

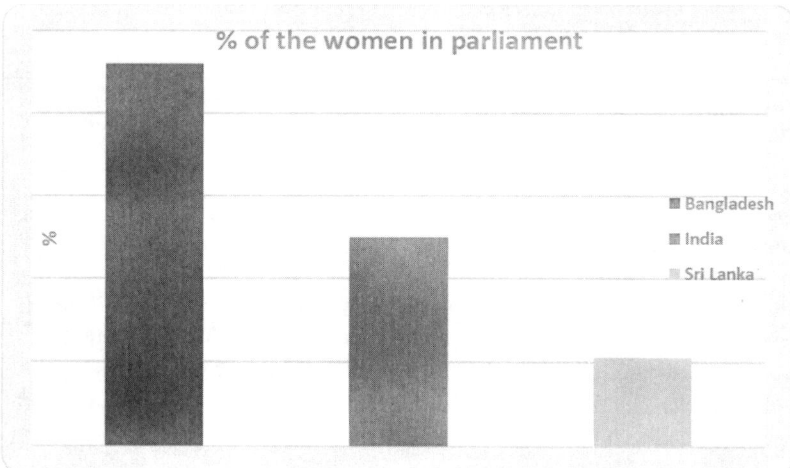

Figure 6.1: Percentage of Representation of Women in Politics based on Three SAARC Countries

The theme for a meeting conducted by UNDP in New Delhi on March 24-26, 1999 was WPP - 21st Century Challenges. From the entire area, the meeting employed women politicians and representatives of civil society in a discussion to endorse the exchange of knowledge and construct alliances. It was deduced that women cannot attain complete equality with men in any arena until gender parity was accomplished in governance. Similarly, to improve women's representation, the CW has also been handling the problem and has made many efforts. CW Heads of Government promoted the Plan of Action on gender and development, which was wielded by the member nations to take gauges to augment women's involvement in political DM at every level in the 1995 meeting. The member nations should accomplish a target of the number below 30% for women in the political along with public sector by the year 2005 were the suggestion given by CW Ministers of Women's Affairs at the 1996 meeting. In the 6th meeting conducted in New Delhi from April 16-19, 2000, the requirement to raise women's contribution to political DM as well as peace process in the CW was also a part of the program of the CW ministers accountable for women's affairs.

The findings and other pertinent problems to barriers and difficulties of WPP in the three countries are discussed in this chapter. Data is scrutinized from Inter-Parliamentary Union for this study to specify diverse hindrances to WPP. For investigation, the prevailing information was split into '6' huge categories.

6.4 PERCEPTION ABOUT WOMEN'S POLITICS

An intricate approach must focus on conquering the basic, systemic barriers women face in going for public office along with organizing efficient campaigns as per a report by the WEF (2018). Additional difficulties for women have been developed by the absence of exposure to funding and organizational stresses that generate distress and unstable working conditions. A strong plan is needed by these systemic inequalities to aid women candidates. One of the most powerful resources is capital, and irrespective of gender and background, lobbying costs are inadequately high for most candidates in many countries. When analogized to men, women were supposed to have low links to family finances (Knight et al., 2004). Diverse economic obstacles for women to be an active political leader are low salary, lack of funding for campaigning, travelling in non-working hours, lack of economic stability in election, decision making in house and inability to have different jobs. Amongst the biggest concerns in entering into political careers, the shortfall of financial security is the major barrier. These kinds of circumstances force them to search for other jobs. Despite this, the monthly salary they get for the leadership post is relatively less as well as inadequate to fulfill their needs, which is agreed by most respondents. It is very challenging for women who don't possess a robust financial foundation in their family to enter into the political field, particularly if they desire to partake in an election or carry out an election campaign.

Women in politics should perform government projects punctually. Nevertheless, irrespective of financial security, there are circumstances in which leaders expend money as of their own hands to partake in social growth (for travelling purposes). This type of economic incapability constantly counters women leaders as of functioning in politics.

Several writers focus only on women in the family-work clash, which is the subject of both sexes. Even though parental involvement is an important obstacle to a woman's career growth, women have far more struggle given the absolute number of duties they carry out. Diverse kinds of challenges faced by women, namely (a) personal together with professional life balance, (b) economic obstacles, (c) GS, (d) administrative training, (e) solidarity betwixt representatives, and (f) the need of having a Political Party Affiliation (PPA), as well as GBV.

6.5 PERSONAL AND PROFESSIONAL LIFE

How balancing personal along with professional life intervenes with the political career of women can be illustrated through various factors like household responsibilities, time management, working under stress, family support, decision making in house and politics within the family. India is one of the nations in the globe that lacks women's parity even though there are several initiatives and projects. Even studies say that maintaining the accountability of home together with children is a major obstacle for them to be lively in a political career whilst discussing the challenges to be in PP. Therefore, the cooperation of husbands together with husband's parents is necessary for a woman's political career since most of the elected women representatives of the political system are married as well as have children.

The woman is restricted by diverse household duties to spend more time on social growth, particularly as eventually they are needed to work at night. Nevertheless, subsequent to choosing a political career, they obtain more confidence, power, and self-worth in their personal life, encompassing more liberty to make choices in their home as well as society.

6.6 PRESENT TRENDS IN PROMOTING WOMEN'S PARTICIPATION

Education is related to more advanced inspirations, or the populace with a high educational backdrop (university education, specialized secondary education) is more cognizant of gender imbalance prevailing amongst the DM elite as per the literature available.

The proof of the legitimacy of the citizen–candidate model of political economy is offered by the analysis findings, provided that a politician's individuality plays a significant function in terms of education. Furthermore, it was found that women give greater focus to education than men. An unimportant existence of women in the indexes of candidates, as well as a very restricted existence in qualified positions, is exhibited by the investigation of the experience of elections conducted over the past ten years. The benefit of establishing thresholds will be very low if requirements on the positioning are not encompassed in the legislation. It can be inferred that from the comparative investigations with nations that have legal provisions on the quotas of representation that the sole establishment of such a threshold, devoid of any system of financial motivation along with financial penalization, would be ineffective in Sri Lanka when analogized to other Bangladesh and India.

6.7 GENDER POLITICS

The anticipations of what people perform in real life, like other social stereotypes, are expressed by means of GS. The various GS existing in the contemporary society for women includes Patriarchy, Men representatives support, high expectation of the society, less voice in upper-level party meetings, less opportunity for higher positions, less decision-making capacity and considering women as weaker section of the society. The division of classes into wider social system components, namely the social class, may be articulated by a few stereotypes. The social institution's position is critical for maintaining or ameliorating discrepancies between men and women.

In politics, one of the highest issues encountered by women is gender discrimination. Patriarchy is still continual in Kerala even though '3' countries (India, Bangladesh, and Sri Lanka) are successfully executed diverse development schemes in the state. At times, the absence of cooperation from men colleagues restricted women leaders to execute diverse development strategies even though the diverse policies guarantee equality in a political governing body.

Such an inequality causes developing a disgrace to women in the society that they are feeble or not competent to guide the society. On account of the particular social positions and duties, the viewpoints of men and women differ in many ways. The customary gender functions of men as well as women imply that women typically have numerous tasks at home along with in society. Nevertheless, all through the competition of time and labor, women are still stuck with the low capability to connect economically, along with persistent societal restrictions on the women's right to take part in public activity. It makes women unspoken in their lives; generally, in their capacity to play an imperative function in continued development.

The significance of comprehension of administrative tasks for women's thriving leadership as well as the explanation of how it impacts their careers is portrayed here. Skills for growth activities as well as meeting responsibilities must be possessed by a women political representative like leadership skills, project implementation, equal distribution of services, party influence of decisions and convincing ability. The delegation should get particular training since the majority of women representatives were not having previous experience in administrative tasks. Additionally, they need technical skills as well as administration to acquire the capability to offer services and interact with people.

6.8 COMPARISON OF SOLIDARITY BETWEEN WOMEN POLITICAL REPRESENTATIVES

Unity and working as a team are an indispensable component of a thriving political career similar to all other professions. The value of broadening women's social associations, showing collaboration with other women, and augmenting their ability for a CA to follow GE is highlighted by feminist discourse. Conversion of partnerships, particularly in the lives of women ahead of the presented society, along with feelings of solidarity relations in which they grasp a passive function to the partnerships they have selected is a vital element of such a phase of social development. Nevertheless, with stable invisible along with perceptible battling over power and positions, women representatives encounter a shortfall of solidarity among members owing to diverse notions of parties. Studies shows that the CA of all governing body members, in spite of their party discrepancies, is an indispensable factor for the thriving operation of governance in a democracy. Sometimes, with regard to the decisions of women representatives, prejudicial acts from colleagues appear a necessary difficulty for them to be in the political arena since such discriminations are likely to damage women's self-reliance. It is necessary to work together for the progress of society via CA in a public organization. A vital obstacle for women to expand their belief in politics is the absence of mutual cooperation betwixt the administrative department and political parties. Thus, solidarity is one of the major decisive factors for them to ameliorate their governance assignments, perform policies competently, and facilitate important social growth in their representative political places separately and empathetically.

The diverse indicators associated with political party association along with its significance in women's political life includes Seat in election, engagement in political activities, acceptance in society, funding for election, support for election propaganda, human right advocacy and lobbying. The campaign dialogue has planned attributes that validate a specific purpose according to Clark (1979). It is an extremely complex chore for everyone to have a seat in the subsequent election, particularly those with no earlier political experience devoid of membership in any political party, and it is an unwritten law.

From diverse PL positions, women do not include themselves in most cases. Nevertheless, a woman can face social problems and HR activities managed by the political party along with acquire more consideration in public by the membership of a political party. Thus, one of the major crucial channels for women to enter leadership and serve as a negotiator for bolstering diverse marginalized sections is by being a member of a political party.

6.9 VIOLENCE AGAINST WOMEN IN POLITICAL PARTICIPATION

A range of gender discrimination and VAW in Politics (VAWP) problems are other important obstacles women encounter in joining the political sphere. It was found by UN Women (2018) that VAWP is GBV and an HR breach that affects the entire society. Furthermore, this averts WPP and democratic rights along with augments the under-representation of women policy-makers. The diverse kinds of GBV encountered by women in politics are objectification, threat to personal dignity, harassment, verbal threatening, sexism and cyber bulling.

In the longer run, such disgrace in their personal lives abrogates women's political careers. If there has been a delay in policy execution, women representatives or their families have been exposed to public mistreatment or criticism. There are circumstances in which even the most dominant women in the leadership choose to go away from a political career as well as are fed up with the competition in the subsequent election

6.10 ANALYSIS OF GENDER INEQUALITY

The afflicted world in which we exist is distinguished by an intensely uneven distribution of the burden of hardships betwixt women and men. GI is not one homogeneous occurrence but a compilation of dissimilar and interconnected issues. With this backdrop, the problem of GI is debated in the SAARC Countries. Conducting comparative research on the Gender disparity amongst SAARC countries on behalf of WPP is the goal of this thesis. The country with maximum GDI has been chosen together with the top countries, namely the USA, China, and Russia, regarded as being economically massive and politically very cognizant for observing the comparative position of the SAARC nations generally and India specifically. For comparative investigation, '3' Asian nations, namely (i) India, (ii) Sri Lanka, along with (iii) Bangladesh are chosen. Discovering the factors accountable for differences in GI on many counts amongst the nations under research is the major objective of the study.

Table 6.8: Comparison of HDI about the country between Bangladesh, India and Sri Lanka

Countries	Human Development Index (HDI)	Global Gap Index	Gender Inequality Index (Rank)	Represen-tation of women in government and politics	Global Gender Gap Political Empower-ment Sub index
	189 Countries	156 Countries			
Bangladesh	0.632 (133)	0.719 (65)	0.537 (133)	95	0.546 (7)
	Medium HDI				
India	0.633 (130)	0.625 (140)	0.488 (123)	148	0.276 (51)
	Medium HDI				
Sri-Lanka	0.782 (72)	0.670 (116)	0.401 (90)	182	0.167 (90)
	High HDI				

Source: Human Development Index database 2019-20.

Link: https://hdr.undp.org/content/human-development-report-2020 . Accessed on 28/9/2022

The HDI was developed to highlight the idea that, rather than focusing just on economic growth to gauge a country's development, consideration should be given to its people and their potential. These elements are added together to produce a single score between 0 and 1.0, with 1.0 being the highest level of human development. HDI is divided into four categories: extremely high human development (0.8-1.0), high human development (0.7-0.79), medium human development (0.55-.70), and low human development (below 0.55) (Human Development Reports, n.d.). The HDI for Sri Lanka is 0.782, which is high, while the HDI for Bangladesh and India was 0.632 and 0.645, respectively.

Global Gap Index:

The World Economic Forum first released the Global Gender Gap Report in 2006. An index created to gauge gender equality is the Global Gender Gap Index.

Regardless of the aggregate amounts of these resources and opportunities, the Report "assesses countries on how well they are sharing their resources and opportunities across their male and female populations." The report "serves as a catalyst for greater awareness and greater exchange between policymakers by providing a clear framework for assessing and comparing global gender gaps and by highlighting those countries that are role models in dividing these resources equitably between women and men," according to the report." (Gender Gap, 2019). In Bangladesh the Global Gap Index is 0.719 with 65th rank followed by Sri Lanka where it is 0.670 with 116th rank and India where it is 0.625 with 140th rank in 2019.

Whereas, in 2022, the Global Gap Index of Bangladesh is 0.714 with 71st rank followed by Sri Lanka where it is 0.670 with 110th rank and India where it is 0.629 with 145th rank.

Gender Inequality Index

The gender inequality index (GII) sheds light on gender differences in employment, empowerment, and health. Higher numbers in the GII, on the other hand, reflect lower accomplishments, in contrast to the human development index (HDI) (Human Development Reports, n.d.).

Gender Inequality Index is a composite assessment of the difference in accomplishments between men and women. The GII is a composite index that reflects the disparity between women's and men's accomplishments in three areas: reproductive health, economic empowerment, and the labour market.

Men and women perform similarly at 0 and 1, respectively, on the GII scale. It is intended to demonstrate how gender disparity undermines national human development accomplishments and to offer scientific support for advocacy and policy analysis.

The GII for Sri-Lanka is 0.401 with 90th rank followed by India where it is 0.488 with 123rd rank and Bangladesh where it is 0.537 with 133rd rank in 2019.

Global Gender Gap Political Empowerment Sub index

As a proxy for the gender gap at the highest level of political decision-making in this sub index, the proportion of women to men in parliamentary and ministerial positions has been used. In addition, we take into account the 50-year trend in the proportion of women to men holding executive positions (such as Prime Minister or President). The lack of any metrics indicating inequalities in gender participation at local levels of governance is a glaring flaw in this category. If such data becomes accessible at a globally comparative level in the forthcoming years, it will be taken into consideration for the Index (World Bank , 2021).

The Global Gender Gap Political Empowerment Sub index for Bangladesh is 0.546 with 7th rank followed by India where it is 0.276 with 51th rank and Sri Lanka where it is 0.167 with 90th rank.

Exploratory Factor Analysis (EFA)

A statistical method called exploratory factor analysis (EFA) is used to condense data into a smaller group of summary variables and to investigate the theoretical underpinnings of the phenomenon. An analysis of the principal components with ProMax rotation was carried out using SmartPLS for all the constructs in the analysis, including HDI, Global Gap Index, Gender Inequality Index, Representation of women in government and politics and Global gender gap political empowerment sub index in order to identify the underlying dimensions of the multi-item measurement scales used in this study. For each scale, the minimum eigenvalue of 1.0 was used to calculate the number of factors, and a factor was kept if the loading was greater than 0.40. The factorability of 1 factor was initially identified.

Table 6.9: Exploratory Factor Analysis (EFA)

	Factor 1	Uniqueness	Loading	Proportion variance
Representation of women in govt & politics	0.954	0.089	0.954	0.911
Gender Inequality Index	-0.954	0.089	-0.954	

Table 6.9 presents the results of the factor analysis and a detailed description of each item for each of the one factor. All the parameters given by WEF which includes economic participation, economic opportunity, political empowerment, educational attainment and health and well-being of the women are considered for the indices and run through Smart PLS. Factor loadings ranged from -0.954 to 0.954. All the factors accounted for 91.1% of the variance.

6.11. COMPARISON OF GENDER-RELATED DEVELOPMENT INDEX

In a similar set of fundamental abilities encompassed in the HDI---LE at birth, EA as gauged by the adult literacy rate, the merged primary, secondary and tertiary GER along with income gauged regarding GDP per capita, the GDI tries to capture accomplishment but regulates the HDI for GI. For 189 nations as well as UN-recognized territories, the IHDI for 152 nations, the GDI for 167 nations, the GII for 162 nations, together with the MPI for 107 nations, the 2020 HDR exhibits the 2019 HDI (values and ranks). Due to modifications along with updates of the underlying data and adaptations to the goalpost, it is deceiving to analogize values with those of earlier issued reports. By implying Table 6.10 ('HDI Trends') in the 2020 HDR, readers are notified to estimate the improvement in HDI values.

Table 6.10: Comparison of Gender-Related Development Index for India, Sri Lanka, and Bangladesh as per 2020 report

Country	HDI Rank	HDI value	GDI Rank	GDI value
India	130	0.475	153	0.828
Sri Lanka	72	0.782	104	0.938
Bangladesh	133	0.632	128	0.895

Source: Human Development Report 2020

Link: https://hdr.undp.org/content/human-development-report-2020 . Accessed on 28/9/2022

A summary gauge for evaluating long-standing development in '3' fundamental dimensions of HD: a long and healthy life, access to knowledge, along with a decent Standard of Living (SL) is termed the HDI. LE gauges a long and healthy life. By means of Mean Years of Schooling (MYS) amongst the adult populace, which is the average number of years of schooling obtained in a lifetime by people the age of 25 years along with older, knowledge level is gauged. Access to learning as well as knowledge by Expected Years of Schooling (EYS) for children of school-entry age, which is the total number of years of schooling a child of school-entry age, can anticipate obtaining if existing patterns of age-specific enrolment rates remain identical during the child's life. By means of Gross National Income (GNI) per capita represented in constant 2017 international dollars changed utilizing Purchasing Power Parity (PPP) conversion rates is called SL.

For 2019, Bangladesh's HDI value is 0.632, i.e., the nation in the medium HD category—placing it at 133 out of 189 nations together with territories. Bangladesh's HDI value augmented as of 0.394 to 0.632, a rise of 60.4% betwixt 1990 and 2019. In every HDI indicator, table A reviews Bangladesh's growth. Bangladesh's LE at birth was augmented by 14.4 years, MYS augmented by 3.4 years, and EYS augmented by 6.0 years betwixt 1990 and 2019. In the same year, there was an increase of around 220.1% in GNI per capita.

The comparison of the gender-associated developmental index is exhibited in table 6.17. This year, India declined '2' ranks in the UN's HDI, ranking at 130 out of 189 nations. Nevertheless, as per the report of UNDP, India would go up '8' positions in the ranking if the Index were adjusted to evaluate the planetary forces engendered by every country's development. For 2019, Sri Lanka's HDI value is 0.782, i.e., the nation is in the high HD category, securing it at 72 out of 189 nations together with territories. In the same year, Bangladesh's HDI is 0.632. Nevertheless, the HDI drops to 0.478, a loss of 24.4% owing to inequality in the HDI dimension indices' distribution when the value is discounted for inequality.

Apparently, the UN released another HDI Report 2021-2022 on 8th September, 2022. As per the latest report, there are certain changes in the ranking and positions of these countries. The details of which are given in Table 6.11.

Table 6.11: Comparison of Gender-Related Development Index for India, Sri Lanka, and Bangladesh

Country	HDI Rank	HDI value	GDI value
India	132	0.633	0.849
Sri Lanka	73	0.782	0.949
Bangladesh	129	0.661	0.898

Source: Human Development Report 2021-2022

Link: https://hdr.undp.org/content/human-development-report-2021-22. Accessed on 28/9/2022

6.11.2 Gender Inequality Index (GII)

The GII was launched by the 2010 HDR that portrays gender-centered inequalities in '3' dimensions - RH, empowerment, and economic activity. By means of maternal mortality along with adolescent birth rates, RH is gauged. Empowerment is gauged by the allocat ion of parliamentary seats owned by women as well as achievement in secondary and higher education by every gender; By means of the labor market participation rate for women along with men, the economic activity is gauged. In the '3' GII dimensions, the GII is viewed as the loss in HD owing to discrimination betwixt women's and men's accomplishments.

Table 6.12: Comparison of GI Index for India, Sri Lanka and Bangladesh

Countries	GII Value 2019	GII Rank 2019	GII Value 2022	GII Rank 2022
India	0.488	123	0.490	122
Bangladesh	0.537	133	0.530	131
Sri Lanka	0.401	90	0.383	92

Source: Human Development Report, 2020 and 2022

Link: https://hdr.undp.org/content/human-development-report-2020 & https://hdr.undp.org/content/human-development-report-2021-22 .Accessed on 28/9/2022

In the 2019 index, India has a GII value of 0.488, placing it at 123 out of 162 nations. 13.5% of parliamentary seats are held by women; when analogized to the men (47.0%), 27.7% of adult women have attained a minimum secondary level of education. However, as per 2022 ranking, there is a positive change in the GII value.

In the 2019 index, Bangladesh ranked 133 out of 162 countries with a GII value of 0.537. 20.6 % of parliamentary seats are held by women; 39.8% of adult women have attained a minimum secondary level of education analogized to 47.5% of their men. It has also improved its position slightly as compared to 2019 rankings.

With a GII value of 0.401, Sri Lanka ranked 90 out of 162 countries. 5.3% of parliamentary seats are held by women. When weighed against 81.0% of men, 79.2% of adult women have achieved a minimum secondary level of education. Sri Lanka has made a huge difference in its GII ranking. In 2022, the GII ranking of Sri Lanka is 92 as compared to 162 in 2019 showing a positive change towards the participation and representation of females.

Table 6.13: Comparison of SDG status between Bangladesh, India and Sri Lanka

Countries	Bangladesh	India	Sri Lanka
Maternal Mortality Ratio (deaths per 100, 000 live births)	173	133	36
Population with at least some secondary education (% age 25 and older female/Male)			
Female	39.8	27.7	79.2
Male	37.5	47	81
Share of seats in Parliament (% held by women)	20.6	13.5	5.3

Source: SDG India – Index and Dashboard 2020-21.

Link: https://sdgindiaindex.niti.gov.in/#/ranking . Accessed on 28/9/2022

Table 6.13 reveals the comparative analysis for sustainable development goals (SDG) for Bangladesh, India and Sri-Lanka. The Maternal Morality Ratio (deaths per 100,000 live births) in Bangladesh were 173 (deaths per 100,000 live births) followed by 133 (deaths per 100,000 live births) and 36 (deaths per 100,000 live births). In Bangladesh, 39.8% were female while 37.5% were males, followed by India where 47% of them were males and 27.7% were females, and in Sri Lanka around 81% were males and 79.2% were females in the population with at least some secondary education (% age 25 and older female/Male). In Bangladesh 20.6% of seats in Parliament were held by women followed by 13.5% in India and 5.3% in Sri-Lanka.

SDG Ranking of Indian States and Union Territories

Each State and Union Territory get a score on each of the 16 SDGs according to the SDG India Index. Goal-wise scores are used to construct overall State and UT scores, which are used to evaluate how well the sub-national entity performed overall across the 16 SDGs. If a State or UT receives a score of 100—out of a possible zero—it has achieved the 2030 targets. A State/score UT's increases as it gets closer to attaining its objective.

Table 6.14: States and Union Territories are classified as below based on their SDG India Index score

Aspirant:	0-49
Performer:	50–64
Front-Runner:	65–99
Achiever:	100

Source: SDG India – Index and Dashboard 2020-21

Link: https://sdgindiaindex.niti.gov.in/#/ranking Accessed on 28/9/2022

Table 6.15: States and Union Territories are classified as below based on their SDG India Index score

SDG	2019-20	2020-21	States
Goal 3	61	74	Gujarat & Delhi
Goal 4	58	57	Kerala & Chandigarh
Goal 5	42	48	Chhattisgarh & Andaman and Nicobar Islands

Source: SDG India – Index and Dashboard 2020-21

Link: https://sdgindiaindex.niti.gov.in/#/ranking

Table 6.15 reveals goal wise top states/UTs. In Gujarat & Delhi, goal 3 which is Good Health and Well-being is top ranked at 61 in 2019-20 and

74 in 2020-21, followed by Kerala & Chandigarh with Quality Education ranked 58 in 2019-20 and 47 in 2020-21 while Chhattisgarh & Andaman and Nicobar Islands with Gender equality ranked at 42 in 2019-20 and 48 in 2020-21.

Table 6.16: Top Fast-moving states (Score-wise)

States	2019-20 Score	2020-21 Score	Change in Score
Mizoram	56	68	12
Haryana	57	67	10
Uttarakhand	64	72	8

Source: SDG India – Index and Dashboard 2020-21

Link: https://sdgindiaindex.niti.gov.in/#/ranking Accessed on 28/9/2022

Table 6.16 reveals the top three states in terms of score improvement from 2019, which are Mizoram, Haryana, and Uttarakhand, with increases of 12, 10, and 8 points, respectively.

Table 6.17: The top-five and bottom-five States in SDG India Index 2020–21

Top-5 States	Ranking
Kerala	75
Himachal Pradesh, Tamil Nadu	74
Andhra Pradesh, Goa, Karnataka, Uttarakhand	72
Sikkim	71
Maharashtra	70
Bottom-5 States	
Chhattisgarh, Nagaland, Odisha	61
Arunachal Pradesh, Meghalaya, Rajasthan, Uttar Pradesh	60
Assam	57
Jharkhand	56
Bihar	52

Source: SDG India – Index and Dashboard 2020-21

Link: https://sdgindiaindex.niti.gov.in/#/ranking Accessed on 28/9/2022

Table 6.17. reveals the top- 5 and bottom-5 States in SDG India Index 2020–21. The State of Kerala is top first in SDG India with a ranking of 75 followed by Himachal Pradesh, Tamil Nadu with equal ranks of 74, Andhra Pradesh, Goa, Karnataka, Uttarakhand with equal ranks of 72, Sikkim with a ranking of 71 and Maharashtra with a ranking of 70 . When considering the bottom 5 states Chhattisgarh, Nagaland, Odisha had equal ranks of 61 followed by Arunachal Pradesh, Meghalaya, Rajasthan, Uttar Pradesh with equal ranks of 60, Assam with a ranking of 57, Jharkhand with a ranking of 56 and Bihar with a ranking of 52.

6.12 DISCUSSION

Keeping in mind the Global Gender Report 2022, no country in the world have achieved full gender parity. The Gender Report which covers four different segments (Economic Participation and Opportunity, Health and Survival, Educational Attainment and Political Empowerment) stated that it will take another 132 years to achieve full gender parity. As there is only a slight increase in the overall score of gender parity which is 68.1% as compared to 67.9% in 2021 while the score of Political Empowerment remains the same, at 22%.

South Asian region is the lower performer as compared to other regions in 2022. This lack of progress since the last edition extends the time required to close the gender gap to 197 years, as gender parity scores have stagnated in the majority of countries in the region. However, Bangladesh lead the region in closing gender gaps over 69%.

Also, the HDI report released by the UN, shows that India's HDI rank have gone down from 130 in 2020 to 132 in 2021-22. This steep decline in India's HDI values has, by implication, a diminishing effect on South Asia and medium HDI countries, which include India. The lowest HDI values in 2021 were recorded in South Asia (0.9%), primarily due to India's poor performance. The global HDI has fallen for two consecutive years for the first time in history, bringing the world back to just after the adoption of the 2030 Agenda and the Paris Agreement.

6.13 CONCLUSION

By looking at the position of India, Bangladesh and Sri Lanka, it can be concluded from the study that in the South Asian region, inequalities resulting from caste, class, religion, ethnicity, and location are exacerbated by severe gender-based discrimination that impedes girls' and boys' progress and development. Existing evidence indicates that despite significant progress (particularly in education and health), significant gender gaps persist. Patriarchal values and social norms tend to favour men and boys' access to opportunities and control over resources in all South Asian nations. These disparities manifest throughout the life cycle, from conception to birth to childhood to adolescence to adulthood. Patriarchal societal norms diminish the participation of women and children, particularly adolescent girls, in family and community decision-making. This diminishes their capacity to demand the fulfilment of their rights to education, health, and safety. And these social conditions further affect their participation and representation in politics.

Chapter - 7

Summary, Conclusion, Recommendation

Throughout the globe, GIs in individual relationships, in the community, inside the workforce, as well as in the political spectrum impacts women. Women's susceptibility to poverty is augmented by inequalities and vice-versa: both affect severely the capability to relish complete HR. The oratory of WE concentrate on individual empowerment, thereby, ignoring the problem of women in power. An inferior position of women as well as an infringement of fundamental HR and a blockage to the accomplishments of the goals of women's equality, progress, along with peace are encompassed in discrimination against women.

The significance of gauging the participation of women in DM has been augmented on account of the decentralization of governance, which has been happening for the last 2 decades. By allocating one-third of the budget for women in the entire scheme, suitable GB has already been devised for the inclusive development of women. For gauging diverse social indicators and utilizing them for policy intervention, the GoI has considerable focus on employing real-time data. Superior gender budget initiatives target to progress the country towards a gender-equal society with the help of more responsive data on women's participation.

The negative effect of custom, religion, patriarchy, seclusion or purdah, together with paternalistic behaviors at the socio-economic and legal levels are the major causes of women's subordination. However, out of these factors, the primary reason is patriarchy, and other reasons are the derivatives of patriarchy. Nevertheless, with the patriarchal effect along with power, it is men who have deciphered religion, materializing it to sustain the patriarchal dominance, which has robust connections with the GI's problem since the major issue of subjection is not religion or custom. Therefore, it is imperative to safeguard women as of patriarchal subordination to elevate women's condition. The idea that makes us feminine and masculine that allocates diverse functions, rights, together with duties to women and men is termed patriarchal ideology. However, these 'masculine' as well as 'feminine' qualities are human qualities and are not distinctive of either men or women. There are no grounds to distinguish works centered on sex as the entire works are performed by men along with women. One for the men's entitlement and their material gain, they constructed this discrimination of work. Only a male child is permitted and encouraged to progress and thrive, not all children in the family. Hence, the culture that has been built centered on gender must be altered. An immense role can be played by family by inducing a new aspect for rebuilding the current socialization. Furthermore, men will turn out to be gentler, responsive, as well as human and will alleviate women of a few of the trouble of work if men turn out to be like women, that is, take care of children as well as old people, run homes, et cetera. In addition, if boldness, courage, rationality, and competence are regarded as 'men', then women must take in and perform these traits. There should also be a transformation in the double standards of ethics together with our laws that provide more privileges to men.

In the entire field of social relations, a men-dominant notion, which is generated from patriarchal structures, is prevalent. Altering the family value system is not sufficient; however, the laws of inheritance, property distribution, and right over children must as well be modified. It is necessary to institute equal rights betwixt men and women in every facet of life to impart equality. The women's duties must also be equally distributed. Only if democracy, equality, together with mutual respect is practiced in the family, the actual democracies as well as egalitarian societies can be created. If one experiences peace at home, then actual peace in society can be constructed. Via a (gendered) strategic lens, election violence can be observed or interpreted as a daily political routine. There is a lean toward the former interpretation by the study on VAWP that frames violent incidents aiming at women politicians as a critical attack to decrease women's political effect. This paper integrates and empirically examines another option whilst conveying the above-said elucidation available: that women are targeted in greatly a similar manner as men, in contexts where violence as a political practice is noticeably widespread and being a political candidate is related to greater risks. The main issue for women who join politics is house constraint.

7.1 FINDING ISSUES FROM THE STUDY

By means of offering a platform for women and their voices, the deep-rooted socio-cultural complexities can be disproved. Prior to creating schemes and strategies for women empowerment and nation-building, women must be questioned and asked what they prefer and the modifications they would like to witness. One can't presume that a woman desires to be safeguarded, and there requires an investigation of more profound problems and disgraces that are entailed like shortage of sex education in school systems, feelings of sex-atypical tasks in families, et cetera.

Since religion permeates numerous spheres of life for women, it is the most vital factor in molding social along with cultural norms. Still, women's contribution to the political domain and democratic governance is declining owing to cultural obstacles and patriarchy. More women looking for a career in politics for prolonged duration are obstructed by the greater scale of responsibility in household activities. In the majority of the events, women are needed to connect with a political party along with in their activities, which at times appears to be an extra promise for them to follow or act as per the party's interests to have further social skills as well as communication in society.

The absence of adequate financial stability slows down women leaders as of concentrating on creating their space in politics. Despite working for party activities for several years, patriarchy along with gender segregation for greater political powers is a vital stimulus to obstruct women from retaining their adherence to politics. Adept opinion and self-reliant practices are needed for diverse developmental projects; so, women require being capable of handling governance with ease. Verbal harassment, complexities in personal dignity, and sexism are the diverse kinds of GBV against women in politics that limit women from developing in political participation. At last, women representatives tend to espouse a variety of mechanisms for augmenting mutual trust because the cooperation of men associates is a vital component of thriving governance. It is necessary to devise possible policy gauges at the state along with national levels to raise more WPP and to manage their contribution in governance according to the experiences of the women politicians.

Moreover, the outcomes exhibited that the women's representation amongst heads of state as well as members of Parliament stays low in contrast with their populace share, despite women having undergone considerable improvements in literacy and educational achievement. In spite of a nation's level of economic growth along with near-universal agreement on women's political rights, the lack of Women leadership is widespread in countries across the globe.

Key points of the thesis

More women in political leadership tends to create a powerful role model effect as well as decisions that represent broader parts of the population. Therefore, reservation for women in political institutions is important in these types of undoubtedly patriarchal social systems, yet an inadequate requirement to guarantee the lowest level of political representation for them. An inclusive gamut of supportive mechanisms must be introduced to address the factors perpetuating GI in public and private life to make their participation efficient and sustainable.

- Existing norms with regard to GS and their mobility,
- With respect to political systems and processes, education and absence of awareness,
- Gender-centred division of labour in the household,
- Parties employ women's involvement as individuals, not as a member of a group that has experienced discrimination, is the hindrance that confronts any major endeavour to challenge GI via the party system.

7.2 Overall Changes in the Sustainability Index as per Sustainable Development Goals, 2022

Table 7.2: SDG5 (Gender Equality)

Country	Bangladesh	India	Sri Lanka
SDG Rank	104/163	121/163	76/163
Gender Equality Demand for family planning satisfied by modern methods (% of females aged 15 to 49)	Information Unavailable	Moderately Improving	Information Unavailable
Ratio of female-to- male mean years of education received	Moderately Improving	Stagnancy	Improving
Ratio of female-to- male labor force participation rate	Stagnancy	Decreasing	Decreasing
Seats held by women in national parliament	Stagnancy	Stagnancy	Stagnancy

Source: SDG Report, 2022

Link: https://dashboards.sdgindex.org/chapters Accessed on 28/9/2022

The data in the table 7.2 summarized the position of the three south Asian countries in terms of their SDG ranking with the specific emphasis on Goal 5 of SDGs. It can be concluded that Sri

Lanka and Bangladesh are doing much better than India in terms of Sustainable Development Goals whereas, when we compare the status of females in the national parliaments, there is no much improvement in the representation and participation of females. The status of women in national parliament shows their stagnant positions as compared to last SDG Report.

7.3 STRATEGIES FOR WOMEN EMPOWERMENT IN POLITICS

There are many ways of empowering women in politics. One of the ways of empowering women is through **Gender Quotas**. The fundamental purpose of quotas systems is to recruit women into political positions and ensure that they are not merely tokens in political field. These quotas can be provided through reserved seats or as a legal candidate quota or through political parties. Women quotas require that a certain number or percentage of a body's representatives be female, whether it be a candidate list, a committee or the government. The majority of quotas aim to increase women's representation because the issue to be addressed is typically the under- representation of women; this is especially pertinent given that women make up half of the population in any given country.

Besides focusing on the gender quotas, there is a need to strengthen **Gender- Responsive Budgeting.** It does not entail establishing separate budgets for women or exclusively boosting spending on women's programs. Rather, gender-responsive budgeting attempts to ensure that the collection and distribution of public resources are carried out in effective ways that promote gender equality and the empowerment of women.

Modeling Female Leadership is another strategy for women empowerment in politics. There is mounting evidence that the leadership of women in political decision-making processes is beneficial. For instance, research on panchayats (local councils) in India revealed that the number of drinking water projects in regions with women-led councils was greater than in regions with male-led councils. Also, women demonstrate political leadership by working across party lines through parliamentary women's caucuses even in the most politically contentious environments and by championing gender equality issues, such as the elimination of gender-based violence, parental leave and childcare, pensions, gender-equality laws, and electoral reform (IPU, 2008).

Political Training Programs should be regularly conducted. Despite the structural impediments, mentoring, confidence development, media training and political campaign education are all useful methods for increasing adolescent girls and women's political goals and effectiveness (UN Women, In brief: Women's leadership and political participation, 2013).

7.4 ROLE OF GLOBAL POLITICAL INSTITUTIONS IN EMPOWERING WOMEN

Apart from the individual efforts of the countries, the UN is playing a pivotal role in merging the gap between gender inequality. It calls for a balanced political participation and power-sharing between women and men in decision-making as a target set in the Beijing Declaration and Platform for Action (UN, 1995).

The UN has created a UNGA Platform of Women Leaders in the year 2021 from a meeting between the women heads of state and government. The event, with the theme "Transformative solutions by women leaders to today's interlinked challenges", emphasis that women's full and effective political participation and decision-making are essential for addressing global priorities effectively, decisively and inclusively. As per the UN data, only 28 of the 193 UN member states have elected female heads of state or government. While progress has been made in many nations, the global proportion of women in other levels of political office has a long way to go: 21% of the world's ministers, 26% of national MPs and 34% of elected local government positions. At the current rate of advancement, equal representation in parliament would not be realized until 2062, according to a new UN assessment.

The aim of the UNGA Platform of Women Leaders is to enable women in key political leadership roles gain prominence. It is clearly proven that women's leadership is crucial to the 2030 Agenda for Sustainable Development. Countries with a greater proportion of female political leaders tend to prioritize health, education, infrastructure and the elimination of violence against women. Even in reaction to the pandemic, women leaders advocated for measures that addressed the social and economic effects of the pandemic on the most vulnerable communities. In conflict-affected environments, evidence indicate that women's participation in public life enhances the legitimacy of peace processes and negotiations, hence contributing to the unification of fractured communities. The presence of more women in positions of authority has also been found to improve girls' educational and professional aspirations (UN Women, Press release: New platform of women leaders meets at UN General Assembly, 2022).

Therefore, South Asian nations should focus on UN agendas along with adopting various other practices followed by other nations. For example- European Union plays a major role in women empowerment and gender equality in political decision making. Bangladesh, India and Sri Lanka along with other South Asian countries should adopt specific political measures to bridge the gap between gender inequality and to promote women empowerment. For instance, France, which has the highest growth in the promotion of female EU lawmakers, has enacted legislation promoting gender equality in elected positions. In political situation with limited freedom, such as one-party or dominant-party systems, it is however debatable how much participation of women in governments or parliaments advances women's agenda and interests.

Also, the "Strategic engagement for gender equality 2016-2019" of the European Commission encourages members states to adopt measures to increase the gender balance in political and public-making positions. And the EU gender action plan 2016-2020 mainstreams women empowerment and gender equality in EU external policies that aims to facilitate women participation regarding their voting procedures at all the levels of governance.

For a broader outlook, Women's political empowerment necessitates a diversified strategy. For example, preventing violence and harassment towards women during elections should be a top emphasis. Additionally, greater efforts are required to recruit more women, particularly young women, into political parties, to train women leaders, and to enhance women's abilities to actively participate in elections as candidates and voters. This is vital in the current political climate, which is characterized by citizen's dissatisfaction in politics.

7.5 LIMITATIONS OF THE STUDY

As the secondary research used the existing data to answer the research questions. Therefore, while conducting the study, the researcher has gone through a number of limitations, which are as follows:

- **Covid phase:** As the research is majorly conducted during the corona period, it was impossible for the researcher to conduct field study, due to which the study lacks public opinion regarding female participation in politics.
- **Lack of data**: There is very less data available in the area of women political participation and representation due to which analysis process became more complicated. And further, the focus

of the study shifted from research question-driven approach to data-driven approach.

- **Issue of biasness:** As the study of the focuses on women, due to which there are many variables which are not available that are important part of the study. Also, the data which is available is more male specific as compared to the females.
- **Social obligations**: Keeping the cultural aspects of the three countries in mind, there were certain social obligations for the researcher due to which certain topics are not brought into the limelight. For example: Role of religion in Politics.
- **Ethical Issues:** Ethical issues which are concerned with this secondary study includes the security and confidentiality. At the same time, researcher dealt with the validity and reliability of the data available and used for the study.
- **Scope of discussion:** Because of the time constraints and nature of the study, the scope and depth of the discussions is compromised in many ways as compared to the works of experienced scholars.

7.6 AREA OF FUTURE RESEARCH

Despite the importance of incorporating concerns encountered by varied cultures into existing research on women and politics, future research projects must be designed in such a way so that women's experiences are not the exclusive basis for generating research questions. Therefore, we require research that begins with the experiences of women. For a comprehensive understanding of the political engagement of women and their contributions, it is often necessary to pose novel questions, such as those concerning the roles of religion and indigenous community groups. And there is a need to conduct primary study in order to get answers to the question like "To what extent do women and men perceive the political arena to be accessible to them?".

Finally, chances for women to conduct research on women and politics must be expanded. While researchers of women and politics must be more sensitive to the unique experiences of women, this is not sufficient. Moreover, we must discover ways to encourage, enable, and fund the participation and research of women interested in researching women and politics.

Reference

Abbas, A. & Muneer L. (2019). Women empowerment in south Asia: role of women in development of Pakistan. *International Journal of Research in Humanities and Social Studies*, 6(2), pp. 42-49. https://www.ijrhss.org/papers/v6-i2/6.pdf

Abbas, S., Isaac, N., Zia, M., Zakar, R., & Fischer, F., (2021). Determinants of women's empowerment in Pakistan evidence from Demographic and Health Surveys, 2012–13 and 2017–18. BMC Public Health, 21, pp. 1-14. https://doi.org/10.1186/s12889-021-11376-6

Abdi, J. J. (2021). Women political participation in somaliland challenges and opportunities. *International Journal of Engineering Applied Sciences and Technology*, 6(1), pp. 106-116.

Abesekera, N. (2021), "COVID-19, Universal Disaster Poverty Cycle and Sri Lanka", Experimental Findings.

Abidi, A. (2013). Muslim women and their representation in South Asian politics. *Islam and Muslim Societies A Social Science Journal*, 6(2), pp. 11-27. https://www.muslimsocieties.org/Vol6_2/Muslim_Women_and_their_Representation.pdf

Acharya, B. N. (2019). Are men and women really equal or is equality defined differently. https://timesofindia.indiatimes.com/readersblog/straighttalk/are-men-and-women-really- equal-or-is-equality-defined-differently-4120/

Adler, E. (1997). Seizing the middle ground constructivism in world politics. *European Journal of International Relations*. pp. 319-363. https://doi.org/10.1177%2F1354066197003003003

Afridi, F., Iversen, V., & Sharan, M. R. (2017). Women political leaders, corruption and learning evidence from a large public program in India. *Economic Development and Cultural Change*, 66(1), pp. 1-30. https://doi.org/10.1086/693679

Agarwal, B. (2009). Does women's proportional strength affect their participation? governing local forests in South Asia. *World Development,* 38(1), pp. 98-112. https://doi.org/10.1016/j.worlddev.2009.04.001

Agbalajobi, D. T. (2016). Electoral violence and women's participation in electoral processes challenges and prospects for future elections in Nigeria. *Unilag Sociological Review*, 12(2), pp. 73-94.

Aggestam, K., Rosamond, A. B. & Kronsell, A. (2018). Theorising feminist foreign policy. *International Relations*, https://doi.org/10.1177/0047117818811892

Ahmed, J., Angeli, A., Biru, A., & Salvini, S. (2001). Gender issues, population and development in Ethopia. Depth studies form the 1994 population and housing census in Ethiopia. Retrieved from https://www.irpps.cnr.it/etiopia/pdf/Gender_Issues_Population_and_Development.PDF

Akhtar, S., (2015). Time for Equality, United Nations publication, New York, PP. 1-132.

Alexander, A. C., Catherine Bolzendahl & Farida Jalalzai (2016). Defining women's global political empowerment theories and evidence. *Sociology Compass*, 10(6), pp. 432-441. https://doi.org/10.1111/soc4.12375

Alternative Report to the 65th session of the UN Commission on the Elimination of Discrimination Against Women, 2016.

Alvarez, M. L. (2013). From unheard screams to powerful voices a case study of women's political empowerment in the Philippines. *12th National Convention on Statistics (NCS) EDSA*, Mandaluyong City, Philippines.

Amrita, B. (2005). Women, political parties and social movements in South Asia. *United Nations Research Institute for Social Development*, Geneva. https://www.unrisd.org/80256B3C005BB128/(httpProjects)/72A65D864B4041EBC1256E4E00575F52?OpenDocument

Anagol, P., (2008). Agency, Periodization and Change in the Gender and Women's History of Colonial India, *Gender & History*, 20(3), pp. 603-627.

Andrew, B. and Freeman, M. (2012). The impact of the cedaw convention paths to equality. *World Development Report*. https://doi.org/10.1017/CBO9780511755910.011

Ann E. Towns (2010). Women and states norms and hierarchies in international society. *Social Forces*, 93(3), pp. 647-650. https://doi.org/10.1017/CBO9780511779930

Ann Tickner J (1992). Gender in international relations feminist perspectives on achieving global security. *Columbia University Press*. https://www.ces.uc.pt/ficheiros2/files/Short.pdf

Arif, Sardar M. A.W. K., Bashir, T., & Fatima, K., (2019). Perspectives on economic, social and cultural rights of women in azad Jammu and Kashmir a legal analysis. *Liberal Arts and Social Sciences International Journal* (LASSIJ), 3(2), pp. 65-73. http://dx.doi.org/10.47264/idea.lassij/3.2.9

Asiedu, E., Branstette, C., Babulal, N. G., & Malokele, N. (2006). The effect of women's representation in parliament and the passing of gender sensitive policies.

Atske, S., Geiger A. W and Scheller, A., (2019). The share of women in legislatures around the world is growing, but they are still underrepresented. *Pew research centre*.

Avinash G. Mulky (2013). Distribution challenges and workable solutions. *IIMB Management Review*, 25(3), pp. 179-195. https://doi.org/10.1016/j.iimb.2013.06.011

Bajpai, R., (2015). Multiculturalism in India an exception. Institute on Culture, *Religion & World Affairs CURA*, https://www.bu.edu/cura/files/2015/06/bajpai-paper-formatted.pdf. http://dx.doi.org/10.1525/luminos.73.g

Baker, S. (2006). Sustainable development. London Routledge, ISBN: 9780415522922. https://www.routledge.com/SustainableDevelopment/Baker/p/book/9780415522922

Bannor, B. (2019). An analysis of women's political participation in ghana under SDG5. Thesis, University of Ghana. https://ugspace.ug.edu.gh/bitstream/handle/123456789/36331/An%20Analysis%20of%20Women%E2%80%99s%20Political%20Participation%20in%20Ghana%20under%20S DG5.pdf?sequence=1&isAllowed=y

Bartolomeo, A. D. (2008). Gender inequality and Female political participation in Great Britain. Working Paper, University of Teramo.

Batliwala, Srilatha (2007). Taking the power out of empowerment an experiential account. *Development in Practice*, 17 (4–5), pp. 557–565. https://www.jstor.org/stable/25548253

Bayeh, E. (2016). The role of empowering women and achieving gender equality to the sustainable development of Ethiopia. *Pacific Science Review B: Humanities and Social Sciences*, 2(1), pp. 37-42. https://doi.org/10.1016/j.psrb.2016.09.013

Bayer, L. A. S., & Mishler, W. (2005). An integrated model of women's representation. *The Journal of Poliotics*, 67(2), pp. 407-428. https://web.pdx.edu/~mev/pdf/SchwindtBayer_Mishler.pdf

Baylis, J., Owens, P. & Smith, S. (2008). The globalization of world politics. *USA Oxford University Press*, ISBN: 9780198825548.

Beauregard, K. (2016). Women's representation and gender gaps in political participation do time and success matter in a cross-national perspective? Politics, Groups and Identities, 6(2), pp. 237-263. https://doi.org/10.1080/21565503.2016.1207548

Beauvoir, S. D. (1949). The Second Sex.

Beijing and its Follow-up (1995). https://www.un.org/womenwatch/daw/beijing/

Benschop, M. (2002). Rights and reality are women's equal rights to land, housing and property implemented in East Africa. *UN-Habitat*, ISBN: 9211316634.

Bhalotra, S., Irma Clots-Figueras and Lakshmi Iyer (2016). Pathbreakers? women's electoral success and future political participation. Harvard Business School Working Paper.

Bhat, R. A., (2015). Role of education in the empowerment of women in India. *Journal of Education and Practice*, 6(10), pp. 188-191. https://files.eric.ed.gov/fulltext/EJ1081705.pdf

Binjha, P., (2020). Challenges and prospects of empowerment of tribal women with reference to Jharkhand. *International Journal for Research in Engineering Application & Management (IJREAM)*, 6(7), pp. 231-236. http://ijream.org/papers/IJREAMV06I0767067.pdf

Bird, K. (2005). The political representation of visible minorities in electoral democracies a comparison of France, Denmark, and Canada. Nationalism and Ethnic Politics, 11, pp. 425- 465. https://doi.org/10.1080/13537110500379211

Bjarnegard, E., Hakansson, S., & Zetterberg, P. (2020). Gender and violence against political candidates Lessons from Sri Lanka. *Politics & Gender*, 18(1), pp. 1-51.

Bonner, M. (2019). Media and Gender equality.

Booth, A. (1999). Initial conditions and miraculous growth why is south east Asia different from Taiwan and south Korea. *World Development*, 27(2), pp. 301-321. https://doi.org/10.1016/S0305-750X(98)00126-0

Bossel, H. (1999). Indicators for sustainable development theory, method, applications. Winnipeg: International Institute for Sustainable Development.

Bowie, K. (2010). Women's suffrage in Thailand a southeast asian historiographical challenge. *Comparative Studies in Society and History*, 52(4), pp. 708-741. https://doi.org/10.1017/S0010417510000435

Branisa, B., Klasen, S. & Ziegler, M. (2013). Gender inequality in social institutions and gendered development outcomes. World Development, 45, pp. 252-268.

https://doi.org/10.1016/j.worlddev.2012.12.003

Bridging the digital gender divide (2018). https://www.oecd.org/digital/bridging-the-digital- gender-divide.pdf

Bruggemann, A. (2018). Empowering female councilors in Srilanka. https://www.iri.org/news/empowering-female-councilors-in-srilanka/?utm_source=www.democracyspeaks.org

Bruggemann, A., (2018). Empowering Female Councilors in Sri Lanka, https://www.iri.org/news/empowering-female-councilors-in-sri-lanka/

Burchi, F. & Singh, K. (2020). Women's political representation and educational attainments a district level analysis in India. *Journal of South Asian Development*, 15(1), pp. 7-33.

Burke, M. J. and Stephens, J. C (2017). Political power and renewable energy futures a critical review. *Energy Research & Social Science*. 35, pp. 78-93. https://doi.org/10.1016/j.erss.2017.10.018

Burroway, R., (2012). A cross national analysis of sex specific HIV prevalence rates and women's access to property, land, and loans in developing countries. *International Journal of Sociology*, 42(2), pp. 47-67. http://dx.doi.org/10.2307/41739551

Butler, J. (1993). Bodies that matter on the discursive limits of sex. *New York and London: Routledge*, ISBN: 9780415610155.

Buvinic, M. & Nichols, R. F. (2014). Promoting women's economic empowerment what works. *The World Bank Research Observer,* https://doi.org/10.1093/wbro/lku013

Carver, Terrell., (2003). Gender and International Relations. *International Studies Review,* 5, pp. 287-302. https://www.ces.uc.pt/ficheiros2/files/Short.pdf

Chakrabarty, B. (2008). Indian Politics and Society since Independence. *Taylor & Francis e- Library,* ISBN 0-203-92767-2. https://www.hkrdb.kar.nic.in/documents/Downloads/Good%20Reads/Indian%20Politics %20and%20 Society%20Since%20Independence%20-%20Bidyut%20Chakrabarty.pdf

Chandrika, A. M. M. (2019). Feminism and emancipation influence of feminist ideas on women's socio-economic and political liberation in Sri Lanka. *Sociology Mind*, 9, pp. 302-315. https://doi.org/10.4236/sm.2019.94020

Chattopadhyay, Raghabendra., & Duflo, Esther., (2004). Women as policy makers: evidence from a randomized policy experiment in India. *Econo metrica*, 72(5), pp. 1409–1443. https://www.jstor.org/stable/3598894

Chawdhury, F. D. (2009). Problems of women's participation in Bangladesh politics. The Round Table, 98, pp. 555-567. http://dx.doi.org/10.1080/00358530903151748

Child Marriage. https://www.unicef.org/protection/child-marriage

Children with Disabilities are Just Like Other Children (2022). https://www.worldbank.org/en/home

Choi, N. (2018). Women's political pathways in Southeast Asia. *International Feminist Journal of Politics,* 21(2), pp. 1-25.

Chowdhury, F. D. (2009). Problems of women's participation in Bangladesh politics. *The Round Table,* 98(404), pp. 555–567. http://dx.doi.org/10.1080/00358530903151748

Chukwurah, D. C., Nduba J. O. & Izunwanne, G. N. (2020). Gender equality and women political participation and representation in Nigeria. *International Journal of Academic Accounting, Finance & Management Research*, 4(7), pp. 52-59.

Clavero, S., & Galligan, Y., (2005). A job in politics is not for women' analysing barriers to women's political representation in CEE. *SociologickyCasopis/Czech Sociological Review*, 41(6), pp. 979-1004.

Collins, A. (2019). Contemporary Security studies, 6th Edition.

Cornwall, A. & Anyidoho, N. A. (2010). Introduction Women's empowerment contentious and contestations. *Development*, 53(2), pp. 144-149.

Cornwall, A. (2016), Women's empowerment what works. Journal of International Development, 28, pp. 342-359.

Dahlerup, D. (2020). Women in decision-making in public life. https://www.unwomen.org/sites/default/files/Headquarters/Attachments/Sections/CSW/6 5/EGM/Dahlerup_TSMs_EP3_EGMCSW65.pdf

Dahlum, S., Knutsen, C. H., & Mechkova, V., (2022). Women's political empowerment and economic growth. *World Development*, 156, pp. 1-19. https://doi.org/10.1016/j.worlddev.2022.105822

Deka, J. (2019). A critical study of Gandhian approach to woman in the light of Sujata Patel's essay construction and reconstruction of woman in Gandhi. *International Journal of Scientific & Technology Research*, 8(10), pp. 2422-2427. https://www.ijstr.org/final-print/oct2019/A-Critical-Study-Of-Gandhian-

Approach-To-Woman-In-The-Light-Of- Sujata-Patels-Essay-construction-And-Reconstruction-Of-Woman-In-Gandhi.pdf

Dhungel, D. (2004). South asian association for regional co-operation (SAARC) prospects for development. *The Pakistan Development Review*, 43, pp. 933-941. https://www.jstor.org/stable/41261035

Dietrich, L., Skakun, Z., Khaleel, R. & Peute, T. (2021). Social norms structuring masculinities, gender roles, and stereotypes. *Oxfam Research Reports*, https://reliefweb.int/sites/reliefweb.int/files/resources/rr-masculinities-misconceptions-women-girls-empowerment-310821-en.pdf

Dubey, K. K. D., & Singh, G. N. (2021). Role of women in politics and national development. *NIU International Journal of Human Rights*, 8(3), pp. 159-169.

Elshtain, J. (1987). Women and war. *Chicago the university of Press*. https://press.uchicago.edu/ucp/books/book/chicago/W/bo3646038.html

Empowerment of Women (2006). Report, Ministry of women and child development Government of India.

Enloe, C. (1989). Bananas, Beaches and Bases. ISBN: 9780520279995

Equality Rights. https://iitr.ac.in/internalcomplaintscommittee/annexure.pdf

Fanny, K. R. & Oluwasanumi, A. A. (2014). Women education and political participation in the south west region of Cameroon an empirical analysis. Public Administration Research, 3(2), pp. 144-153. http://dx.doi.org/10.5539/par.v3n2p144

Farzana, H., Hasan, A. K. M. B. & Musa, H. (2018). Women empowerment model strategies to overcome challenges. *Journal of Fundamental and Applied Sciences*, 10(1), pp. 1068- 1083.

Fernandez, M. L. & Valdes, L. F. V. (2016). The international relations theory under a feminist approach. Revista de Relaciones Internacionales, Estrategia y Seguridad, 11(1), pp. 45-61. http://dx.doi.org/10.18359/ries.1366

Fiaccadori, E. (2006). The question of nature what has social constructionism to offer feminist theory. *Goldsmiths University of London*. https://research.gold.ac.uk/id/eprint/8356/1/fiaccadori_booklet.pdf

Figueras, I. C. (2012). Are female leaders good for education evidence from India. American Economic Journal Applied Economics, 4(1), pp. 212-244. https://doi.org/10.1257/app.4.1.212

Finnemore, M. & Sikkink, K. (2001). Taking stock, the constructivist research program in international relations and comparative politics. *Annual Review of political science*, pp. 391-416.

Franceschet, S., & Piscopo, J. M., (2008). Gender quotas and women's substantive representation lessons from Argentina. *Politics & Gender*, 4, pp. 393-425. https://doi.org/10.1017/S1743923X08000342

Fulu, E. & Miedema, S. (2015). Violence against women: globalizing the integrated ecological model. *Violence Against Women*, 21(12), pp. 1431-1455. https://doi.org/10.1177%2F1077801215596244

Galligan, Y., (2020). Women MPs from Northern Ireland: challenges and contributions, 1953– 2020. *Open Library of Humanities*, 6(2), pp. 1-46. http://dx.doi.org/10.16995/olh.591

Gebru, S. G., & Demeke, M. A, (2014). The millennium development goals and the status of gender disparity in Ethiopia achievements and challenges. *American Scientific Research Journal for Engineering, Technology, and Sciences*, pp. 56-78. https://www.asrjetsjournal.org/index.php/American_Scientific_Journal/article/view/600/504

Gender and Land Rights Database (1978). https://www.fao.org/gender-landrights-database/country-profiles/countries-list/national-legal-framework/en/?country_iso3=LKA

Gender Gap.(2019). Retrieved from https://gem-report-2019.unesco.org/gender-report/

General Assembly resolution 2200A (1966). International covenant on economic, social and cultural rights. https://www.ohchr.org/en/professionalinterest/pages/cescr.aspx

Ghatak, S., (2016). The role of political exclusion and state capacity in civil conflict in South Asia. *Terrorism and Political Violence,* 30(1), pp. 74-96. https://doi.org/10.1080/09546553.2016.1150840

Ghatak, S., (2016). Willingness and opportunity a study of domestic terrorism in post-cold war South Asia. *Terrorism and Political Violence*, 28(2), pp. 274-296. http://dx.doi.org/10.1080/09546553.2014.902813

Gill, A., & Rehman, G. (2004). Empowerment through activism responding to domestic violence in the South Asian Community in London. *Gender and Development*, 12(1), pp. 75-82. https://www.jstor.org/stable/4030604

Goertz, G. & Mazur, A. G. (2008). Politics, Gender and Concepts. ISBN: 978-0-521-89776-1. https://doi.org/10.1017/CBO9780511755910.011

Gupta, D (2014). Gender equality and women's empowerment an analysis of Jammu and Kashmir. *Asian Resonance*, 3(1), pp. 117-123.

Guyo, F. B. (2017). Colonial and post-colonial changes and impact on pastoral women's roles and status. Guyo Pastoralism Research, Policy and Practice, 7, pp. 1-19. https://doi.org/10.1186/s13570-017-0076-2

Guzzini, S., (2000). A reconstruction of constructivism in international relations", *European Journal of International Relations*, 6(2), pp. 147-182.

Guzzini, S., (2005). The concept of power a constructivist analysis. *Journal of International Studies*, 33(3), pp. 495-521. https://doi.org/10.1177%2F03058298050330031301

Hakura D., Hussain, M., Newiak M., Thakoor, V. & Yang, F. (2016). Inequality, gender gaps and economic growth comparative evidence for sub-Saharan Africa. *International Monetary Fund*. https://www.imf.org/external/pubs/ft/wp/2016/wp16111.pdf

Halpern, H. P. & Jenkins, M. P. (2016). Parents' gender ideology and gendered behavior as predictors of children's gender-role attitudes a longitudinal exploration. *Sex Roles*, 74(11), pp. 527-542. https://doi.org/10.1007/s11199-015-0539-0

Hasan (1974). Towards Equality, Report of the Committee on the status of women in India, pp. 1-199. https://pldindia.org/wp-content/uploads/2013/04/Towards-Equality-1974-Part- 1.pdf

Henry, C. & Adams, J. (2018). Spotlight on sexual violence and harassment in commercial agriculture lower- and middle-income countries. International Labour Office, https://www.ilo.org/wcmsp5/groups/public/---dgreports/--- inst/documents/publication/wcms_630672.pdf

Hillman, B., (2017). Increasing women's parliamentary representation in Asia and the Pacific: The Indonesian experience. *Asia and the Pacific Policy Studies*, 4(1), pp. 38-49. https://doi.org/10.1002/app5.160

Holzner, B., Neuhold, B. & Ganger, W. A. (2010). Gender equality and empowerment of women policy document. *Federal Ministry for European and International Affairs, Vienna*. https://www.entwicklung.at/fileadmin/user_upload/Dokumente/Publikationen/Leitlinien/ Englisch/PD_Gender_2017_EN.pdf

Huis, M. A., Hansen, N., Otten, S., & Lensink, R. (2017). A three-dimensional model of women's empowerment: implications in the field of microfinance and future directions. *Frontiers in Psychology*, 8, pp. 1-14. https://doi.org/10.3389/fpsyg.2017.01678

Human development report (2015). https://hdr.undp.org/sites/default/files/2015_human_development_report_1.pdf

Human Development Reports. (n.d.). Retrieved from https://hdr.undp.org/data-center/human- development-index#/indicies/HDI

Human Development Reports. (n.d.). Retrieved from https://hdr.undp.org/data-center/thematic- composite-indices/gender-inequality-index#/indicies/GII

Inter-Parliamentary Union (2008). A survey of women and men in parliaments. Reports and Documents n° 54, ISBN 978-92-9142-379-8. http://archive.ipu.org/pdf/publications/equality08-e.pdf

IPU. (2008). Equality in Politics: A survey of men and women in parliaments.

Islam S k, Tauhidul., & Islam, Emadul., (2012). Barriers and scope of political participation of women in local government of Bangladesh Union Parishad perspective. *Journal of International Social Issues*, 1(1), pp. 71-85.

Israr, M. & Naz, A (2021). Female illiteracy and political participation Pakhtun women at crossroad of culture, religion and democracy. *ACTA ISLAMICA*, 9(2), pp. 39-62.

Issues related to women empowerment in India. https://vikaspedia.in/social-welfare/women-and- child-development/women-development-1/issues-related-to-women-empowerment-in- india

Iwanaga, K. (2008). Women's political participation and representation in Asia. NIAS Press, ISBN: 978-87-7694-016-4.

Iwanaga, K. (2008). Women's Political Participation and Representation in Asia Obstacles and Challenges. NIAS, ISBN: 978-87-7694-016-4.

Iwanaga, K., (2008). Women's Political Participation and Representation in Asia Obstacles and Challenges, *NIAS Press*, 1st Edition, ISBN: 978-87-7694-016-4, PP. 1-336.

Jackson, E. (2010). Feminism and Contemporary Indian Women's Writing. *Palgrave Macmillan London*, 1st Edition, ISBN: 978-0-230-23627-1. https://doi.org/10.1057/9780230275096

Jahan, R. (1987). Women in south Asian politics. *3rd World Quarterly*, 9(3), PP. 848-70. https://doi.org/10.1080/01436598708420004

John, C. D. & Kraay, A. C. (1998). Consistent covariance matrix estimation with spatially dependent panel data. *The Review of Economics and Statistics*, 80(4), pp. 549-560. https://www.jstor.org/stable/2646837

Jung, H. (2019). The evolution of social constructivism in political science past to present. *SAGE Open*. 9(1), pp. 1-10. https://doi.org/10.1177%2F2158244019832703

Kamlasi A. Y., Marzuki & Murdiono, M. (2021). Women's participation in politics as efforts to achieve gender equality a case study in Kupang City, Indonesia. *International Journal of Business and Applied Social Science* (IJBASS), 7(7), pp. 9-15. http://dx.doi.org/10.33642/ijbass.v7n7p2

Kardam N. (2004). The emerging global gender equality regime from neoliberal and constructivist perspectives in international relations. *International Feminist Journal of Politics*, 6, pp. 85- 109. https://doi.org/10.1080/1461674032000165941

Kardam, N. (2002). The emergence of a global gender equity regime. *International Journal,* 57(3), pp. 411-438. https://doi.org/10.2307/40203676

Kardam, N. (2017). Turkey's engagement with global women's human rights. Taylor & Francis. Routledge, 1st Edition, ISBN 9780815398691.

Karen, R., (2011). The vagina dialogues essentialist and constructionist views of female sexuality in contemporary feminist theology. *Thesis*, University of Dayton.

Karim, M. (2013). Socio-economic and political development of South Asian countries: in Bangladesh perspective. *International Journal of Humanities and Social Science Invention*, 2(2), pp. 29-43.

Kassa, S., (2015). Challenges and opportunities of women political participation in Ethiopia. Journal of Global Economics, 3(4), pp. 1-7. http://dx.doi.org/10.4172/2375- 4389.1000162

Katiyar, S. P., (2016). Gender disparity in literacy in India. *Social Change*, 46(1), pp. 46-69.

Khalid, K. A. T. (2014). Women and politics social construction and a policy of deconstruction. *Journal of Social Sciences*, 10(3) pp. 104-113. http://dx.doi.org/10.3844/jssp.2014.104.113

Khan, M. J. (2014). Discrimination against women in social and political fields in Azad Kashmir. *2nd semester University: University of Cyprus*, https://doi.org/20.500.11825/388.

Khodair, A. A. & Hassib, B. (2015). Women's political participation in egypt the role of the national council for women. *International Journal of Political Science and Development*, 3(7), pp. 326-337. http://dx.doi.org/10.14662/IJPSD2015.042

Kim, H. J., Atteraya, M. S. & Yoo, H. Y. (2018). Women's agency freedom through empowerment against domestic violence evidence from Nepal. *International Social Work*, 62(17), pp. 1- 16.

Kodikara, C. (2009). The struggle for equal political representation of women in Sri Lanka. Report, *Ministry of Child Development and Women's Empowerment.*

Krook, M. L. (2017). Violence against women in politics. *Journal of Democracy*, 28(1), pp. 74- 88.

Kumar, P. (2017). Participation of women in politics worldwide experience. IOSR Journal of Humanities and Social Science, 22(12), pp. 77-88.

Kumar, Rajesh., (2016). Women empowerment through education in India since independence. *International Journal of Advanced Educational Research*, 1(6), pp. 40-42.

Kundu, A. & Mohanan, P. C. Employment and inequality outcomes in India. https://www.oecd.org/employment/emp/42546020.pdf

Kunovich, S., & Paxton, P., (2005). Pathways to power: the role of political parties in women's national political representation, American Journal of Sociology, 111(2), pp. 505-552. https://doi.org/10.1086/444445

Lama, S. T. (2001). The Hindu Goddess and women's political representation in south Asia Symbolic resource or feminine mystique. *International review of sociology*, 5-20. https://doi.org/10.1080/03906700020030956

Lasna, K. S., & Haque T. M., (2014). Women's political participation in Bangladesh: rhetoric and reality. IPSA Conference.

Locher, B. & Prugl, E. (2002). Feminism and Constructivism worlds apart or sharing the middle ground. *International Studies Quarterly*. 45, pp. 111-129. http://dx.doi.org/10.1111/0020- 8833.00184

Logan, M. (2017). Conventional and unconventional political participation democracy in action. https://www.utc.edu/sites/default/files/2021-01/crcloganm2.pdf

Mahamud, M., Chowdhury, S. A., Shahinuzzaman K., & Uddin, N. (2021). Participation of women in politics an evidence from local level politics of Bangladesh. *International Journal of Engineering Science and Computing*, 11(4), pp. 27819-27823.

Malami, M. & Kenworthy, L. (1999). Gender inequality in political representation a worldwide comparative analysis. *Social Forces*, 78, pp. 235-68. https://doi.org/10.2307/3005796

Malhotra, A., Schulte, J., Patel, P. & Petesch, P. (2009). Innovation for women's empowerment and gender equality. *International Center for Research on Women.*

https://www.icrw.org/publications/innovation-for-womens-empowerment-and-gender- equality/

Manas, G. M. (2014). Women empowerment through higher education in India. *Research Journal of Philosophy & Social Sciences*, 40(1), pp. 1-9.

Manjunatha (2016). Political empowerment of women problems and prospects. *International Journal of Creative Research Thoughts* (IJCRT), 4(1), pp. 931-935. https://www.ijcrt.org/papers/IJCRT1133750.pdf

Matland, Richard, E. (1998). Women's representation in national legislatures developed and developing countries. *Legislative Studies Quarterly*, 23(1), pp. 109-125. https://doi.org/10.2307/440217

Mel, D. & Pathmala, S. L. (2009). Political and economic policy priorities in supporting post conflict peace and development in Sri Lanka. http://web.worldbank.org/archive/website01241/WEB/IMAGES/SRILANKA.PDF

Menchik, J. (2017). The constructivist approach to religion and world politics. *Comparative Politics*, 49(4), pp. 561- 581. https://www.bu.edu/pardeeschool/files/2017/07/Menchik.pdf

Ministry of Agriculture & Rural Development (2008). Rural capacity building project gender mainstreaming guideline.

Mittal, S., & Singh, T., (2020). Gender-Based violence during COVID-19 pandemic a mini- review. Frontiers in Global Women's Health, 1, pp. 1-7.

Mittal, V. & Dutta, J, (2019). Important Aspects of Women Empowerment in Assam and India. *Arts and Social Sciences Journal.* 10(2), pp. 1-9.

Mlambo, C. & Kapingura, F. (2019). Factors influencing women political participation the case of the SADC region. *Cogent Social Sciences,* 5(1), pp. 1-13. https://doi.org/10.1080/23311886.2019.1681048

Mohamed, A. M. (2017). Women political participation and decision making in Somali. Report, *Hope University.* http://www.somalilandlaw.com/Somaliland_women_political_participation_khadar_disse rttion_0813.pdf

Mondal, S., (2020). A comparative study of gender gaps among SAARC nations. *International Journal of Research and Review*, 7(4), pp. 481-486. https://www.ijrrjournal.com/IJRR_Vol.7_Issue.4_April2020/IJRR0062.pdf

Mosse, D. (2018). Caste and development contemporary perspectives on a structure of discrimination and advantage. *World Development,* 110, pp. 422-436. https://doi.org/10.1016/j.worlddev.2018.06.003

Munir, S., Shehzad, H., & Sahi, A., (2014). Media analysis of women's participation in politics. *Journal of Mass Communication and Journalism*, 4(3), pp. 1-11. http://dx.doi.org/10.4172/2165-7912.1000183

Muzaffar, M., IqraJathol & Yaseen, Z. (2017). SAARC an evaluation of its achievements, failures and compulsion for cooperation. *Global Political Review* 2(1), pp. 36-45.

Nagar, C. B. (2016). Feminism in international relations conceptual analysis. *International Journal of Humanities and Social Science Studies*, 3(3), pp. 174-184. https://oaji.net/articles/2016/1115-1480921760.pdf

Nabanita Bera (2016). Women empowerment through education. *International Journal of Humanities & Social Science Studies*, 2(6), pp. 184-190. https://oaji.net/articles/2016/1115-1464938174.pdf

Nazneen, S., (2004). Gender relations in Bangladesh: the household and beyond dowry, *women's property rights and Salish.* http://doi.org/10.13140/RG.2.2.18601.39521

Nazneen, S., Hossain, N., & Chopra, D., (2019). Introduction contentious women's empowerment in South Asia. *Contemporary South Asia*, 27(4), pp. 457-470. https://doi.org/10.1080/09584935.2019.1689922

Nelson, B. J. & Chowdhury, N. (1994). Women and politics world-wide. *Yale University Press.*

Niaz, U. (2003). Violence against women in south Asian countries. Achieves of Women's Mental Health, 6(3), pp. 173-184. http://dx.doi.org/10.1007/s00737-003-0171-9

Nipu, N. J. (2021). Power distance, women and political participation in Bangladesh Union Parishad perspective. *Public Affairs and Governance*, 9(1), pp. 42-61.

Niyonkuru, P. & Barrett, H. (2021). Gender and intergenerational challenges to Women's economic empowerment initiatives in Rwanda. *World Development Perspectives*, 23, pp. 1-13.

Non-standard employment around the world (2016). https://www.ilo.org/wcmsp5/groups/public/@dgreports/@dcomm/@publ/documents/pub lication/wcms_534326.pdf

Norris, P. (1997). Passage to power legislative recruitment in advanced democracies. *Cambridge University Press.*

Norris, P. (2006). The impact of electoral reform on women's representation. *Acta Politica*, 41, pp. 197-213.

OECD (2008). Gender and sustainable development maximizing the economic, social and environmental role of women a report to the UNCSD. https://www.oecd.org/social/40881538.pdf

Omvedt, G. (2005). Women in Governance in south Asia. Economic and Political weekly, pp. 4746-4752.

Oudshoorn, N. (1994). Beyond the natural body an archeology of sex hormones. New York and London: Routledge.

Page Nand Czuba C. E (1999). Empowerment what is it.Journal of extension, 37(5), 1-5. https://www.joe.org/joe/1999october/comm1.php/comm2.php

Palladino, L. (2020). Exploring barriers to women's political representation in Thailand. *Rice University*, https://doi.org/10.25611/ytvt-b171.

Park, S., & Liang, J., (2019). A comparative study of gender representation and social outcomes the effect of political and bureaucratic representation. *Public Administration Review*, 81(2), pp. 321-332. http://dx.doi.org/10.1111/puar.13092

Parsuraman & Somaiya, M. (2016). Economic empowerment of women promoting skills development in slum areas. https: //wcd.nic.in/sites/default/files/Final%20 Report-TISS- %20Skill%20in%20slums.pdf

Paul, TV., (2019). When balance of power meets globalization China, India and the small states of South Asia. *Politics*, 39(1), pp. 50-63. https://doi.org/10.1177%2F0263395718779930

Patel, Vibhuti (1991). Getting Foothold in Politics, Mumbai: Research Centre for Women's Studies (RCWS), Smt. Nathibai Damodar Thakersey Women's University. https://openlibrary.org/books/OL1251206M/Getting_a_foothold_in_politics

Paxton, P. (1997). Women in national legislatures a cross-national analysis. *Social Science Research*, 26(4), 442-64. https://doi.org/10.1006/ssre.1997.0603

Paxton, P., Hughes, M. M. & Green, J. L. (2006). The international women's movement and women's political representation. *American Sociological Review*, 71, pp. 898-920. https://doi.org/10.1177%2F000312240607100602

Peltonen & Hannes (2017). A tale of two cognitions: The Evolution of Social Constructivism in International Relations. *Revista Brasileira de Política Internacional*, 60(1), pp. 1-18.

Place, K. R. and Winter, J. V. (2017). Where are the women? An examination of research on women and leadership in public relations. *Public Relations Review*, 44(1), pp. 165-173. https://doi.org/10.1016/j.pubrev.2017.10.005

Pokharel, S., (2008). Gender Discrimination Women perspectives. *Journal of Development and Rural Studies*, 5(2), pp. 80-87. https://www.researchgate.net/publication/215457309_Gender_Discrimination_Women_P erspective

Political Participation of Women, https://asiapacific.unwomen.org/en/focus- areas/governance/political-participation-of-women .

Powell, A., Hassan, T., Dainty, A., & Carter, C. (2007). Strengthening women's participation in construction research in Europe. Project Women-CORE.

Prathiba, L., (2017). A study on issues and challenges of women empowerment in India. *Global Journal for Research Analysis*, 6(9), pp. 138-140. https://www.worldwidejournals.com/global-journal-for-research-analysis- GJRA/special_issues_pdf/September_2017_1507115716 61.pdf

President (2011). Statement by the Prime Minister Dr. Manmohan Singh at the General Debate of the 66th Session of the United Nations General Assembly. https://mea.gov.in/SpeechesStatements.htm?dtl/287/Statement_by_the_Prime_Minister_Dr_Manmohan_Singh_at_the_General_Debate_of_the_66th_Session_of_the_United_Nat ions_General_Assembly

Price R. M., (2006). Detecting ideas and their effects. *The oxford handbook of contextual political analysis*, PP. 252-265. http://dx.doi.org/10.1093/oxfordhb/9780199270439.003.0013

Prodip, M. A. (2021). Cultural obstacles to women's political empowerment in India and Bangladesh a comparative perspective. *Asian Journal of Comparative Politics*, http://dx.doi.org/10.1177/2057891121990742

Rahman, H. M. & Siddiqui, S. A. (2015). Female RMG worker economic contribution in Bangladesh. *International Journal of Scientific and Research Publications*, 5(9), pp. 1-9. https://www.ijsrp.org/research-paper-0915/ijsrp-p4579.pdf

Rahman, M. (2014). Perceptions and major challenges of women leaders in the lowest level local government in Bangladesh unheard voices and realities from the grassroots. *Journal of Public and Private Management*, 21(2), pp. 1-5. http://dx.doi.org/10.14456/ppmi.2014.5

Rahman, S, H., Khatri, S., & Brunner, Hans-P., (2012). Regional integration and economic development in south Asia. Edward Elgar Publishing Limited, ISBN 978 1 78100 327 5.

Rai, P., (2017). Women's participation in electoral politics in India silent feminization, *South Asia Research*, 37(1), 58-77. http://dx.doi.org/10.1177/0262728016675529

Rajput, P. & Singh, M. (2022). Role of Self-Help Groups (SHG) In Gender Equality: A Case Study of Jammu. *Journal of Positive School Psychology*, 6(4), pp. 3589-3590.

Rameez, A. (2018). Political participation of women in local governance: a case study of selected local government bodies in eastern Sri Lanka. *Journal of Asian and African Studies*, 53(4), pp. 1-19.

Ranked and mapped which countries have the most women in parliament (2017). https://apolitical.co/solution-articles/en/which-countries-have-most-women-in-parliament

Rati, SaifaT., & Ferdush, K. T., (2021). Evaluating the social, political and economic reasons behind gender-based violence in South Asia a case study of Bangladesh. *International Journal of Law Management and Humanities*, 4(4), pp. 3351-3374. https://doij.org/10.10000/IJLMH.111727

Riggin, J. (2011). The potential impact of Cedaw ratification on U.S. employment discrimination law lessons from Canada. *Columbia Human Rights Law Review*, 42(2), pp. 541-611. https://biblioteca.corteidh.or.cr/tablas/r26395.pdf

Rocha, K., Palazzo, J., Teczar, R. & Clark, R. (2018). Does breaking through the "final glass ceiling" really pave the way for subsequent women to become heads of state. *Sociology between the Gaps*, 4, pp. 1-15. https://digitalcommons.providence.edu/cgi/viewcontent.cgi?article=1040&context=sbg

Rubery, J. & Koukiadaki, A. (2016). Closing the gender pay gap a review of the issues, policy mechanisms and international evidence. ISBN: 978-92-2-131295-6.

Rule, W., & Zimmerman J. J., (1994). Electoral systems in comparative perspective their impact on women and minorities. *Greenhood Press*. ISBN: 9780313036255

Saher, N., Matloob, T. & Ali, S. S. (2014). From representation to political empowerment analyzing the role of political parties and women leadership in azad Jammu and Kashmir. *Journal of Basic and Applied Scientific Research*, 4(5), pp. 90-96.

Sahu, T. K., & Yadav, K., (2018). Women's education and political participation. *International Journal of Advanced Education and Research*, 3(6), pp. 65-71. http://dx.doi.org/10.22271/educatin.2018.v3.i6.15

Saidon, N. R., Daud S. & Samsudin, M. (2019). Leadership and gender women's political participation in Malaysia (1980-2013). *The European Proceedings of Social & Behavioural Sciences*, 68, pp. 1-10.

Sanín, J. R. (2020). Criminalizing violence against women in politics innovation, diffusion and transformation. *Politics & Gender*, 18(1), pp. 1-32. https://doi.org/10.1017/S1743923X20000173

Schaeffer, K. (2020). Key facts about women's suffrage around the world, a century after U.S. ratified 19th Amendment. Pew research Centre, October 5, 2020.

Schwab, K., Samans, R., Zahidi, S., Leopold, T. A., Ratcheva, V., Hausmann, R. & Tyson, L. D. A. (2017). The global gender gap report. World Economic Forum.

Sen, G. & Ostlin, P. (2007). Unequal, unfair, ineffective and inefficient gender inequity in health why it exists and how we can change it. *World Health Organization* Report, http://www.who.int/social_determinants/resources/csdh_media/wgekn_final_report_07.p df

Shakti, B. S. (2017). Tackling violence against women a study of state intervention measures. https://wcd.nic.in/sites/default/files/Final%20Draft%20report%20BSS_0.pdf

Shakti, Bhartiya. S., (2017). Tackling Violence Against Women: A Study of State Intervention Measures, pp. 1-357. https://wcd.nic.in/sites/default/files/Final%20Draft%20report%20BSS_0.pdf

Sharma, M. & Zangmo, D. (2017). The participation of women in local government in bhutan a study of Sarpang District. *International Journal of Economic Research*, 14(20), pp. 673- 679.

Sharma, M. K. & Jain, S. (2013). Leadership management principles, models and theories. *Global Journal of Management and Business Studies*, 3(3), pp. 309-318. https://www.ripublication.com/gjmbs_spl/gjmbsv3n3spl_14.pdf

Sharma, P., (2015). Oligarchic patriarchal political culture of women participation in south Asia with special reference to India, Bangladesh, Pakistan. *Research Reinforcement*, 2, pp. 79-85. http://www.researchreinforcement.com/issue3/16.pdf

Shehzad, H., (2003). Politics and Power: A Gendered Perspective from South Asia. *Journal of Mass Communication and Journalism*.

Shukurana, M. & Adamu, J. (2017). Challenges and prospects of women empowerment in small scale enterprises in Yobe State of Nigeria. *Journal of Business and Economic Development*, 2(2), pp. 87-93.

Sicangco, M. C. T., & Azis, Z. A. (2021). Court companion on gender-based violence cases. ISBN 978-92-9269-046-5, 2021. https://www.adb.org/sites/default/files/publication/735941/court-companion-gender- based-violence-cases.pdf

Sindhuja, P., & Murugan K. R., (2017). Factors impeding women's political participation – A literature review. *International Journal of Applied Research*, 3(4), pp. 563-565.

Sindhuja, P., & Murugan K. R., (2017). Gender disparity in political participation. *Petals of Humanities and Language Studies*, 2(1), pp. 58-64.

Singh, D. (2016). Political participation of women in the state of U.P an analytical study for women status in PRIs. *VSRD International Journal of Technical & Non-Technical Research*, 7(5), pp. 89-96.

Singh, S., (2013). Women empowerment in modern india. https://philarchive.org/archive/SINWEI

Singla, P. & Tulsyan A. (2020). Violence against Women. https://ssrn.com/abstract=3584526

Sjoberg, L. (2012). Gender, structure and war what Waltz couldn't see. International *Theory*, 4 (1), pp. 1-38.

Sohail, M. (2014). Women Empowerment and Economic Development-An Exploratory Study in Pakistan. *Journal of Business Studies Quarterly*, 4, pp. 163-170.

Srivastava, S., (2021). Issues and challenges of women empowerment in India. *International Journal of Education, Modern Management, Applied Science & Social Science*, 3(1), pp. 184-186. https://www.inspirajournals.com/uploads/Issues/694693530.pdf

Stamarski, C. S. & Hing L. S. S. (2015). Gender inequalities in the workplace the effects of organizational structures, processes, practices and decision makers' sexism. Frontiers in Psychology, 6, pp. 1-20. https://doi.org/10.3389/fpsyg.2015.01400

Staniland, P. (2020). Political violence in south Asia the triumph of the state. https://carnegieendowment.org/2020/09/03/political-violence-in-south-asia-triumph-of- state-pub-82641

State of the world's indigenous peoples (2009). *United Nations publication*, ISBN 92-1-130283- 7.

Stevens, C. (2010). Are women the key to sustainable development. *Sustainable development insights*. 3, pp. 1-8. Retrieved from http://www.bu.edu/pardee/files/2010/04/UNsdkp003fsingle.pdf

Stockemer, D., & Byrne, M. (2012). Women's representation around the world the importance of women's participation in the workforce. *Parliamentary Affairs*, 65(4), pp. 802-821. https://doi.org/10.1093/pa/gsr063

Strengthening women's political participation (2016). United Nations Development Programme.

Stromquist N. P. (1991). Educating women, the political economy of patriarchal states.

International Studies in Sociology of Education, 1, pp. 111-128.

Suleman, D., Arafah, B., Abbas, H. & Delukman, A. (2021). Women discrimination in Malaysia examining the gender agenda from the viewpoint of lenoremanderson's

women, politics, and change. *Linguistica Antverpiensia*, pp. 2204-2222. http://dx.doi.org/10.2139/ssrn.3849824 .

Sultan, M. (2018). Women's representation and participation in local government in Bangladesh new openings and remaining barriers, *Palgrave Macmillan, Cham*, 1st Edition, ISBN: 978- 3-319-57474-5, pp. 1-17.

Sultana, A. (2010). Patriarchy and women's subordination a theoretical analysis. *The Arts Faculty Journal*, 4, pp. 1-18. https://doi.org/10.3329/afj.v4i0.12929

Sundstrom A., Paxton, P., Wang Y., & Lindberg, S. I. (2015). Women's political empowerment a new global index, 1900-2012. *Working Paper*, University of Gothenburg. http://dx.doi.org/10.1016/j.worlddev.2017.01.016

Talukdar, I. H., Osterman, K. & Bjorkqvist, K. (2021). Cultural hurdles and family restrictions on female political participation among representatives to the Union Parishads of Bangladesh. Techniu m Social Sciences Journal, 18, pp. 306-316.

Theys, S., (2018). Introducing Constructivism in International Relations Theory. https://www.e- ir.info/pdf/72842

Thompson M. R., (2007). Presidentas and people power in comparative asian perspective. *Philippine Political Science Journal*, 28(1), pp. 1-32. http://dx.doi.org/10.1080/01154451.2007.9723500

Thompson, M. R. (2005). Frauen an der machtdynastien und politischefuhrerinnen in Asien women in power dynasties and political leaders in Asia, *Universitat Passau*, ISBN: 9783933509291.

Tipu, N. A. & Rahman, M. S. (2012). Problems of women's participation in decision making process of local government a study on Nine Union Parishads. *The Jahangirnagar Review*, 36, pp. 1-13.

Towards Equality, Report of the Committee on the Status of Women in India (Government of India, 1974): in Vina Mazumdar (ed.), Symbols of Power (1978), Allied Publishers.

Towards inclusive democracy in Sri Lanka by supporting female politicians, https://demofinland.org/en/towards-inclusive-democracy-in-sri-lanka-by-supporting-female-politicians/.

True, J., Niner, S., Parashar, S., & George, N., (2012). Women's political participation in Asia and the Pacific. *Conflict Prevention and Peace Forum*. https://iknowpolitics.org/sites/default/files/undpa-womens-political-participation-in-asia- and-the-pacific.pdf

UN (1992). Rio declaration on environment and development. Retrieved from Convention on Biological Diversity. https://www.cbd.int/doc/ref/rio-declaration.shtml UN. (1995). Beijing Declaration and Platform for Action. Retrieved from https://www.unwomen.org/en/digital-library/publications/2015/01/beijing-declaration

UN Women. (2013). In brief: Women's leadership and political participation. Retrieved from https://www.unwomen.org/sites/default/files/Headquarters/Attachments/Sections/Library/ Publications/2013/12/UN%20WomenLGThemBriefUSwebrev2%20pdf.pdf

UN Women. (2022). Press release: new platform of women leaders meets at UN General Assembly. Retrieved from UN Women: https://www.unwomen.org/en/news-stories/press- release/2022/09/press-release-new-platform-of-women-leaders-meets-at-un-general- assembly

Un Women (2021). Facts and figures Women's leadership and political participation. https://www.unwomen.org/en/what-we-do/leadership-and-political-participation/facts- and-figures

UNDP (2013). Gender mainstreaming made easy handbook for Programme staff. Retrieved from http://www.undp.org/content/dam/somalia/docs/Project_Documents/Womens_Empower ment/Gender%20Mainstreaming%20Made%20Easy_Handbook%20for%20Programme% 20Staff1.pdf

UNESCO World Report (2009). Investing in cultural diversity and intercultural dialogue (2009). United Nations Educational, Cultural and Scientific Organization, ISBN 978-92-3-104077- 1.

United Nations (1995). Report of the fourth world conference on women. Beijing, 4-15 September 1995.

United Nations (2018). Strategy for gender equality and the empowerment of women. https://www.unodc.org/documents/Gender/UNOVUNODC_Strategy_for_Gender_Equali ty_and_the_Empowerment_of_Women_2018-2021_FINAL.pdf

United Nations (2020). International day for the elimination of violence against women - a pandemic of abuse COVID-19 and gender-based violence. https://www.adb.org/news/events/international-day-elimination-violence-against-women-pandemic-abuse-covid- 19#:~:text=More%20than%2037%25%20of%20women,hands%20of%20their%20intima te%20partners.&text=Indeed%2C%20during%20the%20COVID%2D19,increases%20in %20gender%2Dbased%20violence .

United Nations (2021). Technology and Innovation Report. ISBN: 978-92-1-113012-6, https://unctad.org/page/technology-and-innovation-report-2021

United Nations publication (1994). Report of the International Conference on Population and Development. Cairo, 5-13 September 1994

Universal declaration of human rights (1948). https://www.un.org/en/about-us/universal- declaration-of-human-rights

Varghese, T., (2019). The impact of women's political empowerment policy a perspective from the idukki district of Kerala. *Viesoji Politika Ir Administravim as Public Policy and Administration*, 18(3), pp. 59-72. http://dx.doi.org/10.5755/j01.ppaa.18.3.24710

Varghese, T., (2020). Women's political participation and leadership in India examining the challenges. *ViesojiPolitikaIrAdministravimas Public Policy and Administration*, 19(1), pp. 111-125. http://dx.doi.org/10.5755/j01.ppaa.19.1.25228

Victoria Dauletova, Houchang Hassan Yari and Zainab Hussain (2022). Political Empowerment of women and the mediating role of political awareness the case of Oman. Journal of International Women's Studies, 23(1), pp. 115-130.